D1611944

DATE DUE

Studies in European Culture and History
edited by
Eric D. Weitz and Jack Zipes
University of Minnesota

Since the fall of the Berlin Wall and the collapse of communism, the very meaning of Europe has been opened up and is in the process of being redefined. European states and societies are wrestling with the expansion of NATO and the European Union and with new streams of immigration, while a renewed and reinvigorated cultural engagement has emerged between East and West. But the fast-paced transformations of the last fifteen years also have deeper historical roots. The reconfiguring of contemporary Europe is entwined with the cataclysmic events of the twentieth century, two world wars and the Holocaust, and with the processes of modernity that, since the eighteenth century, have shaped Europe and its engagement with the rest of the world.

Studies in European Culture and History is dedicated to publishing books that explore major issues in Europe's past and present from a wide variety of disciplinary perspectives. The works in the series are interdisciplinary; they focus on culture and society and deal with significant developments in Western and Eastern Europe from the eighteenth century to the present within a social historical context. With its broad span of topics, geography, and chronology, the series aims to publish the most interesting and innovative work on modern Europe.

Published by Palgrave Macmillan:

Fascism and Neofascism: Critical Writings on the Radical Right in Europe
by Eric Weitz

Fictive Theories: Towards a Deconstructive and Utopian Political Imagination
by Susan McManus

German-Jewish Literature in the Wake of the Holocaust: Grete Weil, Ruth Klüger, and the Politics of Address
by Pascale Bos

Turkish Turn in Contemporary German Literature: Toward a New Critical Grammar of Migration
by Leslie Adelson

Terror and the Sublime in Art and Critical Theory: From Auschwitz to Hiroshima to September 11
by Gene Ray

Transformations of the New Germany
edited by Ruth Starkman

Caught by Politics: Hitler Exiles and American Visual Culture
edited by Sabine Eckmann and Lutz Koepnick

Legacies of Modernism: Art and Politics in Northern Europe, 1890–1950
edited by Patrizia C. McBride, Richard W. McCormick, and Monika Zagar

Police Forces: A Cultural History of an Institution
edited by Klaus Mladek

Richard Wagner for the New Millennium: Essays in Music and Culture
edited by Matthew Bribitzer-Stull, Alex Lubet, and Gottfried Wagner

Representing Masculinity: Male Citizenship in Modern Western Culture
edited by Stefan Dudink, Anna Clark, and Karen Hagemann

Remembering the Occupation in French Film: National Identity in Postwar Europe
by Leah D. Hewitt

"Gypsies" in European Literature and Culture
edited by Valentina Glajar and Domnica Radulescu

Choreographing the Global in European Cinema and Theater
by Katrin Sieg

Converting a Nation: A Modern Inquisition and the Unification of Italy
by Ariella Lang

German Postwar Films: Life and Love in the Ruins
edited by Wilfried Wilms and William Rasch

German Postwar Films

Life and Love in the Ruins

Edited by
Wilfried Wilms
and William Rasch

palgrave
macmillan

GERMAN POSTWAR FILMS

First published in 2008 by
PALGRAVE MACMILLAN®
in the United States—a division of St. Martin's Press LLC,
175 Fifth Avenue, New York, NY 10010.

Where this book is distributed in the UK, Europe and the rest of the world,
this is by Palgrave Macmillan, a division of Macmillan Publishers Limited,
registered in England, company number 785998, of Houndmills,
Basingstoke, Hampshire RG21 6XS.

Palgrave Macmillan is the global academic imprint of the above companies
and has companies and representatives throughout the world.

Palgrave® and Macmillan® are registered trademarks in the United States,
the United Kingdom, Europe and other countries.

ISBN-13: 978–0–230–60825–2
ISBN-10: 0–230–60825–6

Library of Congress Cataloging-in-Publication Data

German postwar films : life and love in the ruins / edited by
Wilfried Wilms and William Rasch.
    p. cm.—(Studies in European culture and history)
    ISBN 0–230–60825–6 (alk. paper)
    1. Rubble films—Germany—History and criticism. I. Wilms,
Wilfried. II. Rasch, William, 1949–

PN1995.9.R83G47 2008
791.430943'09045—dc22   2008007997

A catalogue record of the book is available from the British Library.

Design by Newgen Imaging Systems (P) Ltd., Chennai, India.

First edition: December 2008

10 9 8 7 6 5 4 3 2 1

CONTENTS

Introduction: Looking Again at the Rubble

William Rasch

In 1952, at the beginning of West Germany's much praised *and* much maligned *Wirtschaftswunder* (economic miracle), Heinrich Böll looked back fondly and defensively at the literature written during the years immediately following World War II. *Trümmerliteratur* (rubble literature) it was called, *Kriegsliteratur* (war literature), *Heimkehrerliteratur* ("coming home" literature, to evoke the title of a Vietnam War era film of a similar nature), and disparagingly so; but Böll wished to wear these labels, especially *Trümmer*, as a badge of honor. Why? Because, he wrote, "in truth, the people about whom we wrote lived in rubble, emerged from the war damaged, men and women to an equal degree, and children too. And they had a keen vision: they saw things" (339). Writers, Böll contended, identified with the rabble from the rubble, with the black-market profiteers and their victims alike, the refugees and all those who were homeless, in short, with an entire generation who miraculously found their way back from a war that seemed like it would never end. And so the writers of *Trümmerliteratur* wrote, without blinders, about what they saw, or rather, about what that damaged war generation saw.

Böll gives examples. He invites us to assume that the eyes of a writer spy a man in a cellar, a baker in the early hours of the morning making bread. This man smokes cigarettes, goes to the movies, has lost a son in Russia who is buried 3000 kilometers away in a grave that has been leveled and ploughed under, adorned with no cross or reminder of his existence. All this—the man's daily pleasures and his lingering pain—belongs to the vision of the baker in the cellar. And the same goes for the young woman we happen upon in the factory who makes buttons for our clothes. She smokes too, wears lipstick and also goes to movies, and can on occasion be seen walking with a young man who repairs cars. But what an author who has eyes to see must also notice is the fact that her mother lies buried in a city under a pile of unmarked rubble also slated eventually to be cleared away. Once a year this young woman places flowers on the pile of concrete and mortar that stands in for her mother's tombstone (341–42).

All around these individual scenes the author who has eyes to see also finds new buildings going up, but they look like mere facades to him, stage scenery; and the people in them do not really live there, they are merely sheltered, stored, administered. To see these things should be the task of the writer, Böll notes. Like Balzac, like Dickens, recording the reality that lies before one is to be preferred over the manufacture of false idylls, the facades of literature that hide reality from our eyes and our consciousness. The name of Homer, Böll concludes, is revered throughout Western culture. "Homer is the father of the European epic, but Homer narrated the Trojan War, the destruction of Troy, and the homecoming [*Heimkehr*] of Odysseus—war literature, rubble literature, literature of the returning soldier. We have no reason to be ashamed of these terms" (343).

What Böll says of rubble literature could also be said of the films of that time. Made under trying conditions, subject to Allied censorship, and executed with a minimum of resources, these films too dealt with the ever-present effects of the war and its aftermath in the ruins of Germany's major cities, especially Berlin. Like Böll and his fellow authors, German (and Italian, American, and British) filmmakers looked around and saw people trying to survive in a present that was burdened by the past and not yet redeemed by the promise of a better future. The cast of characters—returning soldiers and those at home with memories of soldiers who would never return—and the scenery—rubble—were the same. And like Böll and his fellow authors, these filmmakers soon saw that once a possible political and economic future appeared on the horizon in the form of currency reform and state formation, rubble had to be cleared from the screen as fast as it was cleared from the streets. Yet they too felt they had no reason to be ashamed.

Barely two decades later, the generation of former rubble children begged to differ. Well, they didn't actually beg, they spat out their disagreement, their contempt, their disgust. No longer interested in what the war generation saw, they fixated on what that generation should have seen but did not. That baker, for instance. How did he get his first bakery? Had it once been owned by a Jew before 1938? And what might his son have done in Russia before he was killed—or that factory worker's boyfriend? And is that young woman herself as innocent as her lipstick and chaste walks would lead us to believe? Not to mention her mother, who probably died trying to save her fur coat or *Biedermeier* furniture! These would be the questions the " '68ers" would have asked and are the questions we still ask today. Indeed, we have learned to ask them not only of the characters the authors observe—ever so partially, we suspect—but of the authors themselves. Böll wrote of his war experiences in fictional form. And we have his wartime letters home. But did he write about everything he saw? We know now that even the self-styled paragon of virtue Günther Grass didn't. We have learned to imagine the worst; indeed, we *love* to imagine the worst. It is in our blood. Our reading of Germans reading their past—especially, in the 1940s and 1950s, their immediate past—has become an enactment of the classical hermeneutical trope of understanding authors better than they understood themselves. Only now it is not so much a question of knowledge, but of *Gesinnung* or moral outlook. Armed with our historical knowledge of the Third Reich, we are confident that we know what the war generation knew, or should have known; thus we know what they should have seen, should have said, should have felt, should have done. And when they do not see what we see, we find them wanting. It is as if their eyesight were not as keen as Böll assumed because a mote, nay, an immoral beam obstructed their view.

In his indispensable study of German rubble films—the immediate postwar genre to which the present collection of essays is devoted—Robert Shandley writes: "The rubble films' treatment of the past is far from morally satisfying to today's viewers." This assertion sets the tone for his book. Viewers of rubble films are asked to stand in moral judgment of them, as if it goes without saying that our prime duty as examiners of literary or visual texts is to act as judge, jury, and, ideally, executioner. Aesthetic categories—which, in their own way, might lead one to find many of these films inferior, especially when compared, say, to the neorealism of Rossellini—are subordinated to a catalog of typical German sins. "These films," Shandley notes, "only rarely confront the institutions, traditions, and assumptions that led to the catastrophe that was postwar Europe. At best, they mention them; at worst, they lie about them." He goes on: "Most of the films treat the question of guilt as just one problem among many in the postwar period. Worse yet, the rubble films often conflate the wrongs committed during the Third Reich with the Germans' own postwar suffering." Finally, the filmmakers were "so emotionally involved in the hardships of life in postwar Germany that they were largely blind to other concerns such as personal or collective responsibility for the crimes of the war" (4–5). Certainly, when described in this way (and one may leave aside for the moment the accuracy of Shandley's characterization), these films *are* "far from morally satisfying to today's viewers," or at least to the way today's viewers have been trained to view such German cultural productions. In fact, one wonders whether the claim is not somehow tautological. Today's viewers know that Germans in 1945 were supposed to hold clear and unequivocal positions about their unique guilt and deserved suffering, positions identical to those held by the Allies who conquered them,[1] and today's viewers know this because of a 60-year discourse of postwar Germans' singular moral failings. In a sense, rubble films, like all other postwar German cultural products, are *by definition* morally unsatisfying. One approaches them largely to confirm their status as documents of German moral failings. They attest to what we already know, to what we have always known. To watch them, actually *watch* them, would seem to be superfluous.

But watching the German and non-German films set in the destroyed cities of late 1940s Germany can be instructive, even enjoyable, in a variety of ways. They need not simply serve as lessons that give rise to Sunday sermons. It may indeed be true that rubble films were "largely blind" to what concerns today's viewers. Nevertheless, what concerned the editors of this volume and thus motivated this collection of essays is a different, if related, question: To what in these films are today's viewers largely blind? What, in other words, does the all too familiar story of German evasion, silence, and moral blindness hide from *our* sight, no matter how pure our moral pedigree may be? We asked well-established and up-and-coming scholars in German and film studies to look again at the films of the 1940s and tell us what they saw. This volume is a result of that invitation and, we hope, a partial answer to our guiding question.

We know we cannot claim to be the *Stunde Null* (year zero) of *Stunde Null* scholarship. There is no clean slate, no pristine vision of the past. Nor do the authors represented in this volume wish to claim moral or political neutrality. That would be absurd. We have all either gone through or arrived upon the scene after the moral purgatory of the 1960s. We are all "'68ers" or their heirs. While some of us have made the long march through the institutions and thus have helped shape the following generation, others were born after the Eichmann trials and the mythical month of May, 1968. We all are saturated by the language and the outlook given such emphatic voice in Shandley's introduction. We do not wish to renounce what we have learned, nor can we deny that much in postwar German films may embarrass us because of our moral and political training. Nevertheless, we feel that these films deserve another and a sympathetic look. We are curious and we feel that curiosity—intellectual, aesthetic, even moral curiosity—ought to have its moment in the scholarly sun too. We are curious about Böll's baker and factory worker, as well as the butcher and the candlestick maker, the widow and amputee, the refugee and survivor of concentration camps, the former Nazi and anti-Nazi Germans.

What movies did they watch and what of themselves or others did they see in these movies? Are there truths about total war—and it seems we have only total wars anymore—in these movies that we have lost sight of? Are there aesthetic solutions to the vexed problem of the representation of destruction, annihilation, and suffering that we might rediscover? Where does humor and parody fit? What role does genre play? Is it appropriate, effective, enlightening to broach the question of persecution using the techniques of film noir? What similarities are revealed when one actually engages in comparative analyses? Was the bombing war urban renewal by another name? Can one, as former president Bill Clinton is famous for saying, "feel your pain," or is pain—intense hunger, cold, injury, mental disorientation, and insanity—like politics itself only local?

We are not as sure as some are of the answers to these and a host of other questions that could be raised. But we believe that if we're attentive to what Böll's baker and button maker saw when they slipped into the darkness to look at that always fascinating play of shadows and light projected on wall, bed sheet, or "silver screen" during the second half of the 1940s, we just might learn something we didn't already know.

Note

1. Some Germans now like to claim they were "liberated" by the Allies. The Allies were proud of their liberation of France, Holland, Belgium, Poland, and other European territories overrun by the Germans; but they took even greater pride in their conquest of Germany, and rightly so. It was a tremendous military, logistical, and public relations feat. Given the litany of failures by the former Allies since 1945, one should not trivialize this accomplishment with phony language.

Chapter One
"…When Everything Falls to Pieces"—Rubble in German Films before the Rubble Films

Erhard Schütz

Rubble must be a dramatic argument, final and without concession, otherwise it becomes mere decoration, and then it is nothing but unenlightening and oppressive.[1]

Rubble in Those Days

When the catch word "contemporary film" was heard in those years automatic associations arose: rubble, bunkers, everything demolished, but then, all at once, heave-ho!, construction, democracy, renewal…The performers: well-known stars, who took pains to look as shabby and [yet] as renewed as possible. The offspring: rare and weak. A new cliché. Soon no one wanted to see this anymore.

Thus, influential film critic Gunter Groll was already looking back in 1950 on "those days" that had hardly passed.[2] Even if W.G. Sebald's speculations and Jörg Friedrich's problematic docu-epic *Der Brand* have since initiated an enduring and intense obsession with the postwar era inside and outside the rubble, the postwar Germans'contact to a life in and under the rubble remains quite remarkable. The rubble was incorporated into everyday life, quickly announcing itself as normalcy, and it disappeared from public perception while continuing to be fully conspicuous. This applies not just to the general but to the immediate environment that was perceived as wretched and ruined in the immediate postwar era:

> Good God! How bad misery can be! Sometimes when one is going through the streets, one is hardly able to look at the wretchedness. Between the smart American uniforms, the well nourished figures of our occupying powers, the first German soldiers, prisoners of war, reappear, ragged and haggard, shyly looking around like guilty sinners [...] As strolling ruins they stumble about, legless and armless, diseased, abandoned, lost.[3]

Rubble appeared as normalcy in everyday life; in film, however, it quickly became an anomaly. Even when a critic gushes about *In jenen Tagen*—"Igor Oberberg's camera is superb. It knows the beauty of idylls past, and presents Hamburg's authentic backdrop of rubble, before which a large part of the shoot took place, with an audacious severity. Without any sort of set construction, with a minimum of technical resources."[4]—it is precisely the absence of set construction and minimum of technical resources that makes rubble's disappearance from films most understandable. The disappearance is not due so much to a specific disposition of the audience, but simply to the push of producers to work again in the accustomed opulent, artificial, that is, perfectly controllable ambience as soon as possible. Decidedly, more noteworthy is the way the bombing war and rubble were handled during the war, when the line from the infamous SA song "[...] When everything falls to pieces [...]" started proving true. This treatment will be pursued here.

Käutner's *In jenen Tagen* can serve as a road sign: After the demonstrative exposition of the rubble landscape—in which both of the rubble people, war survivors, salvage a wrecked car, immediately paging through episode after episode of humane acts between 1933 and 1945 on the screen—it takes pretty long until ruins appear at all in the interior narrative, namely, only after the journey through the Russian snow. "I went underground, as it was called at the time," says the car and remains standing with a repainted license plate before the decorative rubble facades of Berlin. A bombing raid is signaled through sounds of explosion and the flak spotlight's fingers of light reflected in the windshield. With its new passengers, the car leaves the city, in order to represent in a Bethlehem-esque setting ass and ox in a stall with hay and straw and a presently unholy holy family. In the feature films before 1945, the German's own rubble and ruins also appeared very late in the game. Of course the ruins were already there before 1945—but as the rubble of others.

The Rubble of Others

If one follows the trail of stones in those days, then one must take into consideration that the process of destruction and ruination took place not "suddenly" but bit by bit, initially just creeping along. It can be read not only from the observations of foreign correspondents,[5] but also in the diaries of the resident population, for example, in the notes of Ruth Andreas-Friedrich.[6]

Thus the war's first bomb siren on September 1, 1939, came across rather "embarrassingly and seemed to us nearly a disgrace." In return, the city now appears most romantic:

> On the way home we see stars over Berlin for the first time. Not sad and dim behind the brightly lighted advertisements, but rather sparkling in festive clarity. The moon casts a milky glow over the surfaces and steep roofs. Not one artificial ray of light intrudes on the streets. "The metropolis returns to nature," smiles Andrik. "One could almost become a romantic."

One year later Andreas-Friedrich will still note the number of alarms in the meantime, visibly unnerved by their seeming superfluity:

> Last night we had the thirty-eighth air raid alarm since the end of August. The most unpleasant thing about the nightly disruptions are the many hours lost They hardly ever let us out of the cellars in less than three or four hours. Only very rarely is there shooting. If the damage done doesn't increase in the future, we needn't worry ourselves seriously about this specter of the war.[7]

Of course, worry would soon arrive.

Early on, when Germany could believe it was on the way to the peaceful and comfortable modernity promised by the Nazis, one was already confronted with rubble, not only the rubble of the last war but also the ruins of the others' wars. It should not be overlooked that in the time before the beginning of the Second World War reports about air bombardments from numerous conflicts across the world—from Manchuria to Abyssinia, from Tangiers to Palestine—were present in the media, especially in illustrated journals and newsreels. Not to mention Spain, already subjected to the German Luftwaffe's involvement. And when one watches a film like Gustav Ucicky's 1933 *Flüchtlinge*, one finds impressive scenes of people marching through a demolished city landscape, which have a nearly documentary presence.

The population had been systematically engaged in the air defense since 1933. Air-defense exercises belonged to everyday life—in the schools and on the job, in the community and across the Reich. The press, newsreels, and educational films, even novels like Ernst Ohliger's *Bomben auf Kohlenstadt* (1935), propagated air defense. By 1936, the Reich Air Defense League [*Reichsluftschutzbund*], with over eight million members, was the largest nonmilitary organization in Germany.

A new twist emerged with Germany's decision to go to war. In addition to the news reels, the propagandistic "documentaries" and feature films now had to interpret the German war and make visible the victories and their consequences for the ostensible enemy. On April 6, 1940, Hans Bertram's *Feuertaufe* (Baptism of Fire) was presented for the first time as a documentary of the Poland Campaign and, at the same time, as an ode to the young Luftwaffe. Introduced with the reassuring authenticity "the shooting took place during combat operations. The images are authentic and simple. Hard and unrelenting like war itself." In addition, authenticated through a roster of war reporters who fell in the line of duty for "Folk and Fatherland," the film delivers a staccato of destruction in a "type of two-level narrative. Above are the Germans with their technology in orderly formations, below are the Poles in chaos."[8] It is a film of the Luftwaffe, its test case, indeed its very "baptism of fire." ME 111s and Stukas are relentlessly deployed and, right from the start, devotedly commented on: "The point of the German sword stabs deeply into Poland's heart." Meanwhile, it is emphasized that only "military targets" are at stake: "deployment routes, train lines, air fields, supply columns." The subsequent sequences illustrate this with aerial shots from a bird's eye view that alternate with oblique shots of planes next to each other: "Attention, deployment route! Clear the way!" Or: "Rail junction," "Ready. Go!" Hits are initially shown only from a bird's eye view and described: "In a storm of steel the concentrated force of German air power is unleashed. [. . .] Mission accomplished." Gradually the configuration begins to expand to animated map images or ground views of the air squadrons: "We are in enemy territory. We want to find out for once what an air attack looks like from the ground." Underscored with solemn music, accompanied by pithy sayings, a panorama of destruction is shown from the perspective of the ground. Then once more faux-Wagnerian music and sayings like "And now onward to wrack and ruin!"—"Bombs are raining from the heavens. A hail of steel."—Sequence after sequence of downright industrial-strength destruction: fly, drop, load, fly, drop. Now the field is expanded once again and civil damages are accounted for indirectly: "Through the devastated streets the wind carries fire from house to house."—Close-ups of burning facades, smoldering rubble, silhouettes of ruins. Smoke clouds. Again and again copious panning shots of the rubble. Of the images of burning houses, it is now said explicitly: "large cities and villages burned in battle or retreat. And of the houses, only the chimneys are still standing, like tombstones on a field of graves." The air attack on Warsaw forms the climax: "The drama of a city comes to an end. In the early morning, the bombardment begins." The image of the theater of war now transforms itself metaphorically as well. The scene becomes a spectacle of a divine tribunal, the spectators gaze down on the stage from the loges of the gods: "After a few hours, a cloud of smoke drifts over the sea of houses like a gray-black curtain." Extended aerial shots of the burning city are explained by the "reason" for the bombing, that is, the "crime" that the open city had been turned into a fortress. Further flight with lofty, solemn music. Interchanging plumes of smoke and clouds, burning ground, Luftwaffe, ground, Luftwaffe, in constant alternation. In the pathos of sublime nature: "The sun stands glaringly on the white cumulus clouds, which, raised high by the burning heat to steep towers, loom like a gigantic mountain range. Below lies hell." The capitulation is illustrated through long ground shots panning over the destruction and images from a flight over the city: "Herr Chamberlain should accompany us on this flight." Further images of the destruction from the aerial view underscored with solemn music: Clouds of smoke, rubble, ruins. For seven entire minutes. In order, subsequently, to announce the continuation of the war as tribunal against England as well: "This is how it goes when the German Luftwaffe strikes. It also knows how to hit the guiltiest of the guilty as well." The film appears totally geared to the Luftwaffe, if need be in cooperation with the army. It is the violence of machinery that is staged here, an industrial annihilation complex. Hitler appears only briefly and hardly central in the inspection of the victory parade. In any event, Herman Göring, as the one responsible for the Luftwaffe, is allowed to look into the camera at the end and vaunt the Luftwaffe's heroic deeds, "which will be forever immortal." And announce that this Luftwaffe will also "meet, defeat and annihilate the enemy" in England and France. Thereupon, renewed ascent and flight, accompanied by the song: "Bomben auf Engelland" (Bombs over Angel-land).

This filmic crescendo of a first total destruction, amplified further through a lofty soundtrack, through an overly conspicuous backdrop of noise—of howling engines, MG-salvos, and soldier songs—had a thoroughly ambivalent effect. For instance, Joseph Goebbels noted on April 6, 1940: "The film comes across grandiose, but in its overreaching realism, somewhat grueling. In the end, a corresponding mood."[9] The mood, the SD (Security Service) report agreed, was markedly depressed in the female audience in particular.[10]

Hans Bertram delivered here the most expansive documentary depiction of the air war and its effects. Subsequent depictions would keep more to the proven model of the newsreels, paying closer attention to changes in tempo and phases of calm. With his very next feature film on the Poland campaign, *Kampfgeschwader Lützow* (Battle Squadron Lützow), Hans Bertram himself delivered a version that desisted from being massively overwhelming and was decelerated to a certain extent. The plot—the rivalry of two buddy pilots over one woman—connects directly to the fighter pilot movie, *D III 88,* which he directed. And he drew his documentary material mainly from *Feuertaufe*. However, in this film, closer attention is paid to dialogue and humorous scenes to counterbalance the battle scenes. The propagandistic argumentation that the "Polish Campaign" dealt solely with the protection of the German people and the attack of military objectives is placed solely in the center.

Right from the beginning the martial continuity is emphasized, when Colonel Mithoff, who is taking over Battle Squadron Lützow, remarks on his career: "World War, the Baltic, a bit of China, Spain and now Poland," all illustrated by an air attack on a Polish airfield or a dogfight with anti-quated biplanes. However, that the Luftwaffe is here to protect "ethnic Germans," is expounded upon in particular. During the return flight two protagonists see how a group of ethnic Germans is being pursued and mishandled by Polish soldiers. "Here you intervene immediately and promise: 'In two days German troops will be here.'"

Another significant sequence shows four pilots, who, having made emergency landings, are trying to get back to a rail line. In the immediate vicinity a Stuka is flying a bombing mission over a bridge: "My good men. From below, the matter certainly can have a dark side!" What in *Feuertaufe*, through the intensity of the destruction's images, had led to the discomfort of the audience is here addressed and deflected through cheekiness.

For the French Campaign there is a pair of similar films, the documentary propaganda film *Sieg im Westen* and the propagandistic feature film *Stukas*. Since Sven Noldan's symbolically pregnant *Sieg im Westen,*[11] shown first on January 31, 1941, sets the Panzer attack as its center piece, the appearances of the Luftwaffe were reduced. Aside from this, however, the film has a different rhythm, because it begins with a particularly strong exposition of ideological justification. In addition, the insertion of didactic animated maps interrupts the flow again and again. For our context, two sequences are of main significance. The first is noteworthy through omission. Rotterdam appears through a map but not one word is wasted regarding the city's bombardment.

The second scene touches on a theme that has weighed heavily on the German Wehrmacht since the First World War, namely, the accusation of cultural barbarism, the destruction of hallowed cultural sites. Here too there is an immediate provocation: On November 14, 1940, during an air attack on the industrial city Coventry and its tightly integrated living and manufacturing areas, the medieval cathedral St. Michaels was also destroyed. Thus the counterargument now appears here propagandistically: Amidst organ music German soldiers reverently enter a cathedral. A German soldier devoutly plays the organ there. And images of Rouen are explained in the following manner: "The exertions of German soldiers are successful in saving the magnificent cathedral from destruction." Of particular symbolic power in this regard is a scene from *Wunschkonzert*, which premiered on December 30, 1940. In it a musically gifted soldier, who had been left behind, plays Bach's Toccata in D minor on a church organ, indicating the way back to his comrades who are lost in a minefield. Meanwhile the French do not shy from reducing the church to rubble. The musically gifted soldier dies, sacrificing himself for his comrades, but not without leaving behind a song as his legacy for the Wunschkonzert: "Gute Nacht, Mutter."

The feature film on the Western Campaign connects again to the overpowering dramaturgy of *Feuertaufe*. *Stukas*, by Karl Ritter, the most stalwart of Nazi directors, premiered on July 27, 1941, five days after the invasion of the Soviet Union began. In varying a single basic model, he almost completely abandons any conventional dramatic plot. Framed by opening and closing credits, the planes take off as the alarm sounds, close formation, intercut with the pilots in close-up, the Stukas tilt down, from their perspective the viewer sees the present target, until the plane climbs again. The detonation follows—usually from a ground perspective. Variations offer images of bombs being released from their racks or falling to the ground.[12] Only the targets change: port facilities and ships at Dunkirk, French positions, a rail bridge, tank formations, fleeing ground troops—in the meantime enemy planes, again and again. Thus the film presents itself as an experience of audiovisual intoxication with suggestively intensified repetition. Furthermore, here as in no other film, German casualties are shown. In sequence after sequence more and more comrades are lost—through crash landings, injury, and death. As with a running gag of the film—the cook always places an especially tasty delicacy in view right before the alarm is sounded—the comrades thus return, in person or in memory. At times lofty, while quoting Hölderlin's *Tod fürs Vaterland*: "Like young gods, one keeps them always in memory." At times intimate: "Children, you were away a long time. Now you are finally home again." Especially penetrating is the protracted sequence in which a hero who has become depressive is reanimated by a nurse with the aid of Wagner's music in Bayreuth. He is then conveyed to his squadron, choreographically reforming itself to the strains of Wagner, and flies with them against "Angel-land" at the end.

The Mood in Berlin

After the twenty-third alarm we climb together out of the cellar. This night the shooting was heavier than normal. "They are rehearsing," says Frank, indicating the red glow that colors the western sky. We go to him by the window. In the distance we hear the sirens of fire trucks. "I will obliterate their cities," Hitler had threatened, and began a month ago with Coventry. You call the total annihilation of a city "Coventri-fy." Bragging about coining the word and forgetting how brutally it can return against us one day. "They are rehearsing," says Frank once again. And like a shudder his words strike our hearts.

This is from Andreas-Friedrich on December 16, 1940.[13] Her premonitions were not unwarranted. Yet while the air attacks and their effects continually intensified, people went about business as usual in Berlin. Yes, one even played with the bombardments in the relevant propaganda. In January 1941, *Signal*, the Wehrmacht's legendary illustrated magazine intended for foreign audiences, presented photos of houses in ruins and asked in three varied headings whether British bombs had hit here. Three times "no" and on the following page the riddle's solution—in the move to remodel Berlin into Germania the house of German Tourism is being built: "With undiminished energy work continues on the new shape of the Reich's capital in spite of the war."[14]

However, foreign correspondents increasingly noted a mood reversal. Thus Howard K. Smith recorded how with the war against the Soviet Union—and with the British bombs over Berlin—the habits of Berliners change. If before they were enthusiastic consumers of the newsreels, they are now weary of them, as well as propaganda films like *Kampfgeschwader Lützow* oder *Stukas*, and instead prefer "second-rate" comedies like *Der Gasmann*, starring Heinz Rühmann.[15] While newsreels and war films continued to present the rubble of others, there was still no rubble to been seen in the contemporary films about Berlin.

Georg Zoch's comedy, *Der dunkle Punkt*, (The Dark Point) first shown on October 26, 1940, takes place in a Berlin boarding house in 1939 during the first months of the war. Here, downplayed humorously, one learns of ration cards and coal scarcity, that private taxi rides are forbidden, and one experiences an intact sightseer's Berlin from a cozy horse-drawn coach, a perspective similar to the one Volker von Collande presented in his 1941 *Zwei in einer großen Stadt*. An unruly tenant is teasingly threatened with the concentration camp and the air-raid alarm is referred to merely as a "test alarm" to which people drum on sinks and bathtubs. The cellar corridor appears as burlesque chaos. The caretaker has confused the alarm date; the new "block supervisor" warns: "If it happens one more time I will have to report you."

Rolf Hansen's *Die große Liebe*, which premiered June 12, 1942, was one of the greatest film successes of those years. Goebbels praised it specifically because it succeeded "in incorporating a personal plot into the great events of the war, and truly with great aptitude."[16] There is an air-raid alarm here as well. The film takes place in the time between March and July, 1941, and ends with the incursion into the Soviet Union. The alarm is now serious. Air warnings on the radio—"Radio Germany interrupts its program for the time being"—sink beneath the party racket. In front of the house people are surprised by the howling sirens. And so it comes to pass that the celebrated *Scala*-Star Hanna Holberg (Zarah Leander) and the ace pilot Paul Wendlandt (Rolf Hansen) get to have their one-night stand, and thereafter, through constant separation, their Great Love arises.[17]

> *Him:* "Now you have to take me with you into the cellar."
> *Her:* "Into the cellar with all the appalling people."

Quarreling household figures appear. A father holds a family roll call, some house residents promise themselves a cozy little chat in the air-raid shelter. Since Wendtlandt isn't allowed to take his little mascot, a young dog, into the shelter—"strict regulations"—they bring him into her apartment.

> *Her*: "So. And now turn the light off."
> *Him*: "Gladly. Why?"
> *Her*: "Because I want to open the window. Say, are you sure you aren't really from the moon?"
> *Him:* "Nah, not quite. But close."

A gaze out on the darkened city. On the horizon, the *Siegessäule* is discernible.

> *Him*: "Gosh! Beautiful, isn't it?"
> *Her*: "Like in a fairy tale."
> *Him*: "No. Much better: Like in reality."
> *Her*: "Well, that's why we need to go down in the cellar. Because in reality there's flak."
> *Him*: "And in spite of that, reality is beautiful. Even when there's danger. Maybe because there's danger."

In the cellar now, where he is devotedly playing Parchese with her and a small boy, there is real coffee: "are we a people's community (*Volksgemeinschaft*) now or what?" And the notorious grumbler—with hat, bowtie, little beard, rimless glasses, and a hooked nose, sketched as an unfeeling intellectual—is unmasked.

There is only danger for the pilot, whom she visits at the end in a mountain military hospital, from where both gaze trustingly at a formation of planes. In the homeland, which profits romantically from the blackouts, it is however not the bombs that are threatening, but merely flak shrapnel. A more realistic discussion of the bombing war's consequences will begin only in 1943, namely, in educational films.[18]

Desecration of Culture

On March 2, 1943 Andreas-Friedrich notes a

> massive attack on Berlin, the likes of which had not been seen until now. It is said that 160,000 people are homeless. The city is burning, as are all western and southern suburbs. The smoky air is sulfur-yellow. Hounded people stumble through the streets. With bundles, suitcases and housewares. Can't comprehend that someone has played them so foul—them of all people. From cause to effect is a long way. Only very few know how to go it. Hardly anyone understands that the consequence of today can be the provocation of yesterday. The provocation of Coventry, the provocation of Dunkirk, the provocation of Jewish atrocities, obliterating cities and concentration camps. The broom that sweeps Germany pure of the Jews, doesn't want to return to the corner. And the spirits that were conjured will not go away now.[19]

The ruins can no longer be overlooked. The allied air attacks come by day the same as by night. On Christmas of the same year Albert Speer's publicist and coworker, Gert H. Theunissen, announced that the "modern cities" should be rebuilt more broad-mindedly: "Certainly never before have the requirements for accomplishing the construction tasks been more favorable as they are in Germany today."[20]

At the same time, Goebbels commissioned a feature film about the destruction of Lübeck by British air attack on March 19, 1942, after having forbidden in October 1942 that "the old beautiful Lübeck be compared to today's demolished Lübeck," since the audience might be too deeply shaken.[21] First shown in Lübeck on July 6, 1944, *Die Degenhardts* was shot by Werner Klinger under the guidance of Ewald von Demandowsky, head of production at *Tobis,* who Goebbels, regardless of all Party factionalism, attested to being the "real Nazi" among the heads of production and the one who also "takes on political matters." Goebbels was satisfied with the result: "For the first time the theme of the air war is addressed here, and does so truthfully and in a very tactful and psychologically intelligent fashion."[22]

This film is completely tailored to the theme of cultural barbarism. The destruction of the Lübecker cathedral stands center stage—and once more the musically gifted German is among the protagonists. In this case it is the loyal civil servant Degenhardt, played by Heinrich George, and his music-making, deeply introspective family. The sixty-fifth birthday of the patriarch on August 28, 1939—symbolic of the day on which 25 years earlier he received his "baptism of fire" in the Battle of Tannenberg—gives cause for an extended walk through the city, in order to demonstrate the medieval beauty of Lübeck. Picturesque corners, magnificent renaissance gables, the silhouette of the city from the river. Highlights are the church, the painting of the Dance of Death, and "one of the most beautiful organs." The son explains that it is 420 years old and Buxtehude played on it. Meaningful pause: "His pupil, Johann Sebastian Bach, was among the listeners." War has broken out. In the cathedral, civilians and military personnel listen to Haydns *Schöpfung* together. The camera pans over the organ and the Dance of the Death. Crossfade: flames and the burning rafters. Ruins. Voice-over: "1941 [sic!]. The Wehrmacht report announces. During the night of March 28–29 enemy planes dropped numerous explosive and incendiary bombs over a city on the coast of Northern Germany. Above all they decimated artistically prized structures, old churches and other cultural monuments." One sees streams of people moving past empty façades and rubble. In the cathedral, rubble everywhere. The organ is destroyed. A gaze upward through a gaping hole in the roof – into the heavens. The neatly arranged and Hollywood-esque hole in the church roof in *Mrs. Miniver*, a film that Goebbels had recommended to directors as the paradigm for perfect propaganda, attains here its forceful German replica. Through the destruction of their holiest cultural assets, the dispatch asserts, the Germans are bombed by the allies into a properly cohesive community. Thus, per crossfade, Father Degenhardt summons to visual memory all his children who are in military service: "But in our hearts they are all gathered. [...] And even if one of them takes leave from us forever, it is so ordained that another always grows in his place. And so should it be just this way in a great family. And so should it be even more in the greater family to which we belong."

By now one can discern a two-track strategy in film's propagandistic handling of the bombing war: On the "documentary" side, there is a narrative of a technical sportive enterprise, which, in the visually copious savoring of rubble production, is by no means portrayed only as a clinically precise action.[23] On the feature film side, there is the inversion of the charge of the culturally barbaric "Air Terror." While *Die Degenhardts* was playing in the Reich in 150 locations, in *Signal*, the reporter Benno Wundshammer described returning from the front to Berlin and how he saw there only "soot-blackened [...] ruins" instead of the previous brilliance: "It's as if you saw the scars of extreme suffering on the countenance of a loved one." After an emotional portrayal of painful losses, he asks: "What is to be made of this violent destruction of the middle class, this dispossession through bombs and craters? Won't it bring even the ponderous stratum of our people into motion and compel, with force, the last people into the community?"[24]

Alfred Weidenmann's *Junge Adler*, first presented on May 24, 1944, appeals to this community spirit of the young. Apprentices at an airplane factory are gradually welded together into a community, independent of social origin, bodily strengths, or musical aptitude. From a group camp on the Baltic Sea they are in the end hurriedly brought back. Their workshop has not been hit by bombs, rather "there have been fires in the workplace." Later the talk is once more of the "fire that had hit our works." The boys are now working at night too: "Our machines are needed." United with the others they—sons of a cultured people—listen to a concert on the factory floor, which delivers serious music as well as the composition of one their own.

According to the propaganda's argumentation, the community, where it doesn't already exist, is bombed into existence by the Allies. However, according to relevant evidence this communal unity was in no way so united. Rather the "Volk" was held together—with all the inner frictions between privilege, denunciation, plundering, and exclusion of "foreign workers"—by fear of the end and all its consequences. Until the very end Goebbels had film after film produced for the Volk. Their spectrum was strange indeed.

Nothing Works Anymore—Life Goes On

Berlin. Saturday, February 3, 1945

> Heavy daylight raid on Berlin. The city is appallingly battered. Through smoke, soot and cinders, I fight my way to the publishing house. It rains in torrents. The damp strikes the smoke to the ground, which sticks to your soles like hardened porridge. The hiking is laborious. [...] In the editorial office the walls are lying on the desks, the windows on the ground.[25]

While the editorial office of Andreas-Friedrich's newspaper closes, the Babelsberger Studios go on producing. Even Helmut Käutner's *Unter den Brücken* is released—of course, due to the destruction in Babelsberg, it doesn't manage to be shown until the 1946 Locarno Film Festival. A noteworthy bit of film history. A film that so studiously dissimulates the conditions of film production in the last year of the war, near and in the almost totally destroyed city, so that these conditions begin to shine through again as if on a palimpsest. The actual and symbolic center of the plot is the Glienecker bridge, of which exterior shots could still be made during the day. However, the night shots had to be produced in the studio, since a film crew would have become a bomb target because of the lighting. Indeed it begins and leads always to the river landscape of Havel and Spree, to the Landwehr canal or Osthafen, but the more distant view is usually only very brief, immediately brought back to a nearness that is constricting outdoors as well. In addition, the film is limited to mostly dark and gloomy perspectives with only a few sharply lit contours. Suddenly appearing from out of the image: "Here, Berlin!"— Berlin is a rapid sequence of pictures underscored with swing music: the Rummelsberg power plant, the Oberbaum Bridge, Osthafen, the Shell House, the cathedral—signals from an earlier time. There is only very rarely an open, wide horizon. The camera is constantly kept deep in the waterway. Window views are largely obstructed, for example, half filled with a nearby firewall, on which—again significantly—an advertisement for cigarettes, "Juno 3 1/2, plump and round," and next to it a gaze over the city in cutaway—two factory smoke stacks are recognizable. The tight crossfades of port facilities, cranes, and above all the continually alternating bridges do indeed suggest an intact infrastructure. Paddling couples suggest normality. But the city, almost systematically cut out above the line of the riverbank, and the continual underside views of bridges, which additionally reduce the line of sight, communicate more of a bunker atmosphere, the anxiety of an underground existence. It is not without its paradoxes: Where the one film wages every effort to make widespread demolished reality disappear in the exterior shots, the other film aims to simulate the destruction as grandiosely as possible in the studio: The film meant here is Wolfgang Liebeneiner's *Das Leben geht weiter.*

In late summer 1944, *Signal's* international readers find a picture, among others, of two young women striding along elatedly in front of some ruins. The accompanying caption: "Out of the ruins, a new type of person has emerged, who, again reliant on personal strengths, leaves behind everything burdensome and restrictive about conventions of the past. Indestructible, life goes one."[26] That takes up the slogan that Joseph Goebbels had released in 1944: "In the ruins and remains of our bombarded cities, life goes on. It no longer relies on such richly drawn fullness as before. But we stand fast on our feet and never show the slightest inclination of bowing down."[27]

Meanwhile, the newsreels seldom show airplanes anymore, and even more rarely aerial views. On December 21, 1944, there is a sequence that in no way provides an index of the actual situation: "German fighters over the fronts! They are attacking ground targets!" In exchange, allied bomber squadrons are shown from below. "Aerial combat with low-flying enemy planes"—"Sheaves of fire mow through the skies." Burning enemy plane crashes. "An American breaks apart." Almost always it is the air defense that is shown. Until finally, on January 18, 1945, "the first shots of the V2" are shown—for "reasons of secrecy," the camera is far away. Two launches and vapor trails, accompanied by Wagner's *Ride of the Valkyries*. After one-legged skiing and an accelerated course on blowing up tanks, the highlight of January 25, 1945 is a long bunker sequence: field kitchen, administration—everything underground.

At the same time the film that Goebbels had conceived of as fitting his slogan "life goes on" is produced: "I would like for it to depict Berlin during a night of bombardment in a house in the Hansa quarter. The entire house in its individual stories and families should be involved." This from March 30, 1944. "I believe," he then tries to convince himself on July 13, 1944, "one could make a striking film about the nights of bombardment in Berlin from this scenario."[28] Because revising the script according to the constantly changing wishes of Goebbels took longer than predicted, it was first presented in October 1944. Goebbels apparently coproduced this film and intervened in the script even more than normal.[29]

On the Berlin Hansaplatz all residents of a six-family house celebrate the birthday of Gundel Martens, mother of two and S-Bahn employee, with Bundt cake, candle light, and the Fox Trot. Her husband Ewald works as an engineer on a frequency direction finder, with whose help the German night fighter pilots could reconquer the majesty of the skies. Her friend Leonore falls in love with the night fighter officer Walter, who is underway on a secret mission. Among others belonging to the household is Winkler, the obligatory weakling-opportunist, who spreads the rumor that, on September 16, 1943, there will be a massive attack on Berlin. This naturally doesn't occur.

However, the actual heavy air raids of 1943, between November 18 and 22, are meant to be the special subject of the film. Thus, for Gundel Martens' provisional tombstone, the script provided the date November 22, 1943.[30] She, who as S-Bahn employee had so selflessly rescued others from a bombed train station, can no longer be helped out from beneath the rubble of an air-raid cellar. Pilot Walter wants to console the husband: "Helping one another in these times, not abandoning each other, that is certainly just as important as the battle, because life can not come to an end." Afterward follows one of the versions of the film's conclusion.

> While the image slowly fades out, one sees the silhouette of the night-time city as it was earlier under attack. Spotlights circle, some cross. One hears the droning of planes. More and more spotlights cross one another. The droning gets louder and louder, it sounds like bells ringing, then actual bells

do begin to sound. Simultaneously all spotlights from all sides unite into a vault of spotlights, which we know from our celebrations of peace. The sound of bells becomes powerful festive music. With its final notes the image also fades out, and the word END appears.[31]

The search lights of the air defense had always evoked the cathedral-of-light effect from the pre-war era.[32] Now the flak spotlights should unite as a cathedral of light and thus blur war and peace together. But this end with the cathedral of light was not the only one planned for the film. In the draft that came from the Ministry of Propaganda,[33] the film seems to have been constructed as a mixture of *Kolberg*, the earthquake film *San Francisco*, and *Wunschkonzert*. The conclusion suggested by the Ministry, which works like a Berlin variation of *Kolberg*, suggests that perhaps the film is less intended to secure belief in "final victory," as to pass down the ostensible perseverance heroism to future generations. In doing so, the challenges to persevere were sufficient. Leonore, who waits so stalwartly for her night fighter Walter, is supposed to say to Ewald Martens: "We've gotten involved in something, Ewald, that is so monstrously huge, that is about life and death, and too much blood has been spilled already so that no one could still say, it was just for fun, now I don't want to play anymore...and could you respect a man who thought that way?" The tireless cancer researcher Professor Hübner explains war as the same as a natural catastrophe: "And war is just a natural catastrophe, like an earthquake, because you don't know WHY it happens. The only thing that matters is that we need not be ashamed afterwards when we look in a mirror."[34]

From the following finale, the authors from the Ministry of Propaganda apparently hoped that it would later allow them to be able to look in the mirror without shame:

In the rubble life begins again. Berlin pits itself against the terror. (as much documentary material as possible.) [...] We see the scorched street cars, high voltage wires hang onto the pavement, a collapsed overpass with tracks, a city rail station that's been hit. There is no traffic. From this train station, a little column of people begins to march, heading toward their workplace. Against the airborne ash and soot, most have put on glasses, kerchiefs or even gasmasks. Here and there someone is still wearing an army-issue helmet. [...] The column empties into a main street. It has become continually larger, broader, and longer. A choir sounds hymn-like, similar to in "San Fransisco." [...] The head of the column appears over an incline. Camera shoots from below. The people do not sing. Their step is not in sync. But the powerful choir still roars over them. [...] Endlessly the column flows. Because life goes on.[35]

Measured against this *Kolberg* reminiscence, Wolfgang Liebeneiner's version was marked by downright intimate melancholy:

> 534: Total:
> The iron cemetery gate. Behind it a long lane of poplars.
> Leonore and Ewald approach. Ewald opens the gate, lets Leonore out, exits himself, closes the gate, then remains standing and looks for a long time at the cemetery.
> Slowly Leonore walks on and waits for Ewald at some distance. The latter turns and leaves—the camera zooms on the gate—so that only the long poplar lane remains in the picture, down which Leonore and Ewald walk.
> Fade out!
> END![36]

It is noteworthy that the film, in so late a stage, used as its theme the bombing war in its various aspects—from the evacuation to death in the ruins. People no longer speak nebulously of a fire, as in *Junge Adler*; rather, even the laboratory, in which Ewald Martens mans his miraculous direction finder, receives a direct hit.[37] However, it is somewhat grotesque that the film draft called for a multitude of locations, which even in peace time would have posed a great challenge. Also grotesque is that the late 1943 destruction of the city through air raids had to be replicated and pyrotechnically staged only a year later in the Babelsberger Studio because in the meantime Berlin had been completely reduced to ruins.[38]

The simulation of bombs dropping is said to have been especially effective—Heinz Pehlke, assistant cameraman at the time, remembers that they wanted to show bombs falling from the bomb bays by hanging mock-ups from the studio ceiling, and moving through them from below with the camera, so that the illusion of bombs falling around you was produced.[39]

The sequence in which Gundel Martens should show her superhuman valor was a highpoint of drastic events, in that she saved a small child near the corpse of his dead mother, while all around them the S-Bahn station was being demolished by a hail of bombs, and shrapnel was whistling by. Karl Ritter's corresponding storyboard has been preserved[40] At the end of the sequence the uprooted rails, fallen telegraph poles, and roof beams twist into a decorative ornamentation of total destruction.

Of course the topos of the romantic night is not missing here: Gundel: "How beautiful the night is." Ewald: "Mm-hmm, you know, in peace time you couldn't even see it with all the lights on the street." Gundel: "Yes, truly! And it was so loud here with all the cars." Statement: "At this moment a siren on the adjacent roof begins to howl."[41] And the evocation of community is certainly not forgotten. Hübner: "I had no idea that so many people live in our house." Leonore: "Because you never go in the air-raid cellar. Until the war I didn't know it either, but now that we have trembled together so often we have formed bonds." Pilot ace Walter: "If we stick together, then we'll be stronger than anything, but only then."[42]

Originally the deadline had been planned for February 1945. At this point in time the studio was relocated from Babelsberg to an airbase near Lüneberg; an end of shooting was not yet in view. Accommodated in a nearby village, shooting proceeded until the English took Lüneburg on April 18, 1945. Approximately two-thirds of the planned project were shot then. The unedited material was stored in Bardowick Cathedral. What happened with it is unexplained. The UFA Film No. 205 remains missing till today. In the transcripts, two witnesses stated that they had fooled about with the film material and that, in the process, a large part of it burned.

In the subsequent rubble films, children had to symbolize the promise of a new beginning again and again. Here, in the reality of those days, children, in whose play life went on, would have thus seen to it that the continuity of the rubble films was interrupted by protecting the real postwar backdrop of rubble from its demon, the staged rubble of the war's end within which the war should find no end.

Notes

Translated by Todd Cesaratto

1. Erich Paetzmann, "Neuer Film auf alten Wegen," *Westdeutsche Allgemeine Zeitung* (October 14, 1948). Quoting Ursula Bessen, *Trümmer und Träume. Nachkriegszeit und fünfziger Jahre auf Zelluloid* (Bochum: Studienverl. Brockmeyer, 1989), p.98.
2. Gunter Groll, "Deutscher Nachkriegsfilm—Klamauk oder Welträtsel," *Neue Zeitung* (September 27, 1950).
3. Ruth Andreas-Friedrich, *Schauplatz Berlin. Tagebuchaufzeichnungen 1945–1948* (1962; reprint Frankfurt am Main: Suhrkamp, 1985), p.88.
4. *Der Spiegel* 24 (June 14, 1947). Quoting Bessen, *Trümmer und Träume*, p.145.
5. See Oliver Lubrich, ed., *Reisen ins Reich 1933 bis 1945. Ausländische Autoren berichten aus Deutschland* (Frankfurt am Main, 2004). Also see Erhard Schütz, "Ersatzwelt mit Ameisen. Berlin unter Bomben. Literarisch-journalistische Deutungsmuster 1940 bis 1945," in *Zeitschrift für Germanistik*, N.F., 15 (2005), 2: 352–376.
6. Ruth Andreas-Friedrich, *Der Schattenmann. Tagebuchaufzeichnungen 1938–1945*. Mit einem Nachwort von Jörg Drews (Frankfurt am Main: Suhrkamp, 1986).
7. Ibid., pp.62,74.

24 / ERHARD SCHÜTZ

8. Manuel Köppen, *Das Entsetzen des Beobachters. Krieg und Medien im 19. und 20. Jahrhundert* (Heidelberg: Universitätsverlag Winter, 2005), p.330.
9. Felix Moeller, *Der Filmminister. Goebbels und der Film im Dritten Reich.* Mit einem Vorwort von Volker Schlöndorff (Berlin: Henschel, 1998), p.235.
10. Ibid., p.234. See also Klaus Kreimeier, *Die Ufa-Story. Geschichte eines Filmkonzerns* (München, Wien: Hanser, 1992), p.362.
11. Produced by Fritz Hippler, directed by Sven Noldan and Fritz Brunsch.
12. See Köppen, *Das Entsetzen*, p.323.
13 Andreas-Friedrich, *Schauplatz Berlin*, p.74.
14. "So sieht Berlin aus...!," *Signal* 2.2 (January 1941): 27.
15. Howard K. Smith, *Last Train from Berlin* (London: Cresset Press, 1943), p.157.
16. Quoted in Moeller, *Der Filmminister*, p.266.
17. See Eric Rentschler, *The Ministry of Illusion. Nazi Cinema and Its Afterlife* (Cambridge, MA: Harvard University Press, 1996), p.140.
18. Such as *Brandbomben und Entstehungsbrände* (1943), *Erst löschen, dann retten* (1944) and *So wird's gemacht* (1944). See also Kay Hoffmann, "Mobilisierung der Heimatfront," in *Geschichte des dokumentarischen Films in Deutschland*, 3 vols., ed. Peter Zimmermann (Stuttgart: Reclam, 2005), 3: 634–644, 639.
19. Andreas-Friedrich, *Schauplatz Berlin*, p.103.
20. Gert H. Theunissen, "Die zerstörten Städte und ihr Wiederaufbau," *Kölnische Zeitung* 64.65 (Reichsausgabe, December 25–26, 1943): 3.
21. Quoted in Moeller, *Der Filmminister*, p.288.
22. Ibid., pp.143, 288.
23. This contra the thesis of Gerhard Paul, *Bilder des Krieges. Krieg der Bilder. Die Visualisierung des modernen Krieges* (Paderborn: Schöningh [u.a.], 2004), pp.234, 238.
24. Benno Wundshammer, "Unter dem stählernen Teppich," *Signal* 5.15 (August 1944): 18, 18 n., 19.
25. Andreas-Friedrich, *Der Schattenmann*, p.195.
26. Walter Kiaulehn, "Von den Grenzen des Erträglichen," *Signal* 5.16 (August/ September 1944): 35–37.
27. Reichsminister Joseph Goebbels, "Das Leben geht weiter," *Das Reich* (April 16, 1944): 1–2.
28. Moeller, *Der Filmminister*, p.290.
29. See Hans Christoph Blumenberg, *Das Leben geht weiter. Der letzte Film des Dritten Reichs* (Berlin: Rowohlt, 1993); as well as the DVD-documentary *Das Leben geht weiter. Der letzte Propagandafilm des Dritten Reiches* (Polar-Film, 2003). The following depiction is based on both.
30. See Blumenberg, *Das Leben geht weiter*, pp.49, 91.
31. Ibid., p.175.
32. On this compare Köppen, *Das Entsetzen des Beobachters*, p.313.
33. See Blumenberg, *Das Leben geht weiter*, p.37.
34. Quoted in ibid., pp.180, 183.
35. Quoted in ibid., p.29.
36. Quoted in ibid., p.181.
37. See ibid., p.172.

38. See ibid., pp.68, 82, 108.
39. See ibid., pp.79, 81, 87–89.
40. Ibid., pp.96–97.
41. Ibid., p.142.
42. Ibid., pp.97, 204.

CHAPTER TWO

RUBBLE WITHOUT A CAUSE: THE AIR WAR IN POSTWAR FILM

Wilfried Wilms

Trümmerfilm owes its existence to destruction and death. Oddly enough, death and destruction are by no means at its center. While most rubble films, as their backdrop, feature the ruins of destroyed cities, civilian death, and hopelessness, and zoom in for brief moments on disease and hunger as the necessary consequences of erasing urban civilian habitation on an unprecedented scale, the films mostly depict a new humanism coming from the shared experience of living in the rubble. In other words, we are hard-pressed to find even the beginnings of an extensive reflection on what caused the rubble, namely, the area bombing of German urban centers and their noncombatant inhabitants. The films give little account of how Germans processed, or perhaps even debated their experiences, of how a "coming to terms with" what caused this radical transformation of Germany's cities to ruins took place—no evidence of conversation in local pubs, for example, or discussion in the privacy of their "Behelfsheime" (makeshift homes) or "Kellerwohnungen" (generally a euphemism for a cave-like space in the ruins), on a market place, or anywhere else.[1] Rubble films contribute little to the public memory of these harrowing events. Yet not all was quiet on the Western front of the soon emerging Cold War. While silence was the standard response to the bombing war, it was not the only one. It is the intention of this essay to pursue some of the traces of the air war in two rubble films, ... *und über uns der Himmel* (1947) and *Der Ruf* (1949)—both directed by Hungarian filmmaker Josef von Baky.[2]

To explain this overall discursive paucity, we typically escape into the psychological provinces of taboo and repression that often mystify as much as they enlighten. The tendency is to assume that the Germans remained silent out of shame or guilt, out of some sense of complicity that, in turn, they were unable to confront, maybe due to a psychological (and national) inability to mourn the death of all victims, including neighbors as well as those of the camps. I think the explanation is much simpler. Critiquing or commenting on the bombing war proved to be a tremendous challenge—and not only for the defeated Germans, who, in some ways, had it even easier than the Allies. There was no ambivalence about German guilt. There was no question that their conduct of war, especially after 1941, had jettisoned the conventions of warfare. The punitive wisdom at the time, born out of postwar emotions, was that Germany's population had reaped what it had sown. The demand for an all-encompassing self-purification was thus the only German response considered appropriate. German resentment, when noticed, was condemned, its subjects considered politically unreliable and morally inferior. The roots of the resentment required no elaborate investigation as the German "disease" had been diagnosed already. That the German people as a whole needed to be reeducated was indeed the perceived necessity. Yet the Allies, apparently lacking pride in their accomplishment, responded with a silence of their own.[3] The bombing war over Europe and Japan was *not* the stuff for gallant tales on the silver screen. Hollywood quickly realized that and preferred to send John Wayne and his men onto the beaches of Iwo Jima or Normandy. The good war had happened there, not in the skies over densely populated cities. The end result was that, even though the consequences of the war and the bombing were visible each and every day for many years, they nevertheless fell into a dark hole with one party (the Germans) unable to make the destruction an issue of public discussion, and the other party unwilling to do so.

What we see and do not see in the majority of rubble films is possibly the product of German pride and prejudice, a prevailing attitude that all too often prevented acknowledgment of guilt and complicity from surfacing and one that swiftly dismissed culpability for the sake of a palpable self-pity that strikes us today as distasteful. Yet what we see and do not see in these films is also the result of active reeducation and reorientation in a tightly controlled and supervised, reemerging German public sphere in which Germans, intent on surviving, *and* Allies, intent on controlling, welcomed certain messages and not others. Peter Stettner's detailed study of the *Junge Film Union* in the British zone of occupation, for example, sheds light on the enormous impact of British film policy on projects pursued or even considered by recently licensed filmmakers—and that despite the fact that the British were generally perceived to be the most lenient of all occupying powers. Why risk one's professional future, not only politically but also economically, on subjects that could incur the wrath of the Allied cultural officer in charge of allotting raw stock or other material support, not to mention giving the project the initial clearance?[4] Given the material and political constraints of the time, does it make sense to look at rubble films solely as a reflection of the deficiencies of the German mentality?

An anecdote by the Swedish author Stig Dagerman might help us understand the dilemma Germans faced during that peculiar early phase of democratization for which, soon enough, they would discover the word *Demokratur*.[5] In the fall of 1946, Dagerman traveled through Germany for the newspaper *Expressen*, talking extensively with its shell-shocked survivors, all the while deliberately avoiding the moral admonitions dispensed by the Allied journalists who were his colleagues. In fact, Dagerman was quite skeptical of what he felt were their dubious practices and was intent, despite advice to the contrary, on seeing the people and their attitudes for himself.[6] "A French journalist of high repute begged me with the best of intentions and for the sake of objectivity" he writes "to read German newspapers instead of looking at German dwellings or sniffing in German cooking-pots." Nevertheless, Dagerman did look and sniff, and what he sensed was a "mood of bitterness towards the Allies" everywhere he went.[7] An incident in Hamburg is of especial interest in our context. Here he observes a crowd reacting with apathy and cynicism as they gather to read placards announcing the executions in Nuremberg and the first free elections. "No one said a word. People read, and passed on. [...] True enough [...] in Hamburg during the night someone had painted '*Shame Nürnberg*' in huge letters; and in an underground station in front of a poster showing a bombing raid a man grasped my arm and hissed: 'Those who did that won't be condemned.'"[8] We must ask whether it is telling that this happened in an "underground station," that it took place out of sight of the Allied observers of postwar German mentalities who, as Dagerman reports with specific reference to an Allied journalist, preferred not to mix too much with the impoverished locals and instead wrote up reports on the ideological state of mind of "the" Germans in the warm hotel over a glass of good German beer. We could also wonder whether it matters that the expressed contempt for the military tribunal in this democratizing new Germany found release "during the night." To be sure, Dagerman points out that this was the exception, reporting that, for the most part, "the" Germans have fallen silent, a contention that competes with what Karl Jaspers found to be the deplorable "inclination to strike back" around the same time, an inclination that Jaspers identified as detrimental to the ultimately desired "self-examination" that was to lead to the "catharsis" of the German soul.[9]

When Germans did talk about the bombing war in the public realm, the issue was quickly raised to a metaphorical, even metaphysical level. A famous case in point is Hermann Claasen's picture book *Gesang im Feuerofen*.[10] Claasen's *Gesang* unites the sensation of an existential abyss and loss of language as well as agency in exemplary fashion. Claasen, born in 1899 in Cologne and a professional photographer since the late 1920s, documented the devastation of his hometown in 1947 with "rubble photography." Besides *Köln—Tragödie einer Stadt*, it was especially the illustrated book *Gesang im Feuerofen* that brought him into contact with the then mayor of Cologne, Konrad Adenauer, who subsequently supported the distribution of Claasen's book. The introduction to *Gesang*, written by Franz A. Hoyer, is carried by one central notion: the hubris of the recent past, caused by the word that became the carrier of the lie, can only be redeemed by the existential decision to return to the everlasting transcendent order of the creator. The beginning of such a homecoming to an order purified of man's hubris begins with a sober glance at the reality of Cologne's ruins. Hoyer stresses repeatedly that the written word is incapable of bringing about the *Entscheidung* (decision) necessary for any further life in these ruins. The written word is discredited not only by the "impudence of Babel," but also by its necessary "failure" in the face of such disaster. "This book contains images," Hoyer writes, "before which language fails. [...] Language, the mirror of everything that is alive and that exists, [...] falls silent at the edge of the chasm; language lies nearly slain from its fall into the abyss; and language, used to set forth that which makes sense, remains silent before the emergence of the senseless." What the book promises is immediate access to the surrounding reality. "Whoever opens this volume and observes the photographs," the introduction begins, "will be granted entrance into a reality that can hardly be grasped more directly in an immediate encounter. What is reflected in these images is certainly not a city anymore. [...] What happened?"

This is the question that the volume sets out to answer. With his photography, Claasen attempts to depict an unmediated reality. However, while he rejects the explanatory and interpretive thrust of language in order to "face reality" and "fight the continued existence of any form of illusion," Hoyer's introduction nonetheless seeks refuge in the Christian master narrative of sin and redemption after their "fall" from grace. The Germans (who seem to represent all of humanity) can reach a "possible purification" only when they decide, in Kierkegaardian fashion, to throw themselves into the abyss, hoping that a forgiving God will accept their humble return into His kingdom. Only "hope" in God's forgiveness will allow redemption for a German population that is "on its way to return to the magnificent order of God's creation."[11] The specifics of the bombing war are not mentioned anywhere, not even the word bomb. Culpability can therefore be generalized, relegated to the realm of myth. His inventive allusions to biblical wrath depict the recent "Flood" that came over Babel (Germany) as the result of Nazi-Germany's hubris and the grandiose presumptuousness of its people. "What happened?" "The demon played a truly demonic game" with the Germans, and did so because of the Germans' nonspecified and nonlocalizable guilt. And God's agents, the British and American policy makers and aircrews, are equally absolved of any particular responsibility. In Hoyer's introduction to Claasen's collection of photographs, the principle of retribution and the rhetoric of fatalism merge into a messianic supernarrative. The very concrete cause and effect of years of area bombing, part of the reality Claasen's *Gesang* intends to capture with photographs alone, vanishes in a mythological construction that ironically verifies his own suspicion about language's feeble power. In a few introductory pages, Hoyer erases the physicality of years of bombing and the resultant mountains of ruins that once was Cologne. The book's images, largely of destroyed churches, point beyond the realities of 1945 to a Christian apocalypse and a hoped for redemption. What remains is not even a "natural" history of destruction but a supernatural one. And it is convenient for all concerned, Germans and Allies: where everybody is guilty, nobody is. Pushed into the public sphere in this spiritual or theological form, the bombing war was acceptable; it could be discussed without self-criticism, without self-pity, and perhaps as significantly, without the threat of censorship.

The enforced silence after the war, mistaken by Sebald as exclusively self-imposed, deprives us today of memories these generations have learned to keep to themselves. By examining two scenes of two very different films under the direction of Josef von Baky, I hope to show that some rubble films do provide a discursive space, however small and restrained, to "discuss" what Germans experienced and may have considered difficult to cope with, yet could not openly express without arousing suspicion. It is the difficult task of talking about the experience of death and destruction through aerial bombardment, including the enduring consequences of living in the ruins.

. . . und über uns der Himmel (1947)

On the surface, *. . . und über uns der Himmel* tells the story of two different responses to postwar Germany's misery, exemplified by Hans and Werner Richter, father and son, who return to postwar Berlin. While Hans quickly makes his peace with the necessities of the time—he becomes proficient as a black-market racketeer, all the while kindheartedly sharing his new riches with those near and dear to him—his idealistic son Werner, once he has recovered from temporary blindness from the war, denies himself the easy pleasures of the black market for the sake of integrity and fairness, the pillars of a future Germany that tosses old ballast. Ultimately, it is the son's idealism that convinces Hans to forsake profiteering, although it means a return to poverty and hardship. Together they will work for a better future; even if doing an honest day's work means hunger nonetheless, as the father claims without being contradicted by his son. While on the surface a test of character, Baky's film distinguishes itself from most other rubble films by the way it records and exposes postwar miseries of life in the rubble. The ruins here are not just the necessary backdrop for a cinema that is forced onto the street because of a destroyed cinematic infrastructure. In...*und über uns der Himmel*, the ruins demand to be explained, and want to be made sense of-but there precisely lies the difficulty, because what was there to say? An early review of the film in the *Darmstädter Echo* by Theo Mackeben underlines this. The film, Mackeben writes, "leads us in a relentlessly documentary manner to the misery of our times. If the first German film after the war was called *In Those Days*, then this one could be called *In Our Days*: black market and marketeers, rubble, hunger, poverty, work; that is the world in which Hans Richter, the returning soldier, begins his life anew." What effect will this "merciless" exposure of Germany's present conditions have on the audience? How will the audience, yearning to escape the misery outside the movie theater, read the filmic arrangement of the ruins? Mackeben sets the tone: "Young Richters reacquaintance with the destroyed Berlin is devastating. Here the camera refuses to spare the spectator and forces onto the audience's conscience the misery of this people of beggars."[12]

In their first encounter, Werner is blind. We hear that Hans Richter's son returned prematurely because he wanted to be "back home." This "home," however, has undergone a radical transformation that Werner, somewhat implausibly, has remained unaware of during his years at the front. Werner's homecoming unfolds in two installments and begins with a flashback. His blindness allows the viewer to contrast the old Berlin that Werner remembers with the new Berlin he gets to see for real. Their drive to an eye specialist provides the opportunity to recall what was lost in years of bombing. Melancholy music accompanies Hans, Edith, and Werner in the car. A close-up shows their sincere faces gazing out of the broken windshield into a broken world, and in a succession of shot/countershot the audience gets to view what they are seeing: ruins at every turn the car takes in a deserted city through which people move like ants; for a brief moment we see what seems to be an American jeep parked on the left side of the road. Edith is the first to break the silence: "The beautiful, old West" she says in dismay. Werner, though, is not paralyzed by the surrounding destruction that is invisible for him and sits motionless. Because the exterior is inaccessible to him, he looks inward. A close-up of Werner's face follows as he inquires: "Where are we now?" Edith's reply "In the Postdamer Strasse" triggers up-tempo music, which carries the audience into a lost past. The ruins are fading out, and on the screen appears prewar Berlin the way Werner recalls it: we seem to see Potsdamer Platz, Gedächtniskirche, the Brandenburg Gate, and Hotel Adler as well as the bustling street cafés on Unter den Linden. In his memories of the past, the streets are buzzing with life, dance, and community. The images provide no indication of Nazi rule, no flags, no uniforms. In fact, the Berlin Werner conjures up dates back to the years of the Weimar Republic, an odd

UND ÜBER UNS DER HIMMEL — Deutschland 1947
Regie: Josef von Baky
Quelle: Deutsche Kinemathek

and again implausible circumstance if we do the math: Werner is about 23 years old in 1945, yet he recalls the Berlin of his childhood and not the formative years of adolescence in which he in all likelihood wore a Hitler Youth uniform. When the music returns to the melancholic title melody and the camera to Hans who has his sharp (yet perhaps unimaginative) eyes set on the realities of postwar Berlin, the images capture the surrounding ruins again. Hans' gaze brings us back to the ugly present, while Werner remains lost in the past. *His* gaze will follow later, and with him we will see the familiar with, literally, new and unaccustomed eyes that, as the film suggests, can also look into a more humane future.

The scenes between Werner's arrival at the clinic and his recovery focus on the need to barter, to be less idealistic and more pragmatic to survive. A brief visit by Edith to the hospital indicates that Werner is recovering and can already see again. So far, though, he has only seen the inside of the hospital. When he finally leaves the clinic the low-angle shot of the damaged Gedächtniskirche, filmed from below and thus threatening to collapse onto the viewers, is an omen of Werner's complete return "home." He steps in front of the camera, towering over film viewers, yet has his back to the church that, in turn, threatens to collapse on top of him. He is excited, happy, and the extreme camera angle corresponds with Werner's equally distorted expectation of what he will find. "I cannot wait any longer" he says to the nurse who has stepped outside with him. And when urged to wait for his father, who promised to come with a car, Werner responds "Nonsense, nurse, I have to walk! I am finally able to see everything myself!" The next shot is already level: the music turns somber, and toward the camera walks an old woman with three small children through the rubble, pulling and pushing a cart overloaded with shabby belongings. We can make out an old mattress full of gaping holes. The next shot—and we are now following Werner's discovery of the new Berlin, again in the form of shot/countershot—shows an ocean of rubble with people digging through the ruins in hopes of finding anything useful or edible. Werner looks on sincerely, taking it all in. What we see through Werner's eyes is documentary footage. The next shot is remarkable: a one-legged, younger woman on crutches limps into the frame from behind. Werner, now in a close-up, follows her with his eyes, takes a deep breath, and seemingly gets upset. He then surveys—a pan shot—the surrounding devastation and misery while the music becomes more dramatic and threatening. We see rubble women cleaning up; the camera zooms in on an older woman working in the debris. A close-up exposes the varicose veins of her calf. Finally, with the music nearing its crescendo, a woman with several children is washing their clothes near a fountain surrounded by wreckage, followed by an old man who walks into the frame, hauling a heavy sack on his shoulders. Everybody is doing whatever necessary to survive in this wasteland. The sequence ends with another combination of scenes: on a post we see an announcement that indicates that one can receive a suit or pair of pants for a certain amount of rags. A note on an advertising column reads "Offer vegetables, need bread." The announcements all speak of the same basic needs of the average German who is trying to cope under extreme circumstances. The message is obvious: Germany's cities in 1945 are a land of rags, poverty, mutilation, and hardship, its cities populated by suffering human beings.[13] It suits the storyline that the surveyed and documented misery of the majority is immediately visually contrasted with the affluence of the few who have no scruples about exploiting the desperate conditions of their fellow human beings. Before returning home, Werner enters the bar his father frequents in hopes of finding him there. The milieu of the racketeers he discovers behind its closed doors appals him as much as the poverty outside. When Werner's father meets him, he asks his son "So, did you have a look at our old Berlin?" to which Werner coldly replies "The new one."

If the Signal Corps photography of Germany's destruction was, as Dagmar Barnouw claims, "expected to answer questions, not to pose them,"[14] the ruins in Baky's film seem to do the opposite: they raise questions, perhaps even pose a challenge to the dominant interpretation that Germany's destruction from

UND ÜBER UNS DER HIMMEL — Deutschland 1947
Regie: Josef von Baky
Quelle: Deutsche Kinemathek

the air and the present suffering of its people are deserved and the necessary consequence of their own deeds. ... *und über uns der Himmel* presents the audience with something like the photography of the defeated with all the pathos that defeat entails. The ruins dominate the individuals, loom over them like the church over Werner, constantly threatening to crush the frail life within them. Where Hans and Susanne in Staudte's *Die Mörder sind unter uns* are able to block out the ruins once they acknowledge their love for one another and join hands in work, Baky's individuals are swallowed up in an unrecognizable moonscape of debris ruled by racketeers and other lawless figures. As in Claasen's *Gesang*, there is no ascription of responsibility for the ruins that we see. Nowhere does the film suggest that what Werner sees (and what many Germans endure) is the just retribution for a war unleashed and supported by the same people we now see digging through the ruins. And the only hint of Allied involvement is the glimpse viewers catch of an American military vehicle parked in the ruins of what was once Potsdamer Strasse. The disgustingly rich profiteers without a conscience are German. The "PX-millionaires" of Billy Wilder's *A Foreign Affair* who "swap cigarettes for castles on the Rhine" and soak their feet in "sparkling Moselle" are absent, and the entire "affair" on the ground seems an exclusively German one—though we do momentarily see a black face in the bar and American rations procured by Mizzi on a kitchen table. What, then, is the German "conscience" supposed to make of the "misery of this people of beggars" that the relentless camera "forces onto the audience" (Mackeben). Is it a coincidence that women, children, and the elderly take center stage as suffering victims of the bombings? How is the audience to understand the cause of the one-legged woman's lost limb? In the narrative of the film these images belong to the very present that Werner will want to overcome with honest work. But are these scenes meant to jumpstart the audience's introspection and acceptance of guilt? A simple reference to Hans' or Werner's Nazi past would have contextualized the rubble accordingly, yet there is neither comment nor image that does so. Are these scenes, then, mere expressions of self-pity or, more likely, contempt for the perceived hypocrisy of the representatives of democracy, which—in his own satirical way—Billy Wilder had packed into *A Foreign Affair* around the same time? Do these scenes question the goodwill of the victorious Allies? The film leaves no doubt that Hans' neighbors take a liking to the blond and sexy Mizzi who begins to distribute Hershey bars to her family, and apparently pays for them with sexual favors. But what about the equally present older couple who die a slow death? Perhaps self-critical Germans would have interpreted what they saw on the movie screen as a direct result of Nazi hubris. Most, however, would have attributed the pain and suffering to the way the Allies conducted the war and subsequent occupation, which, as Dagerman's encounter in the subway tunnel recalls, was not to be criticized in daylight.

Der Ruf (1949)

What Baky's film in 1947 challenges only visually—the relative silence about rubble that seemed to have no cause—he confronts in his next film verbally. It is the only rubble film I know of that does so, even if only in its margins. *Der Ruf* (1949) is generally considered Baky's most ambitious project, yet it was also a financial debacle. The film tells the story of Mauthner (played by Fritz Kortner, who wrote the screenplay and on whom Mauthner is closely modeled), a returning professor of philosophy, who emigrated to the United States in 1933 to avoid persecution as a Jew. Successful and content in California, yet torn between his love for both the old and new home, he is suddenly called back to his former university post. Once there his hopes for a new beginning for Germany are dashed. His lecture on the "Learnability of Friendship"—a lecture whose moral tenor evokes Jaspers' university lectures on collective guilt in 1946—falls on the deaf ears of a German student body still under the influence of brown ideology and prejudice. The rejection he experiences ultimately leads to his death.

It is the subplot within the main story that is of interest here. Mauthner, we learn, used to be married to a gentile, Lina, and together they have a son, Walter, who, according to the temporally vague storyline, must have

DER RUF — BRD 1949

Regie: Josef von Baky
Quelle: Deutsche Kinemathek

been born around 1926. As a soldier, Walter fought in the German Wehrmacht. Sometime around Mauthner's flight in 1933, he and Lina divorced, and Lina raised their son without ever sharing his Jewish heritage with him, making Walter believe, as the film script has it, that he was the son of another man, an Aryan. Over the years, Mauthner attempted to support Lina, sending packages from the United States. He delays his eventual return to Göttingen to look for his former wife in Berlin. Their accidental encounter there and emotional dispute over both Walter's future and Germany's recent past contains a discussion about the bombing of cities that in its frankness is startling for film of the time.

The opening scenes of the film take the audience into exile, that is, to the lush warmth of postwar California, an extraterrestrial space for all those who call Germany's drafty ruins their home. The initial sequence is crucial in building Mauthner's character. His friends there at the soiree, exiles themselves, object vehemently to Mauthner's plan to accept the call. Fraenkel, representing the position of collective guilt, calls all Germans "Menschenfresser" (cannibals) and asks: "Do you not feel any hatred?" Mauthner, though, calmly retorts: "There is neither a people of perpetrators, nor is there a people of heroes." And Mauthner does not stop there but utters a challenge, for he reminds Fraenkel that no one can know what he would have done had he stayed. He further counters what he perceives to be Fraenkel's moral self-righteousness with a proposition: if he, Fraenkel, wants to, he can demonstrate his support elsewhere and stand up for one of the many oppressed people on this planet. Clearly, between 1947 and 1949, much has changed politically. Prior to the emerging Cold War, and the resulting identification of (West) Germany as an ally in the fight against communism, a moral rehabilitation of Germany was at best of secondary importance. While, overall, the film does not shy away from exposing the continued presence of National Socialist thought among Germans—for which the film was heavily criticized in reviews,[15]—the film is equally relentless in its rejection of all generalizations, especially the denunciation of all Germans independent of their actual deeds and memories—even if that rejection has to be uttered by the Jewish émigré in the film and not a local gentile (and thus implicated) German. In 1949 the time is ripe for a less emotive response to Germany's recent past. Or so it seems, because once in Germany, and once confronted personally, Mauthner's benevolence undergoes a temporary transformation.

After having met in a café, Lina and Mauthner quickly begin talking about their respective experiences. She recalls the awful bombings, recalls fleeing over and over again, but finds Mauthner rather unreceptive. He is conciliatory, however, suggesting that after the end of the war enmities have to make room for a new beginning. Their first encounter ends abruptly when Lina, questioned about their son, becomes nervous and runs off.

DER RUF — BRD 1949
Regie: Josef von Baky
Quelle: Deutsche Kinemathek

Mauthner's suspicion that she was awaiting another man is proven wrong when they meet up again later that evening, continuing their conversation in a bar. Mauthner becomes increasingly assertive when he attempts to find out whether his son knows about his (Jewish) identity, and whether Walter will learn the truth about his real father. At this crucial point of the discussion, they are interrupted by another guest. The progressively heated debate about Mauthner's (and, by extension, Walter's) Jewish identity is temporarily suspended. The interlude allows Mauthner to contemplate a different past. The ensuing exchange goes directly to the issue of collective guilt.

> *Mauthner*: I am trying to imagine how things would have turned out if I had been granted custody of the boy. If a child of two had been given to my hands...
> *Lina*: Then you would have taken him along when you had to leave, wouldn't you?
> *Mauthner*: Naturally.
> *Lina*: Then he would have become a soldier over there and...what if he had had to destroy our cities?
> *Mauthner*: That would have been the alternative...."Destroy our cities"...now you are looking at me as if I had dropped the bombs!
> (*Mauthner here seems angry and insecure at the same time*)
> *Lina*: And you look at me as if I were to be blamed for everything that happened here.

Mauthner: [...] So you're not accusing me of actually dropping the bombs personally...but as an American citizen...

Lina: But that's what you are, aren't you?

Mauthner: This is not the only community I belong to, to which you were hostile! (and this he says with his finger raised, as if trumping her own feeling of victimhood)

How would the audience evaluate this moral dilemma of a German woman pointing her finger indirectly at America and its citizens? The accusation is absurd insofar as Mauthner had no influence on the war policies of the United States. But is it possible that the German viewing audience would have been tempted to adopt this stance of impotence and innocence? Is his lack of responsibility for Allied war conduct the same as hers for Germany's deeds? Lina's comment puts the "collective guilt" formula to an intensive test.

Mauthner's admonition, recalling that he is not only an American citizen but also a Jew, brings both characters back to the discussion centering on anti-Semitism that was interrupted by Mauthner's contemplation. His rebuke puts Lina back in her place as a representative of a generation of perpetrators. The discussion swings away from the irrationality of generalizations and back to the experiences of two individuals. However, while Lina's memories and explanations fall silent, it is Mauthner's judgment that will find a voice. In the following exchange, Mauthner shows that he is not willing to contemplate what Walter's youth as a half-Jew growing up in Nazi Germany would have been like, exposed to harassment as an outcast, as Lina reminds him. Mauthner now exhibits traits of the same intolerance he criticized back in Los Angeles. At some point, while he accuses Lina herself of anti-Semitism, she attempts to defend herself and her private memories, claiming that she cannot recall such an attitude, and that she took care of Jewish orphans during the war. Mauthner responds with mockery, and dismisses her individual experience in exchange for the collectively assigned one, maintaining that she is like all the other Germans who are busy excusing themselves, trying to feel better in the face of what happened. The audience—who cannot decide either way—has no chance of investigating the truth or falsehood of her story. After being called "vicious" by his former wife, Mauthner continues infuriated: "It was not only pressure that made you convert the boy to a full-fledged Aryan. [...] You have a genuine drive toward your racial ideals I sensed that I've offended." Close-ups show a face distorted in anger that hovers accusatorily over Lina who looks down at the table, seemingly vulnerable and unable to ward off the barrage. They cannot but eerily take the viewer back to the vilification of "the" Jew in propaganda films like *Jud Suess*. Is Baky deliberately alluding to that? Is he criticizing Mauthner's emotiveness, the execution of his real or perceived moral superiority and outrage into which he withdraws and that is far removed from his otherwise composed demeanor, that is, his advocacy of forgiveness? Or is he challenging the audience's willingness to pigeonhole, to fall back on familiar racial stereotypes? In Mauthner, the audience is, deliberately or accidentally, confronted with a variety of Jewish stereotypes, and hostile reactions to both the character of Mauthner and the storyline accompanied the making of the film in Munich, where students were used as extras. A Munich student paper in October 1948 reports of demonstrations and conflicts during the filming. Some called the film "nonsense" and "Jewish business."[16] But this is only one interpretation. It is equally conceivable that Baky is exposing Lina's position as one of deplorable self-absorption and spineless self-pity. She does not offer an apology, does not show curiosity about Mauthner's years of imposed exile, and does not open the door for a discussion on Nazi tyranny. Surely, Kortner had collected his own share of experiences of this sort. In *Aller Tage Abend*, he remembered his exasperating encounters with non-Jews after his arrival in Germany in the winter of 1947.

> I wanted to express the following: We who stutter around together, embarrassed and more or less competing with each other about the misery we experienced ought now be Christian and Jew again, not Aryan and Jew. Survivors of one and the same catastrophe. And our survival and that which we survived would be somewhat of a common experience. I apparently didn't have much luck with this argument. Most stubbornly stuck with their feeling that no suffering could be as bad as theirs. They probably needed this conscious feeling of having suffered the greatest injustice in order to ease their subconscious.[17]

The strength of Baky's *Der Ruf* is its very ambiguity, that is, the film invites the audience to mull over both positions. To reduce the film's ambiguity to either a simple moral tale or an exculpation of Germans for their complicity in the crimes of their regime diminishes its critical potential.[18] In his posthumously published book *Letzten Endes*, Kortner remembered that the film "wanted to enlighten, to correct and promote understanding. [...] The large majority of the viewing public, however, did not have an opportunity to evaluate the film, yet went along with the inciting rumors about *Der Ruf* and condemned the film."[19] The film manages to maintain a tension between two equally half right and half wrong positions. On the one hand, Baky's films attempt to make room for an experience that was generally considered taboo but begged to be expressed. The smugness of the victor, who declared the rubble an affair made in Germany and imposed silence on those conquered, is challenged by both... *und über uns der Himmel* and *Der Ruf*. Yet both films exhibit the difficulties with which the frightful experiences of millions of Germans during the bombing raids could be addressed in film. On the other hand, the films, especially *Der Ruf*, attempt not to lose sight of the inherent blind spots of a German self-pity that can only call to mind one's own personal suffering. The absence of the air war in most rubble films is symptomatic of a certain orthodoxy with which we have come to remember these years. Baky's films evidently struggle against the construction of a public memory (and, ultimately, history) of these events that presses home that "the" Germans as a whole deserved their fate. The likelihood that these Germans were lured, socialized, or simply cowed into compliance with this interpretation of the surrounding destruction is just one side of the coin. We could go so far as to wonder whether the indignation and condemnation of the war generation and the resulting politics of memory (and, more to the point, Allied cultural politics) may—for all of its efforts to instill a vague sense of German historical accountability—actually have fostered amnesia about the war.[20]

Notes

1. On postwar language as an instrument and filter of these experiences (and perhaps mentalities), see Horst Dieter Schlosser, *Es wird zwei Deutschlands geben. Zeitgeschichte und Sprache in Nachkriegsdeutschland 1945–1949* (Frankfurt am Main: Peter Lang, 2005).
2. Von Baky, born in 1902 in Hungary, became known during the late 1930s for his well-made entertainment. In 1942, he made UFA's anniversary film *Münchhausen*. His postwar career started with two rubble films,...*und über uns der Himmel* (1947) and *Der Ruf* (1949). The latter film, which Baky also produced, was a financial disaster; in the following years until his death in 1966, he returned to what he was known for: entertainment. For *Das doppelte Lottchen* (1950) he received the German Film Prize; with *Die Frühreifen* (1957) he attempted to address social realities of the FRG.
3. See Stephen A. Garrett, *Ethics and Airpower in World War II. The British Bombing of German Cities* (New York: St. Martin's Press, 1993).
4. Peter Stettner, *Vom Trümmerfilm zur Traumfabrik. Die «Junge Film Union» 1947—1952* (Hildesheim, Zürich and New York: Olms, 1992). See also Gabriele Clemens, *Britische Kulturpolitik in Deutschland 1945–1949: Literatur, Film, Musik und Theater* (Stuttgart: Steiner, 1997).
5. "The Germans," writes Volker Koop on the limits of tolerance in that peculiar phase of democratization, "were supposed to think and say whatever they wanted as long as it did not interfere with the interests of the victors." Volker

Koop, *Das Recht der Sieger. Absurde alliierte Befehle im Nachkriegsdeutschland* (Berlin: BeBra 2004), p.32. On "Demokratur," see Ralph Willett, *The Americanization of Germany* (New York: Routledge, 1989), esp. pp.1–15.

6. Stig Dagerman, *German Autumn*, transl. and introduction Robin Fulton (London and New York: Quartet Books, 1988 [1947]), p.2. On his contempt for Allied journalism, esp. pp.5–17.

7. A mood that continued, despite both U.S. support during the Berlin Blockade and the economic recovery for many in West Germany, during the 1950s. See Michael Geyer, "America in Germany. Power and the Pursuit of Americanization," in *The German-American Encounter. Conflict and Cooperation between two Cultures 1800–2000*, ed. Frank Trommler and Elliott Shore (New York and Oxford: Berghahn, 2001), pp.121–144.

8. Dagerman, *German Autumn*, pp.9, 15.

9. Karl Jaspers, *Die Schuldfrage* (Zürich: Artemis, 1946), pp.79, 89.

10. Hermann Claasen, *Gesang im Feuerofen. Köln: Überreste einer alten Stadt*. Introduction by Franz A. Hoyer (Düsseldorf: Schwann, 1947), pp.ix–xiv.

11. A position that finds expression in the written introduction to Rossellini's *Germany Year Zero*. "When ideologies distance themselves from Christian morality and piety, the very foundation of human life, they become criminal folly. Even childhood innocence is tainted and drawn from a horrible crime to a lesser one in which, through its own ingenuity, it believes to find freedom from guilt."

12. Theo Mackeben, "…und über uns der Himmel," *Darmstädter Echo* (April 6, 1948).

13. See Victor Gollancz, *In Darkest Germany* (Hinsdale, IL: Regnery, 1947).

14. Dagmar Barnouw, *Germany 1945. Views of War and Violence* (Bloomington, IN: Indiana University Press, 1996), p.xi.

15. See Helmut G. Asper, "Zurück aus Hollywood. Fritz Kortner und sein Film 'Der Ruf,'" *Film-Dienst* 23 (2000): 52–55.

16. On Kortner, who returned to Germany in December 1947, and *Der Ruf* see Klaus Völker, "'Aufklärung ist wichtiger als Verurteilung.' Zu Fritz Kortner's Film 'Der Ruf,'" *Filmexil* 3 (November 1993): 5–12; see p.10.

17. Fritz Kortner, *Aller Tage Abend* (München: Kindler, 1959), p.561.

18. As Shandley does. His conclusion is too bleak. "He [Mauthner] subjects his homeland to an aptitude test [...] Instead of finding rich belief in the fundamentals of Enlightenment thinking, he finds a land filled with the same prejudices, pettiness, and deceit [...] He had hoped that he could return idealism to a defeated community. Instead, the community defeats his idealism. He is called home only to realize that home is an illusory space." Shandley, *Rubble Films*, p.114. Similarly, Shandley, "Fritz Kortner's *Last Illusion*," in *Unlikely History. The Changing German-Jewish Symbiosis, 1945–2000*, ed. Leslie Morries and Jack Zipes (New York: Palgrave Macmillan, 2002), pp.251–261.

19. Fritz Kortner, *Letzten Endes* (München: Kindler, 1971), p.28.

20. Kaes makes a similar point, but quickly converts it into the common repression thesis: "the denazification program [...] and Allied control of all public media and institutions did more to impede than to promote free discussion among Germans about their own past. It seemed as if even the German past

were now under the jurisdiction of the Allies; it was *their* business. [...] The mounting resentment against the conquering powers could not, however, be articulated in the immediate postwar years. Just like the Hitler era itself, this resentment had to be repressed. It did not surface until thirty or forty years later." Kaes, *From Hitler to Heimat*, p.14.

CHAPTER THREE
A TIME FOR RUINS

Dagmar Barnouw

The English translation of W. G. Sebald's slim volume of reflections on air war and literature, *On the Natural History of Destruction*, took its title from Solly Zuckerman's 1945 project to report on the destruction of Cologne. Overwhelmed by the experience, he never wrote the report realizing that he did not have the language to describe the utter desolation of that "ravaged" city. Over the years, images of Cologne's ruins retreated and he only remembered the "blackened cathedral rising from the stony desert around it," and a "severed finger" he had found on a heap of rubble.[1]

Sebald refers to these images at the end of his first chapter, which contains his most powerful descriptions of Allied air war, indeed a sublime "natural history" of heretofore unknown forces of destruction: mountains, tidal waves of fire, hurricanes of flames, burning skies fusing heaven and hell. He was not interested in the people who experienced these horrors but in the hyperphysical effects of total air war that he reconstructed in a few carefully chosen and rendered details: fields of ruins sculpted by fire, piles of grotesquely shrunk purple corpses cured in its unearthly heat, puddles of their congealing fat. Isolated in their literally "brilliant" representation, they point to the surreally clear incomprehensible mass transformation of the familiar and normal. Writing about air war in the late nineties, Sebald believed himself to be the first writer to really see and represent the monstrous scale and truth of a destruction ultimately justified by a monstrous German past.

Like Solly Zuckerman, Janet Flanner was shocked by ruined Cologne "in the rubble and loneliness of complete physical defeat. Through its clogged streets trickles what is left of its life, a dwindled population in black and with bundles—the silent German people appropriate to the silent city." Quoting Flanner, Sebald comments: "That silence, that reserve, that instinctive looking away are the reason why we know so little of what the Germans thought and observed in the years between 1942 and 1947. The ruins where they lived were the terra incognita of the war."[2] The contemporary observer Flanner saw the black of mourning (there was death in almost every family at the end of the war), the silence of utter exhaustion, and the bundles of the homeless. Half a century later, Sebald found only concealment in the silence and the ruins, an apocalypse lost in forgetting that enabled him to maintain the perspective of sublime distance. It is curious that he used Zuckerman's title since it indicates a very different perspective on the presence of ruins, rubble, and human misery, revealing a destruction so total, unimaginable, and overwhelmingly real that it was beyond human comprehension and language, as if not man-made, the subject of a "natural history" of destruction.

If Sebald's invocation of the sublime would not have been an option for Zuckerman, it was for Margaret Bourke-White and other professional Allied photographers who took "ravishing" pictures of the many flattened cities published in a LIFE photo essay of June 4, 1945, "The Battered Face of Germany." The superhuman sharpness and distance of the camera eye allowed them to see the true beauty of the ruins cleansed of all human life, one-dimensional shapes in visually exciting , immutable constellations. Light-years removed from all human fears and hopes, they were the most obvious witnesses to the justice meted out by the victors' punishment for the vanquished.

The omnipresent ruins and rubble left behind by unearthly storms of fire were not so much a "terra incognita" as a visual and semantic paradox. In the literally "bombed-out" cities with its houses broken up and broken open, what had been visible had now become invisible, and what had been invisible was now visible; what had been public was now private, what had been private was now public. Looking back at the physical, political, and moral devastation of the chaotic early postwar years, the chaos seems most persuasively represented in the incomprehensibly altered cityscapes of rubble that, profoundly disorienting even to the cities' lifelong inhabitants, defied all familiar human meaning. It is not surprising, then, that these ruins were too overpowering to speak for themselves retaining, with the certainties, also the ambiguities of guilt, retribution, and remorse.

Wolfgang Staudte, who conceived and directed the first German postwar film, *Die Mörder sind unter uns* (The Murderers Are Among Us, 1946), responded to this phenomenon when he made the rubble and ruins of Berlin the film's most important protagonist. Staudte had worked for UFA as specialist for comedies almost until the day when Soviet soldiers invaded the Babelsberg studios in the spring of 1945. He wanted above all to get back to filmmaking as quickly as possible to assert his professional and political participation in a new Germany. In November 1945 he attended a meeting in the ruins of the famous hotel Adlon at the Brandenburger Tor where Russian *Kulturoffiziere* and a group of German film makers and writers hotly debated the new antifascist, humanist, democratic, anti-UFA goals and perspectives of German film. Staudte had already sent the Soviet headquarters a mission statement regarding the cultural renewal of German film and contributed to plans for what would become the first postwar German film agency, DEFA. He was, however, not interested in theoretical debates about film or the occupation forces' politics of film production but in how he could make a film now.

His first chance was filming the ruins of Potsdamer Platz and the destroyed subway tunnels where thousands of civilians fleeing from the bombs had drowned when the tunnels were dynamited. Preliminary work for Friedrich Wolf's film project on the last days of the war in Berlin began, but the project ended abruptly and Staudte's footage was lost. But he already had a film project of his own related to an experience in late April when he had told an acquaintance that he was not going to join the *Volks-Sturm*, the Nazi's last insane attempt to draft a militia of old men and teenagers against the invading Allies. Organizing this "storm of the people" in the dangerous and treacherous chaos of the last days of the war could be deadly for those who obeyed and those who disobeyed the call. Almost getting himself shot, Staudte swore revenge—the central topic of his film, at first titled *Der Mann, den ich töten werde* (The Man I Am Going to Kill).

Staudte had obtained a license for a "Wolfgang-Staudte-Filmproduktion" in the British sector and offered his project first to the *Filmoffiziere* of the British occupation forces. They sent him on to the American "Filmsection of the Information Service Control Branch" where he was told that "in the next five years no film will be made in this country except by us"[3]— echoing the sentiments of the American film industry. Until a (hoped-for) successful conclusion of the American denazification program, Germans were to be treated as Nazis incapable of producing worthwhile films.

Ironically, if the Americans had not rejected, without reading, Staudte's 1946 "Exposé Arbeitstitel: Die Mörder sind unter uns," they might have understood that it fully affirmed the official Allied attitude toward vanquished Germany as a collective of guilty perpetrators. Moreover, his narrow perspective on the "unredeemed," "unmastered" German past would not change over the decades. Unlike Harald Braun whose psychologically, if not visually, more interesting film *Zwischen Gestern und Morgen* (Between Yesterday and Tomorrow) was shot two years later in the American sector, Staudte did not want to waste any time with differentiating reflections on the past. He intended to seize *Stunde Null* (Zero Hour), that important point in time when the end of the war would turn into a new beginning. As it turned out, *Stunde Null* was an illusion and the chaotic end would just merge with a no less chaotic and obscure beginning. But, given his pedagogical temperament, Staudte would not have seen that even in hindsight. An immediate "honest confrontation" with the military and moral catastrophe that, in his view, the Germans had brought on themselves was all that was needed now.

Turned down by the Americans, Staudte's last chance was the *Filmoffiziere* of the Soviet occupation. They actually read the script and after three weeks gave him permission to make the film. This fact, as well as the film's early date would be of importance for its positive reception at the time and through the years.[4] In May of 1946, DEFA became the first licensed German film institution, its most important goal the struggle for democratic reconstitution by thorough reeducation of the German population. Film was art by and for the masses, *Massenkunst,* and the core issues were "true democracy," humanity, "inner honesty," "search for truth"—in short, the awakening of a cleansed collective conscience.[5]

These guidelines were fine with Staudte, though he probably had some reservations regarding a narrow interpretation of *Massenkunst,* and he did have to change the ending. The film is set in Berlin, a few months after the end of the war, when the young Dr. Mertens by chance meets his former commanding officer Brückner whom he had last seen badly wounded. Traumatized by his war experiences, the former surgeon has become a cynical, self-absorbed alcoholic drifter. In contrast, the businessman Brückner has had no problems adapting to the new situation and is doing very well. Only Mertens knows that he ordered the shooting of Polish civilian hostages on Christmas Eve 1942; and his desire to take revenge for the inhumanity of war turns into an obsession to kill Brückner. Staudte's script had the film end with Mertens shooting him as an attempt to bring about justice. But despite mounting frictions among the Allies, the Soviet Union accepted the American controlled Nuremberg Trials as a way to mete out justice to authentic war criminals and thereby end the chaotic *Lynchjustiz* of the immediate postwar period.

Given their notoriously brutal conduct in war and as occupation force, Soviet objections to the film's conclusion might appear disingenuous, but Staudte shifted the intended real killing of Brückner to a symbolic level that allowed a choice of interpretations. In the end, Brückner may or may not be judged and sentenced; Mertens may or may not be walking into a better future with Susanne Wallner whose patient love may or may not have redeemed him, though it prevented him from shooting Brückner.

Despite his general focus on an "honest confrontation" with the German past, Staudte was fortunately much less interested in characters or plot than in the visual grandeur of Berlin's horrifying transfiguration. His documentary and artistic vision in this film was not unlike Sebald's attempts, half a century later, to represent as fully as possible the "unbelievable" scope of destruction by invoking the surreal dimension of the sublime. He shot the film from March to July 1946 in the Babelsberg studios and, in an unusual approach, the streets of Berlin. Since they were all lined by the most gorgeous ruins and magnificent mountains of rubble, it would have been silly to build ruins and pile up rubble in the studio, though the first American movies set in early postwar Germany tended to do just that. The journalist Curt Riess who witnessed part of the shooting described the endless lines of ruins, the bombed-out tanks, the ubiquitous machine guns and helmets shot to pieces. It is a shattered world suddenly lit up by the film crew's glaring floodlights that both lured and blinded the people living in the ruins. Emerging from the rubble fearfully, they seem to be drawn back into its darkness, merging again with the ruins. A shadowy, pitiful sight, they are also a disturbance to be shushed away like moths because the film calls for eerily empty streets. But an empty street, Riess remarks, is not as disquieting as a street where "people emerge who no longer exist, who have been dead for a long time, even though they do not know it."[6]

Shot amidst ruins and rubble and under very difficult conditions—the crew's experience of chronic hunger, illnesses, lack of shelter and medical care, constant problems with obtaining enough film and electricity—this early film represents, perhaps better than all other *Trümmerfilme*, the disquieting insubstantiality and instability of the ruined city. What the camera sees is a surreal, hostile world reminiscent of the expressionist sets of earlier silent movies.[7] Werner Fiedler, in a review of 1946, rightly points out the camera's aggressive focus on the "frighteningly beautiful landscapes of ruins. It homes in on shattered lives, creating gloriously gloomy psychic landscapes."[8] The dominant elements of the film are not light and shadow but shadows darkened by the lighting technique, a play with gradations of darkness. A staircase appears as a shaft of shifting darknesses; a human face as a field of blackish rubble, and the slanting camera angle intensifies the sense of disorientation among the mountains of rubble. The effect is a feeling of dizziness, like stumbling and groping amidst a plethora of images turning into "allegories."

A contemporary to the destruction, Fiedler emphasizes the challenge for the director of "this first German anti-fascist film" to "document the new German attitude" and wake up a lethargic German population to sweep away the "rubble of the soul." Yet he thinks Staudte's perspective on the immediate postwar period is too harshly judgmental and selective. There are the overwhelming material and psychological difficulties, but there is also the exhilaration of the new beginning during that famously beautiful summer of 1945 when the sights and sounds of cleaning up, repairing, and establishing order made life seem possible again, even among the ruins. In Staudte's film every character, with the exception of Susanne, cannot but be guilty, deeply flawed or seriously damaged and the dark times of the rubble do not support hopes for the future. Even Susanne's friend, the kindly, helpful old clock maker has to die just before his beloved son returns from the front.

Another contemporary reviewer, Friedrich Luft, had expected a great deal from that first German film after the "small apocalypse of our time" and did not find the "clarification," moral "accounting," and "finally a new view and liberation" needed by 1946 audiences.[9] He did point out Staudte's visual sensitivity to all the filmic possibilities of Berlin's fantastic ruins and rubble. But Luft also criticized him for indulging his cinematic interest to the detriment of dealing with the "deadly serious, extremely important" topic of this film, German guilt and atonement. In hindsight, such high expectations were unrealistic, obscuring the film's cinematic achievements. Yet even Luft was open to the powerful visual immediacy of the film's beginning. With the camera starting at a soldier's grave, like Berlin's ruins an allegory of one of the most terrible battles of that most terrible war in Western memory, a crane shot reveals a huge mountain of rubble, the archetypal representation of this city's near total devastation.

Still, since Luft was mainly focused on a coherent moral-political filmic narrative, he overlooked Staudte's extraordinary cinematic treatment of the omnipresent mountains of rubble as dangerously treacherous living matter. Left behind by the planes and tanks of mid-twentieth century hypertechnological warfare, these mountains are both unyielding and shifting: alien monsters of unearthly proportions having swallowed thousands and thousands of human habitations and everything in them, alive or dead. Right in the beginning there is a traveling shot of a group of small children clambering across a huge pile of rubble in search of something they will probably never find. In a later scene, the camera follows two men rapidly walking across an endless mountainous wasteland of rubble. Mertens, the man in the lead, is disoriented and diminished by the war but he unerringly finds his way in even the most confusing terrain of rubble, as if it were his native ground. He is taking Brückner to one of the places of amusement that have sprung up in the midst of the rubble like poisonous colorful mushroom in stark contrast to their dark, desolate surroundings. Unable to keep up with Mertens, Brückner panics for fear that he will be left behind in this nowhere, a chaotic wasteland without any traces of human cultivation and habitation, with no signs for direction, nothing to establish meaning. The film's most evil character, he seems at the mercy of the rubble whose ominous physical presence is the film's main protagonist. Secretive, inscrutable, unreliable, it distorts and disorients by constantly changing underfoot as if in reaction to the person walking on it—perhaps innocent, certainly fearless like Mertens; guilty and apprehensive like Brückner.

Mertens has intruded into Brückner's well-appointed, well-stocked, cozy apartment, complete with a devoted wife, two obedient children, already restored windows. Without any moral imagination, he is genuinely glad to see Mertens and eager to help him—as he had organized a really nice Christmas celebration for his men right after the shooting of the hostages. Mertens' challenging his authority at that time by trying to talk him out of senselessly murdering women and children seems forgotten or irrelevant. Brückner has managed to separate himself totally from the past war, the time of death, and is now securely connected with the postwar present, the time of life. Staudte gave him immoral innocence, the extreme opposite of Susanne's moral innocence. Not knowing, not caring about the distinctions between good and bad he is, in most situations, without fear or suspicion, and Mertens will have no difficulties luring him into the terra incognita, the postcivilization wilderness of the rubble, where he intends to kill him.

In the complex and difficult reality of the postwar era, both kinds of innocence are too radical and therefore abstract, even if the victors, and then the German elites, would hold up the ideal of radical moral purification as a measure for successful denazification. For Mertens, a slightly more credible character, the past horrors of warfare are still in the present; there seems to be neither rupture nor change. Staudte's perspective at the end of the war appears to balance Brückner's memory gap and Mertens' inability to forget. His own desire for a new beginning and his professional ambition causes him to establish a connection between the failures of the past and the promises of the present. For Staudte, a better future has to be grounded in principled not-forgetting of the evil deeds, the guilt of the German past. Shot in Berlin, the film's visual focus on rubble and ruins is "natural" and, attempting to represent the city's near total destruction "itself," Staudte's cinematography is "naturally" both realistic and surrealistic. It is also fitting that this first German postwar film manages to present, more powerfully than the *Trümmerfilme* after it, the all-enveloping alienness and familiarity of that destruction; its shocking sublime attraction and powerful ordinary repulsion.

In retrospect, perhaps the most remarkable aspect of Staudte's film is the fact that the extraordinary nature of the destruction it documents faithfully and artfully could not be acknowledged again for almost six decades. Until Jörg Friedrich's attempts to do so in *Der Brand* (2002) it remained hidden in the moral history of destruction. The ideological restrictions and selectiveness of this history were in some ways politically helpful, in others culturally harmful. For its early supporters, the West German political and intellectual elites, this was undoubtedly the easiest way to cope with a host of postwar difficulties. But this moral history of destruction would also be used in the American moral and military power politics of the postwar era drawing on the memory of World War II as the "good, clean, just war we won" to justify the unjustifiable wars and warlike conflicts to come. Since the Germans had brought the wholesale destruction of their cities on themselves, it could not have been all that unimaginable. And since, as always, life had to go on, life could not be imagined without wars—even after this war.

Perhaps in spontaneous reaction to the visual power of Berlin's mountains of rubble as a result of the unimaginable destructiveness of World War II Staudte managed to circumvent this moral history of destruction in his recorded "pure" images of rubble and ruins. But in the moral lessons he extracted from his characters, the gloriously horrible rubble served him as an allegory for Germany's bad past never to be forgotten and in bad need of redemption. The moral judgments in *Die Mörder sind unter uns* are too certain and predictable, as if to balance the ambiguities and ambivalences in the images of darkness and shadows. There are sharp if not entirely clear distinctions between good and bad, victim and victimizer, innocence and guilt. Mertens who drowns his nightmare memories of the Eastern front in alcohol may not seem much of a victim until Susanne Wallner begins to love and thereby redeem him. At the end of the war, moral and political innocence goes with the victim status protected by Allied victory and German defeat. Brückner, the evil perpetrator, is beyond redemption even though he may yet escape human justice; it is left to the viewer to decide.

In contrast to these inner Manichean separations, the visible outside world does not allow such distinctions. Like most of the surviving apartments, Susanne's has no windows left; there is no clear distinction between inside and outside and the apartments themselves are constantly invaded by rubble carried in by wind, rain, and snow. When that happens, they cease to give shelter and become what they really are, were it not for their inhabitants' desperate illusions: part of a ruin, half jagged hole in the wall, half recognizable walled-in space; half inhabitable, half almost habitable. Gradually Susanne makes the apartment habitable with the pleasures of order. She does that "naturally" as a woman who does it for her man; but the reestablishing of order, the redeeming of mental and material chaos is also assigned to her as a former KZ inmate punished for the political views of her father. Her innocence allegorized in the delicate blond beauty of the young Hildegard Knef is angelic; and Staudte was rightly blamed by contemporary and later viewers for that ironclad innocence and goodness, if praised for the discovery of Knef's expressive face. But ironclad innocence and guilt is what the bad German past has been about for now more than sixty years.

All the characters are teaching figures, with Mertens as a kind of bridge between victim and victimizer: no matter how much he suffered himself, he is also guilty because he has let things happen and thereby committed the arch-German collective crime of passivity. Staudte's development within less than a year from UFA's comedy specialist to DEFA's political morality specialist is intriguing and also in important ways predictable. In this regard, his connections with what was to become the German Democratic Republic suited him: if he could hold his viewers responsible for the bad German past by "honestly confronting" them with it, he would not himself be tainted by it. He anticipated by two decades the judgmental rigor of the leftist student generation of 1968 who would relentlessly lecture their parents, the war generation of perpetrators, about *their* collective guilt because they themselves were collectively innocent. Staudte did not allow his human characters the shades of gray of their unstable, unreliable war memories; but his filmic representation of the treacherous living rubble with its dangerously ambiguous shades of darkness at the end of that monstrous war is still a remarkable achievement. If the film has been seen as the most important of the German *Trümmerfilme*, it is for the unmediated, unmatched visual power of its literally inhuman protagonist.

German political and psychological preoccupation with guilt and retribution proved to be tenacious, outliving German rubble and ruins by many decades and even surprisingly strengthened by reunification 45 years after the war. However, in their emotional urgency and intellectual openness, discourses of German guilt and remorse appear most nuanced and searching in the immediate postwar years, before the return of a more organized political life that would also politicize and thereby diffuse the powerful physical and mental effects of the German war experience.[10] A good example are Erich Kästner's articles in the American controlled *Neue Zeitung* 1945–1947 in which he tried to develop a more differentiating view of the question of German guilt, to help his readers cope with the moral and psychological aftermath of Nazi rule.

Kästner's description (*NZ* November 1946) of his first visit to the destroyed Dresden, the serenely beautiful, beloved city of his youth, is one of the most effective texts of the immediate postwar years because it interweaves mourning and hope, emotion and reason. There are the devastating images of irrevocable transformation and radical reduction and yet, at the moment of the visitor's speechless despair, they are already retreating into the past. It will be a past that, though painful, will not resist a future gradual normalization, because the war left the Germans with "the two fires of guilt and of pain." Inconsolable, Kästner does not search for a "higher" meaning of the "unspeakable" absence of what was once Dresden. In order to accept the openness of the future, he looks for ways of dealing realistically with the challenges of the past and the present.

Half a year later, in a detailed report on the extreme difficulties of the notoriously cruel winter of 1946/47—hunger, cold, lack of shelter, illness, death on a catastrophic scale—Kästner linked these problems to the questionable Allied self-interest politics of separate sectors (NZ, May 12, 1947). Frustrated by the rigid American media control with its high moralizing interventions, Kästner would soon resign his post as feuilleton editor. It saddened many readers who had found particularly useful his informal, shrewd discussions of how to deal with the Nazi past, among them the advice to recall their own experiences of these years and not settle for what the Allies had told them to remember.

Many of Kästner's readers would also have seen *Die Mörder sind unter uns.*[11] Staudte's reaction to Berlin's destruction, his filmic creation of its transformation into a monstrously sentient rubble protagonist beyond human time and conscience, differs dramatically from Kästner's reaction to Dresden's destruction, his verbal reflections on the political and social meanings in human time of a city's radical transformation into insentient matter. The difference of the medium is as crucial here as is the difference in both men's temperament and experience. The power of *Trümmerfilme* can be to make immediately visible the extreme, amoral nature of war and to shock the viewer into isolating incomprehension: how could it have happened? The power of verbal reflections on the extreme, amoral horrors of war and the moral dilemmas of its aftermath can be to create a shared process of understanding.

Looking back at the time of ruins and moral dilemmas, Stanley Kramer's 1961 *Judgment at Nuremberg* attempted to combine both approaches. It was the year of the Berlin Wall, Cold War tensions were high and Kramer was ready to make a high-serious film about a hot topic. In *Halliwell's Film Guide*, the one-star docufictional film about a 1948 trial of four high-ranking Nazi judges is described as a "courtroom marathon with philosophical asides. All good stuff but too much of it." The cast of stars befitting the moral effort includes Spencer Tracy as the presiding judge, Marlene Dietrich as the attractive widow of a Nazi general hanged by the Allies, Burt Lancaster as the only remorseful Nazi judge, Richard Widmark as the icily passionate prosecutor, Maximilian Schell as the fiery young

German lawyer for the defense, and Judy Garland and Montgomery Clift as Nazi victims. Garland and Schell won academy awards; the film was nominated for best picture. All characters in this morality play know the outcome of the trial: it is a show trial without risks or surprises. Only the judge in his impermeable American innocence, aggravated by Tracy's acting, seems to believe that his judgment would not have already been scripted.

Nuremberg's impressive and omnipresent ruins are an important part of the morality play, but they seem deliberately stagy, invoked rather than documented, visual reminders rather than witnesses of German guilt. Driving by them in the back of a big black official convertible with built-in right-of-way, the judge shows a judiciously mild interest in the scale of the destruction. His handsome head of white hair and attractively weather-beaten face bespeak a calmness troubled only occasionally by some uncommonly evil evidence. Then a close-up of his eyes narrowing intensely is a signal to the viewer to watch out. When the car almost hits an old man trying to push a cart across the road, the young German driver honks too triumphantly for the judge's taste. Surrounded by ruins, he insists on American democratic treatment of vanquished Germans. Since he is uninterested in the reality of the German war experience, the ruins, the rubble, and the squalid people living in them can only be allegories of a defeat so profound that it cannot but call for the victor's justice.

The judge lives in the Nuremberg villa of the executed Nazi general and treats its elderly German caretakers with exquisite politeness. They have lost a son at the front and a daughter in the air raids; as they tell him calmly, a common fate for Germans their age. But they themselves cannot be real to him since they insist on their innocence where it concerns the evil deeds of their regime. Asked by the nice American judge how they feel about Nazi criminality, they appear fearful rather than remorseful, yet his questions make it impossible for them to answer other than evasively— meaning guiltily. When we see him looking at the ruins through the windows of the villa or the court room, the transformation of Germany's cities into rubble seems to have transformed the whole country into evidence against itself.

Tracy's acting affirms the character of the judge from Maine who came to ruined Germany as the good American with impeccable values. His twinkly charm and courteous provincial humility support his unshakeable belief that his judgment will be just in all cases, whatever the circumstances. For later viewers, such relentless goodness would make the character a sermonizing cartoon complementing the two relentlessly evil Nazi lawyers. This might have been Kramer's intention for his teaching drama. But there is also the character of Ernst Janning who, helped by Lancaster's low-key acting, occasionally suggests a professional dilemma. A well-known respected jurist, he cooperated with the Nazi regime and is now deeply remorseful about the results of some of his judgments. While he fully accepts the life sentence, he also pleads with the American judge to believe him that he did not know the full extent of Nazi criminality—evidently to establish some kind of connection with the man whose life had, like his own, been dedicated to the law, but in vastly different ways. The judge rejects all communication and goes home to Maine untainted by Nazi evil and certain that he has done justice to all. At Janning's request, he does take with him a collection of his legal briefs, admires their intelligence and cannot understand how he could have gone so wrong. He never engages in any way with German political and social history that might have given him some clues.

We see Janning settle into his spartan cell, expecting to spend the rest of his life at his narrow desk reconstructing the errors of his professional past. But changes are in the air: Janning's life sentence would not have satisfied the demanding Allied morality immediately after the war, when the general had to hang. But it may seem too harsh a few years later, given the Allies' new political needs, and soon be overturned. The film's endless, inconclusive speechifying is not "all good stuff but too much of it;" it is mostly empty rhetoric on the occasion of putting some Nazi judges on trial. The argument of anachronism in handing down life sentences to civil servants who in obedience to then valid laws made their now criminal judgments is never debated but simply rejected in redundant moral assertions that these laws were monstrously wrong and that adhering to them was a self-evident crime against humanity. The two evil judges are only allowed to demonstrate that they have learned nothing from the country's defeat and will never be able to change. A more complex character who might argue this issue more skillfully, Janning is not scripted to succeed. For the entire trial, he is exclusively focused on the sincerity of his own remorse, has nothing but cold contempt for his colleagues, and openly undermines the sometimes clever strategies of the Defense.

Declaring his guilt, Janning is more interested in making himself morally acceptable to the American judge than in helping him understand some of the reasons for his past acts. Asked to believe that Janning did not know the full extent of Nazi criminality, the judge simply tells him that the first instances of Nazi justice should have shown him what was to come. "You should have known," the Allies' mantra, did not allow any questions; and the new, never clearly defined concept of "crimes against humanity" only hardened the Allies' denial to consider the historical and political contexts and circumstances of past criminal acts. Ideological rather than legal in the modern sense of contextualization and differentiation, the victor's justice should have made it clear to a jurist like Janning that the American judge following Allied political policy simply refused to concern himself with the serious problems of a regime change on a huge scale. In the situation of Germany's unconditional surrender, Janning's character is contradictory to the core: it is precisely the power of his sincere remorse that weakens his plea to be believed that he did not have full knowledge of Nazi criminality, because it implied that he claimed a relative degree of innocence even where he declared himself guilty. The Allied absolute victory literally present in the rubble left by the firestorms of British and American air raids did not allow a halfway realistic relativization of guilt and innocence. Since the innocence of the Nazis' victims was absolute, the guilt of the perpetrators was absolute and it extended to all Germans who would remain tainted by their criminal regime in perpetuity.

The generalizing indictment of German political and moral criminality at the center of the trial, and then of the film, leaves too many questions unasked. How was the film's audience in 1961 to look at the not purely evil character of Janning? Or the shrewd American senator who explains to the judge the political realities of 1948? Is he the opportunist politician, and the judge the good American still striving, like the sheriff protagonist of a Western, for a pure but already anachronistic justice? Are they meant to complement each other? But, then, what about all the heated awkwardly staged debates about Nazi crimes against humanity that *are* the film?

The impending Berlin *Luftbrücke* in 1948, marked for the Allies the end of the time for ruins and rubble as allegories of German collective guilt and remorse. Germans are now needed for fraternal cooperation in the Cold War, hence *Marshallplan*, *Wiederaufbau*, and later the emblematic power of the Berlin Wall. Once omnipresent, the signs of Germany's punishment will now retreat and with them, very quickly, memories of the worst war in Western history. Not, however, of Nazi evil and of the good, clean, just American war, a valuable postwar political commodity for the United States in the postwar era. In East Germany the time for ruins continued, witnesses to the capitalist criminality of both Nazis and Western Allies, though East Germans, too, had to put aside their war memories to avoid clashes with Soviet memories of the good, clean, just war *they* won.

Unlike the earlier *Trümmerfilme*, Douglas Sirk's melodrama *A Time to Love and a Time to Die* (1957) does not allow allegorical associations of guilt and remorse with the rubble and withholds affirmation of the Allies clean and just war. "Haunted" by the fate of his son, a young German soldier killed in the spring of 1944 at the Eastern front, Sirk made his film "an imagined version of the last weeks of his son's life, and invested it with anguish—and hope—and despair."[12] Though the film is based on Erich

Maria Remarque's pacifist novel *Zeit zu leben und Zeit zu sterben* (Time to Live and Time to Die), its premise is not that love is doomed in war but rather that its "time is the war" as "situation and as nourishing soil for an emotion"—hence Sirk's alteration of the title.[13]

On a few weeks' leave from the brutal Eastern front, Gräber, a young soldier, knows that this is all the time he has to live and, falling in love with a young woman he knew as a girl, they both realize that the inevitable brevity of their love is also its intensity: the ecstatic emotion of love is its finitude.[14] There are no limits to their love in the chaos and anarchy of Berlin's transformation into mountains of rubble other than the absolute finitude of his leave. The lovers' story fits Sirk's concept of filmic melodrama with its "intense emotions, controlled by violence and accident, error, and blindness and by the impossibility to influence the lives of others and one's own. An unreal and pessimistic world."[15] For the young lovers in the time of war, the inevitable briefness of their love and the inevitability of death cannot but be inseparable: irresistibly, the time to love flows into the time to die.

Berlin's rubble is for Sirk the natural environment of displaced people, searching for lost relations and friends, moving between ruins and notice boards, without real hope and as if only half alive. Only the lovers are fully alive because their moments of happiness are so rare and precious. When Gräber is called back to the front, they take leave from each other in the house where they had found refuge for their time to love. Following him to the station, she sees him among the other soldiers already crowded together like a pile of rubble in the train carrying them back to the front, the time to die. He does not know that she came to see him a last time; and we see only her reflection in a piece of a broken window pane. Sirk's descriptive cinematic style is remarkably attentive to the characters in their settings, be it the orderliness of middle-class living rooms, or the chaos of war. Consequently, and particularly in this film, the viewer's intense emotion does not come from identification with a character but from the director's montage suggesting complex emotional associations. Sirk's remark that "lighting and camera angles constitute the philosophy of the director" means that he is making films *with* people rather than *about* them.[16] He relies on the camera that "sees things the human eye does not detect," but he is the one who puts it all together in his mind, "matching the mood of scene and characters, of light and length."[17]

Back at the front, reading a letter he just received that tells him that he will be a father, Gräber is interrupted by an order to shoot a group of Russian partisans but instead shoots the SS officer, sets the prisoners free, and throws away the gun. The partisans use it to kill him before he can go on reading in his letter that his parents have survived. Dying, he tries in vain to retrieve it from the river and the camera pans slowly down to the piece of paper floating away from his groping hand, an image of utter futility. Stern comments on the meaning of that famous final shot: "like the air raids, there is really no enemy to blame. Gräber's death, like his three weeks of life, and like the chaos raining from the sky, are all expressions of an absurd fate."[18] But Sirk's stoic pessimism goes deeper. Rightly, he prided himself on his realistic filmic representation of the horrors of the Eastern front. Beyond guilt, retribution, and remorse, but also beyond fatalism and existentialism, his film brings to life the stupefying tragedy of war for the people caught in it, the vanquished as well as the victors.

Notes

1. Solly Zuckerman, *From Apes to Warlords* (London: Hamilton, 1978), pp.352, 322.
2. W. G. Sebald, *On the Natural History of Destruction* (New York: Random House, 2003), p.31.
3. Malte Ludin, *Wolfgang Staudte* (Rowohlt: Reinbek bei Hamburg, 1996), p.123, n.56.
4. See the large number of contemporary reviews listed in *Edition Filme 6. Staudte* (Berlin: Wissenschaftsverlag Volker Spiess, 1991).
5. For the text of the speech see Ludin, *Staudte*, p. 32.
6. Quoted in Ludin, *Staudte*, 34.
7. Ibid., 36.
8. Werner Fiedler, "Der Weg durch die Trümmer," *Neue Zeit* (October 17, 1946, reprint in *Edition Filme 6. Staudte*, pp.176–177).
9. "Der erste deutsche Film nach dem Kriege," *Der Tagesspiegel* (October 16, 1946; reprint in *Edition Filme 6. Staudte*, pp.173–176).
10. See the large collection of documents in Jürgen Steinle. *Nationales Selbstverständnis nach dem Nationalsozialismus. Die Kriegsschuld-Debatte in West-Deutschland* (Bochum: Universitätsverlag Dr. N. Brockmeyer, 1995).
11. Kästner did not write a review, but Luft published his *Tagesspiegel* review two days later in the Berlin edition of *NZ*.
12. *Sirk on Sirk. Conversations with Jon Halliday* (London and Boston: Faber and Faber, 1997), p.3. Sirk told Halliday about searching in vain to "find some trace of my son," even checking "the notice boards" in Berlin (89) that will play a role in the film when Gräber searches in vain for his parents.
13. Rainer Werner Fassbinder, *The Anarchy of the Imagination* (Baltimore: Johns Hopkins University Press, 1992), p.86. Fassbinder, a great admirer of this film, refers to Sirk here as a German director (pp.29–30).
14. On the importance and brevity of the lovers' happiness, and the "relationship between their love and the ruins" see *Sirk on Sirk*, p.144. Sirk was depressed that the film was banned in Israel and Russia for not being sufficiently anti-German, insisting that "it is anti-war, it is against killing, and it is anti-Nazi" (ibid., p.145).

15. Quoted Sabine Pott, *Film als Geschichtsschreibung bei Rainer Werner Fassbinder* (Frankfurt am Main: Peter Lang, 2002), p.69.
16. See Fassbinder, *Anarchy*, pp.80, 77.
17. See *Sirk on Sirk,* pp.99, 110.
18. Michael Stern, *Douglas Sirk* (Boston: Twayne Publishers, 1979), p.179.

CHAPTER FOUR

RUBBLE FILM AS ARCHIVE OF TRAUMA AND GRIEF: WOLFGANG LAMPRECHT'S *SOMEWHERE IN BERLIN*

Anke Pinkert

Since the 1960s critics have used notions of repression and amnesia to describe the difficulty Germans faced in dealing with the Third Reich and the Second World War. Most famously, Alexander and Margarete Mitscherlich argued in their book *The Inability to Mourn* (1967) that in an attempt to shake off guilt the Germans blocked out any capacity for empathy and paid little attention to the losses of the victims of Nazism or their own for that matter.[1] Observing an emotional rigidity in the postwar population, they concluded the Germans did not experience the melancholia or depression that in their view would have been the appropriate affective response to the collapse of the Third Reich, the loss of Hitler, and the confrontation with the Holocaust directly after the end of the war. While this psychoanalytical approach to postwar culture was able to draw attention to the unconscious effects of the past in the present, the Mitscherlichs' focus on the suppression of guilt relied on an all too unitary notion of collective behavior and memory production. Moreover, their investment in a normative perspective of how the Germans should have dealt with the past prevented a further probing of the presumably absent affects of grief and depression. For decades to come, the interpretation of silence as an unconscious expression of moral uncertainty obscured an understanding of the traumatic consequences of mass death and destruction in the postwar population. Turning more specifically toward the deaths the Germans had experienced themselves in the Allied bombings,

W.G. Sebald's 1999 essay "Air War and Literature" reinforced the earlier claims that the German population had emerged from the Third Reich without addressing the human and material losses caused by the war.[2] Rather than sorrow and grief, Sebald identified a persistent silencing of the German deaths in postwar culture resulting from feelings of shame and resentment toward the victors. Although Sebald described the absence of air war memories as a collectively shared secret, in other words, a tacit agreement not to speak about the destruction of German cities and lives, he also invoked a language of traumatic shock to make sense of the emotional numbing and amnesia in the German postwar population.

Since Sebald's essay appeared, new historical accounts of the air war have responded to an evolving public interest in narratives about the German war experience. Jörg Friedrich's highly publicized book, *The Fire: The Bombing of Germany*, has detailed the bombing of German cities and the killing of their inhabitants with a range of archival, literary, and experiential accounts. The historical context of ultimate German responsibility for the war and all its consequences that had come to define the critical approach to postwar memory since the 1960s falls outside the parameters of Friedrich's study.[3] Underlying the contentious responses to this description of the devastating impact of the Allied war are questions about the legitimacy of public memories centered on German suffering rather than perpetration. Instead of asking whether Germans should remember their own historical losses, we need to examine *how* these losses can be integrated into today's memory discourse and public debate. During the 60th anniversary ceremonies for the end of the Second World War, German state officials have offered important public recognitions of "terror and shame" (Koehler) with respect to the mass annihilation of the Jews in the Holocaust. In turn these statements have increased demands for a cultural memory that involves the historical losses the Germans experienced themselves. Without a robust public discourse, however, that conceives of empathy with the self as a potential pathway toward empathy with others, a concern with German suffering will continually relapse into narcissistic or nostalgic engagements with the war past. The popular success and wide distribution of Sönke Wortmann's *The Miracle of Bern* (2003) and Oliver Hirschbiegel's *Hitler's Downfall* (2005), both ultimately told through the narrow personal perspective of a presumed German victimization, attest to the cultural currency of such a sliding toward revisionist notions of relative innocence.

As these recent cinematic shifts toward a collective memory involving German war losses and the collapse of the Third Reich tend to block out historical responsibilities in favor of more intimate (often sentimentalized) points of view, this essay explores possible counterforces to such modified forms of historical numbing that still pervade Germany's public culture today.[4] It is from this perspective that I return to DEFA rubble films, and specifically Wolfgang Lamprecht's Somewhere in Berlin (*Irgendwo in Berlin*, 1946), proposing that modes of melancholic mourning did indeed emerge in early antifascist film. While this challenges the long-standing notion of silence and repression associated with Alexander and Margarete Mitscherlich and, to a certain extent, W.G. Sebald, their concern with the conscious and unconscious modes that shape the past in the present remains crucial for my analysis of cultural and, specifically, cinematic texts. Resulting from competing memory strands and elisions, many postwar productions contain small, peculiar moments that do not quite add up to the overall narrative or visual economy of the film. Instead of an enduring and all-encompassing failure, or even refusal to mourn, however, these textual symptoms reveal continually partial, and often awkward efforts to develop a representational language of grief in Germany's posttraumatic culture. Abandoning a strict distinction between melancholia as a pathological form of grieving, and mourning as the more advanced recuperative memory practice, I account for the various ways in which feelings, or structures of affect, related to loss and trauma impacted early postwar life and the Germans' difficulty to come to terms with the Nazi past.

Crucial to my argument is the notion that DEFA rubble films neither fully attest to the long-standing notion of postwar German flight from death and defeat (the often misunderstood silence or amnesia) nor to a revisionist attachment to German loss and suffering. Instead, these films, devoted to a symbolic language of antifascist renewal, constitute a public archive in which the shifting movements between personal loss and historical transformation can be tracked as an elegiac postwar memory. Here, Ann Cvechovitch's understanding of cultural texts as "archives of feelings," or more specifically, of a wide range of affective responses to traumatic individual and historical experience, helps us rethink the work of grief and mourning in postwar rubble film. Challenging distinctions between collective or political responses and private affective life, she treats cultural artifacts as "repositories of feelings and emotions," which are encoded not only in the content and, I would add, representational choices of the texts themselves, but in the practices that surround their production and reception.[5] From this perspective, rubble films produced shortly after 1945 capture the historical trauma of the Second World War, which refracted outward and produced all kinds of related affective residues, including sadness, shame, anguish, and bereavement and their respective blockage as depression, apathy, and numbing. In other words, the cinematic narratives and their respective elisions, the audience's engagement and the public reviews were all inevitably mired in the emotional experience of people who had lived through the war. Yet, at the same time, the rubble films served as an important public space where these affective responses, not yet solidified into identifiable meanings, were negotiated through cinematic performance and practice. That is, even if we agree with Julia Kristeva that film with its tendency toward spectacle, staging, and the image, produces semantic and sentimental associations that come only as a substitute to the silent exaggeration of grief and depression in literary speech, it is the medium's recourse to artifice, to performative and visual modes, which enables those substitutions and displacements that can give us insight into the precarious presence of death and the postwar crisis of signification related to the eruption of mass death in the Second World War.[6]

After 1945, postwar Germany lacked a viable public sphere of death and grief, in which the experience of war and genocide could have been transformed into more stable forms of discourse and representation. The experience of death was all-pervasive in Germany at the end of the war— around four to five million German men had been killed at the various fronts, which meant that in almost every family one man had died or was missing; 600,000 civilians had lost their lives during the air raids of German cities, continuously requiring emergency burials and makeshift graves that were scattered throughout the rubble of the destroyed urban landscape. Initially, newspapers and film media reported in detail the mass annihilation of the six million Jews in Nazi concentration camps. At the same time, however, the need to confront the immediate effects of material destruction, malnutrition, and bacterial epidemics coupled with a tenuous public sphere of death and a diffuse sense of guilt among the German population fostered a tendency to split off the experience of mass death, let alone responsibility for mass murder. Michael Geyer has put this into helpful metaphors: the outer presence of death did not simply vanish, it "was reduced to a stage whisper, not really repressed into the unconscious, but enclosed between conscious and unconscious—a half-waking presence."[7]

At this time when war death suffused the public sphere in postwar Germany, yet no workable articulations and commemorative practices were available to stabilize this experience, the first films produced by the Deutsche Film AG (DEFA) in the Soviet Occupation Zone, such as *The Murderers are Among Us* (1946), *Somewhere in Berlin* (1946), *Wozzeck* (1947), and *Our Daily Bread* (1949) played an important role in binding war experiences and affective responses to traumatic loss into transformative postwar and increasingly antifascist narratives. In December of 1946,

Lamprecht's *Somewhere in Berlin*, the third DEFA film, was publicly released with a grand opening at the State Opera in the Soviet sector of Berlin. The film continued DEFA's cinematic engagement with economic crisis, psychological struggle, and political transformation by intertwining the story of a group of children roaming in the ruins of Berlin with the exemplary narrative of a returning soldier who successfully recuperates his position in the paternal order and is reintegrated into postwar society. The film's concern with the social and psychological problems of the immediate postwar years received contesting reviews in the local and national newspapers at the time. While some contemporary critics perceived the film's interest in the struggle of returning soldiers, broken families, and neglected children as particularly realistic, others dismissed especially the final scene of the film that portrays nearly all protagonists united in the effort to reconstruct a new humanistic postwar society as melodramatic and politically tendentious.[8] Most reviewers focused on the cinematic depiction of postwar youth dislodged from any stable ethical and social structure rather than the programmatic story of men's displacement and return, thus emphasizing the role played by generational conflict in the restoration of the conventional social and specular position of the postwar male, a position that depended in fact on the affirmation by children.[9]

Rather than centering on the film's recuperative practices, I would like to direct attention to a subplot of *Somewhere in Berlin*, which shapes a representational and affective space for grief and mourning with respect to the German men who died in the war and, tainted by National Socialism, needed to be largely forgotten in a postwar society that lived segregated from its war dead.[10] As the film strives toward closure and postwar beginning, it performs a number of exclusions to support its fantasy of a harmonious social totality in which the postwar male subject can find new meaning. Set against the integrationist narrative of the exemplary returnee, Iller, is the story of another former Wehrmacht soldier, Steidel, who survived the war severely "shell-shocked" and is now receiving maternal care. This story plays an important public role in articulating the social costs and consequences of a potentially irreparably damaged postwar masculinity, participating in the larger discursive efforts in the 1940s that rendered war suffering, and more specifically, war trauma in terms of psychic abnormality and social failure. At the same time, however, and more central to my concern here with the elegiac dramaturgies of early DEFA film, it is the narrative and symbolic overlap of the psychologically impaired returnee with the death of one of the children in the ruins of Berlin that allows for a mediated dramatization of blocked affects concerning the massive loss of German men incurred by the war.

Steidel's delusional presentation of militaristic rituals on the balcony of his apartment separate him from any constructive postwar activities as a madman on the margins of society. Staring blankly into space, this character displays the perceptual paralysis that after the war had come to define the public image of the defeated returnee in the urban landscape of Germany.[11] As the neighbors complain about his seemingly offensive appearance and want him removed from the window, the film disseminates the insight that the mentally impaired returnees, in contrast to the physically disabled amputees, increasingly struggled with blame and shame in the public sphere.[12] Aside from the film's engagement with sociopsychological realities of Germany's transitional postwar culture, there is a notable excess in the performance of Steidel's psychic episodes that situates this figure outside the realist register of the overall film. The deranged soldier appears theatrical, overacted, and, in contrast to the other characters in the film, simply unreal. This is underlined with a stagy and seemingly composed mise-en-scène that makes up the claustrophobic, tactile-sensory interior of the scenes in his room, in which objects and close-ups of the protagonist's face rather than real optical sound situations construct representational meaning. While the outside world seems to be manically moving forward, Steidel's daily life is reduced to the same alternation of sleeping, window watching, and public reenactment of militaristic rituals accompanied by the detachment of his motionless stare. These anachronistic stagings involve a certain passivity and disengagement from the world, but the theatrical excess of the performance also renders Steidel's afflictions as an act or strategy. In other words, the uncanny public appearance of postwar normalcy enabled by the film's overall emphasis on reconstruction, is disturbed by Steidel's displaced enactments of subservient rituals on the balcony above the ruins of Berlin. Here, the war-damaged soldier who is locked in a transfixed gaze and whose deadened body is reanimated through the silent performance of military rituals emerges as one of the most visible locations of historical loss in early postwar cinema. Executing the gestural life of a pantomime, to draw on Benjamin's figure of melancholic mournfulness, the returnee erratically plays out an undiminished inner presence of death that cannot be fully symbolized within the postwar cinematic imagination.[13]

Since the film renders this elegiac performance through a set of psychopathological registers, however, the reviewers transformed the tenuous historically specific meanings entailed in Steidel's mournful display into a larger modern narrative concerned with madness and war.[14] From the dominant display of a facial scar, reduced speech, and quiet sadness to the limpness of facial muscles, soft smile, and diverted gaze, the representational language indexes in great detail the radically altered personality and physical idiosyncrasies psychiatrists in the forties ascribed to those who appeared to suffer traumatic brain injury.[15] This regressive physiological discourse of brain injury, which harked back to earlier organic notions of trauma as bodily damage already challenged by Freud after World War I, legitimized those with brain injuries (*Hirnverletzte*) as the only real remainder of war-related suffering in postwar Germany. Often, however, the general population did not perceive these men as patients who could be treated medically, but rather as mad or severely mentally disturbed. The representational strategies by which Steidel's war damage is constructed as mental debilitation, even idiocy, ultimately sustain these cultural fantasies that evacuate the contingent interrelations between historical violence and transient modes of trauma.

Even as the traumatic flashbacks intruding on Steidel's waking life create some sense of historical causality and linkage, these break-ins of the past are represented through generic war footage borrowed from the National Socialist newsreel *Wochenschau*, which constructed the past as a disembodied history of technological warfare, involving lighting and sound effect rather than human injury and suffering.[16] As we no longer enter the diegesis of a past narrative that addresses crimes, guilt, and perhaps remorse—this was still the case in *The Murderers Are Among Us*—the abstract war footage superimposed on Steidl's face intimates a haunted psychic landscape in which the actual experience of mass death and murder has been blotted out.

In significant ways, these erasures of historical contingencies set the stage for what I call the film's metonymic ritual of bereavement, a sentimental, yet arguably cathected, displaced restaging of the loss of German men at a time when their involvement in the war had been widely discredited. Given the atrocities and mass murder perpetrated on the Jews and peoples of Eastern Europe in the name of National Socialism, those men, dead or defeated, who had fought in the war could not salvage their dignity, let alone honor and respect.[17] Here the film's affective and discursive reworking of the National Socialist ideology of heroism and sacrifice is crucial. Steidel believes in his delusional state that the boy Willi, who climbs up onto the ruin of a bombed-out house to disprove that he is a coward, is willing to sacrifice his life for some higher cause. Even if the film's message lies precisely in conveying that this kind of misunderstood heroism is not only futile but also harmful to the individual and the collective, the film's integrationist plotline relies on the recuperative function of the child with respect to war-damaged masculinity. In fact, Lamprecht's specific articulation of an integrationist narrative requires the death of the boy. A highly stylized staging of the encounter between the exemplary returnee, Iller, and the dying boy, placed toward the end of the film, completes the generational transition from child to paternal subject, restabilizing the social and symbolic hierarchies dislodged across the historical crisis of 1945. In other words, on the film's symbolic level, the child's life is relinquished to repair the social and discursive dispersion under the newly affirmed master signifier, the postwar father. While this imaginary investment indicates just how fragile the familial sociosymbolic structure had become by the end of the war, there is more at stake in the sacrificial discourse played out through the subnarrative of Willi's accident and death. The boy's trial of courage is staged as a public spectacle witnessed by children and neighbors, but through a series of point-of-view shots and a number of visual repetitions and similarities (broken-off facade, balcony/rim), this scene of displaced male strength is also performed *for* Steidel and the ideology of derailed heroism embodied by this character. Witnessing the child, he promptly yells out "Hurray!" "A hero! A hero!"

Given that already during the war the ideology of bravery and sacrifice had ceased to provide cohesive identifications for German males serving in the Wehrmacht, the film's critique of heroism glosses over a significant gap between official Nazi rhetoric and the creation of private meaning (*Sinnstiftung*).[18] Perpetuating a notion of heroic sacrifice whose "positive" relation between identity and war had already been lost before 1945, the lesson to be learned here about abused masculinity and misguided strength attains an overdetermined status. This affirms a general feature in postwar DEFA film, where the complexity of the crimes of genocide tend to be elided in favor of a compensatory attention to and inflation of other moral failings. Albeit underscoring a postwar return to democracy and civility, the film's totalizing critique of a National Socialist war ideology that remained presumably intact and subsumed all subjects until the end of the war seems oddly hollow and defunct. This ideological transfer—the film's tendency to sustain a discourse of heroism that had already become formulaic and bankrupt—contains the knowledge of an ever deeper postwar crisis, namely, the horrific intuition that ultimately most of the men who died in the war did not die *because* they believed in the higher purpose of sacrifice and fatherland but rather that they lost their lives devoid of the affirmative power of this rhetoric.

In that sense *Somewhere in Berlin* is as much about the child's "fall," which ultimately enables the restabilization of a postwar order through the integration of the exemplary returnee, as it is, by way of a number of metonymic shifts, about a kind of commemorative project in response to the collective trauma of the "fallen soldiers," the men who did not survive the war or who were indelibly wounded.[19] For a brief moment, the boy's accidental fall tears apart the precarious sociosymbolic structure of this postwar community. Especially in light of the film's concern with the reinvigorating power and universal innocence of children, the sudden fall comes as a shock. This alteration of pedagogical conventions points to the relatively flexible nature of the trope involving the child as savior in cinematic production of the immediate postwar years. When the body cuts through the frame, dropping into the inner crater of the ruin (viscerally marked by the eerie absence of the otherwise predominant music score) the film's integrationist postwar project comes to a halt, until only seconds later, as the witnesses approach Willi's body, the overall narrative picks up, quickly rearranging and repairing the ruptured postwar sociosymbolic order.

The scene of Willi's unrelenting fall reveals the full impact of injury and historical, if not foundational loss. Here the dispersive meanings produced by the associations of body, child, ruins, bombing, and modern warfare are reined in by sliding the open impulse action, resonant with neorealism, into the strongly composed interior space of the Steidel scene, linked with the traditional studio-film aesthetic. In contrast to the emergence of empty and fractured spaces in the scene that engenders Willi's accident, the setting associated with Steidel is already specified and determines certain actions (i.e., the couch on which he rests only for his flashbacks, a window and balcony for his mad enactments, and the war paraphernalia to be touched). While the airy cinematography associated with Willi's accident extends the visual field into an imaginary impending space out of frame, the composed claustrophobic interior in Steidel's room is strongly defined by the presence and arrangement of objects (i.e., the military helmet that does not seem to sediment in time, a picture of a soldier). The deliberate handling of the objects, carefully positioned, together with close-ups of the protagonist's tormented face, control the viewer's affective response. The film's attempts to articulate war death and grief can be made out in the jarring breaks between these two different types of images and styles that are symptomatic of a larger crisis of the old realism in European cinema after 1945. Whereas the circumscribed staging of the war-damaged soldier confines the shattering effects of violence and death, the boy's accident exposes the voids in the ruins without addressing their specific historical meaning. Shifting between naturalist set and neorealist setting, overacting and enacting, predefined affect and unanchored emotion, the film searches for a representational language that can articulate war suffering. It is then by creating an inner diegetic link between the two characters that a mourning ritual is dramatized.

In order to fully situate the child in the enclosed space of the mentally impaired returnee, a narrative intervention is required. An orphaned resettler, Willi, had been forced to leave his temporary home and is now also in the care of Steidel's mother. This insertion of the ailing child into the scene associated with Steidel entails a ritual that gives meaning to war death through temporal deferral. In a carefully structured scene of mirroring and doubling, Willi's injured body (bathed in light and with no visible wounds) is literally displayed on the bed where Steidel rested earlier. That this sickbed scene already resembles a last viewing of the body is articulated by Steidel's mother who conveys to the model returnee Iller that her son guards the child all day long (*Wache stehen*). Particularly, the verticality of the previous accident scene, established through extreme camera angles and the marked horizontality of the "wake" scene, casts this sequence through a semantic field of *Fallen*, the sublimational circumscription of the soldier's death ubiquitous in both official and private discourse.[20]

The visual composition of the sickbed/deathbed scene is reiterated in a second sequence that dramatizes the child's actual death. Almost imperceptibly, the scene has been located to a different room of the house. Obviously this marks the passing of time, but more importantly, the left/right positioning of Steidel and Willi has been inversed, which secures the symbolic entwinement of the two figures. Seconds later then, Steidel manically repeats at the sight of the child's suffering "Soldiers are dying! Soldiers are dying!". The lighting and strong composition of these two scenes suffuse the child's death with a stagy style reminiscent of UFA studio film. The act of dying dramatized here implies a ritual ceremony where an extensive waiting period culminates in a final moment of death, which will give retroactive meaning.[21] Even if no religious iconography is invoked in this DEFA film (as was common after the war in the West), the visual signification of the "laid out body" resonates with the solemn rituals associated with dead soldiers in World War I and also, if to a lesser extent, throughout World War II.[22] These auratic connotations help preserve the distance between object/body and viewer and thereby suspend the visceral violence of vulnerable bodies annihilated, mutilated, torn up, and dismembered by modern warfare into a language of pathos. Through dramatic high-contrast lighting of Willi's face, slow pace, and a swelling music score, this scene resembles the "death kitsch" of UFA films, as Shandley put it.[23] Some reviewers who saw the film when it was first released critically remarked how out of place the prolonged and excessively melodramatic staging of Willi's deathbed scene appeared.[24] And Mückenberger is right when she describes this scene as a foreign element (*Fremdkörper*) within the overall more realist and sober visual economy of the film.[25]

My argument is this, however: through a series of substitutions and displacements, the "wake" scenes establish a public space in which feelings of loss and grief concerning dead German men could hover. Although the film's ideological program is to dismantle war heroism and to establish a reintegration narrative for the former Wehrmacht soldier, the metonymic deathbed segment reveals a public need to address war suffering and death. The aggrandizing emotive and visual registers of the scene certainly edify the dying displayed here. In contrast, for example, the 1947 neorealist film *Germany Anno Zero* by the Italian director Roberto Rossellini also involves the death of a boy in the ruins of Berlin, but the film ends the very moment his discarded body is found by a random passerby. This is not to say that Lamprecht could or should have used such minimalist, yet deeply disturbing display of suffering; but rather that the generic language of auratic, even sacrificial death opens associations with the loss of German men, revealing the absence of other, more usable commemorative strategies in postwar Germany. That is, instead of simply avoiding or neutralizing pain (the common argument about formulaic postwar expressions), Lamprecht's film indicates an impasse on the level of collective representations. Enmeshed in a larger discursive network through which the public memory of war death was continually suppressed (if never fully), the film falls back on melodramatic conventions to elicit the viewer's identification. David Bathrick has identified the reemerging UFA style in early postwar film as a traumatic acting out of the past, even a first necessary step toward working through it.[26] That these formulaic representations show a tendency to surmount individual pain and devastation points not only to the structure of melodrama itself but also to the lasting effects of the treatment of loss under National Socialism.

The death cult of the Third Reich had absorbed genuine affective responses to loss, including grieving and crying, within a ritualized display of pride and sacrifice whose totalizing orchestration surpassed traditional militaristic ceremonies. As Sabine Behrenbeck has shown, especially since 1941, the Nazis had strictly regulated the meanings of war-related deaths. Funeral rituals and symbols that traditionally secured the recognition of loss and passing were overridden by a public aestheticization and mystification of death that hindered the recuperative work of releasing the departed. This also meant that private burial ceremonies organized by the church were increasingly discouraged in Nazi Germany. As people turned into the spectators of the official commemorations of heroic sacrifice, individual sadness was to be dissolved within the communal experience of conquering death itself. Although during World War I, women had played a significant role in commemorating those who had died, they no longer had an active place in the stagings of proud grief conducted by the Nazis. Those who grieved had to exercise will power and self-discipline, expressions of pain and despair were not permissible within the heroic spectacles of sacrifice and triumph. The wearing of black or the use of black ribbon as public significations of mourning were increasingly restricted and already forbidden in 1939.[27] Subsequently—and in stark contrast to a public culture after World War I, where the dead and disabled were acutely present in films, paintings, and psychological discourse—no viable debate about how to remember the war dead took place in Germany after 1945. Even civilian victims were hastily burned and buried in mass graves. The uniform small wooden crosses and provisional enclosures of temporary cemeteries could barely conceal the tenuous relation between the living and the dead. One year after the end of the war, the Allies ordered the demolition of war monuments and museums built by the Nazis as well as those monuments that lent themselves to militaristic glorification.[28] While cemeteries for dead soldiers continued to be built in the western zones, the commemorative practices in the Soviet Occupation zone centered on the members of the Red Army who had lost their lives in a war that had killed 25 million of their own people. More than 5,000 Soviet soldiers who died in the final military actions were buried at the cemetery Berlin Treptow, where between 1946 and 1949 a monument park was built, at the center of which the gigantic overtowering sculpture of a Soviet soldier carrying a German child symbolized the liberation of the Germans by the Russian Army.[29] Even as the empty tombs to "Unknown Soldiers" and the public ceremonial reverence for such monuments have become emblematic of modern nationalist cultures, few marked burial sites or memorials existed in the eastern zone for German men who had died in World War II.[30]

The discursive vacuum concerning the dead German soldiers (subsumed under victims but whose loss cannot be signified) in the transitional postwar culture of the Soviet Occupation zone, is the context in which the displaced dramatization of dying/death, the strong corporeal rendition of this scene in Lamprecht's DEFA film unfolds its excess and sinks into the cliché of cinematic melodrama familiar from UFA productions. Deleuze reminds us, however, that it is in the cliché,

> where all the powers have an interest in hiding something in the image. [...] at the same time, the image constantly attempts to break through the cliché, to get out of the cliché [...] Sometimes it is necessary to restore the lost parts, to rediscover everything that cannot be seen in the image, everything that has been removed to make it "interesting." But sometimes, on the contrary, it is necessary to make holes, to introduce voids and white spaces, to rarify the image by suppressing many things that have been added to make us believe that we are seeing everything. It is necessary to make a division or make emptiness in order to find the whole again.[31]

Surrounded by Steidel, his mother, and a group of children, including Iller's son Gustav, the boy, Willi, suffused by light, is dying. The camera alternates between the child's pure ailing face and medium shots of the other characters watching the child. If there is any expression in their faces at all, it is a kind of solemn numbness (*getragene Starre*), an emotional paralysis underlined by the pathos in the music score, which lays itself like a patina over this scene, keying the audience into a feeling of loss that the psychically disconnected characters seem barely able to feel.

Even if this melodramatic displaced restaging of dying in DEFA's third film after the end of the war does not give way to new workable representations of death, grief, and mourning, two brief sudden outbursts of Gustav's voice tear "holes" in the tight visual and affective linkages of the scene. There is a rawness in the uncontrolled and desperate utterances of this child that runs counter to the prefabricated emotional cues of this scene. These words are of course scripted and memorized by the child actor, that is, they are as performative in nature as any of the other visual or sonic elements; but whether intended or an unconscious effect, within this constructed field of meaning the distress in the voice of the boy carries an authentic quality. While everybody stares in detached silence at the body of the child, Gustav, the son of Iller, is the only one who cries out: "Will he…?" "Will he…?" Unable to fully take the words of death into his mouth, his voice reveals the "choking back of sorrow" that underlies the deathbed scene, a lockage in the state of grief rather than the refusal to mourn that we have come to associate with the postwar era. Steidel picks up the child's fragmented speech and yells out in unchanged madness "Soldiers die!" "Soldiers die!" The camera cuts to a reaction shot of Steidel's mother, who appears unable to respond or intervene. At this point, the child's desperate voice punctures the traumatic ties between the characters by pointing to the seemingly obvious: "But he is *not* a soldier, he is a small boy." This interjection establishes a difference between past and present, war and postwar situation, loss of lives in war combat and in the ruins left over by the war, unsettling the "permanence of numbing" related to the experience of mass death that in many respects became the primary characteristic of the postwar period.[32] When the death displayed on the screen is markedly recognized for what it is—the passing of a child and not that of a soldier—then there also opens up an alternative space, in which the war death of German men as well as the vulnerabilities of those who lived on could be addressed without the support of the metonymic apparatus and transcending pathos supplied by this inset.

But the dead and those who suffer from their loss are glossed over in the film's overall linear narrative program of recuperation and moving on. The next scene quickly moves the loss associated with Willi/Steidel into the past and erases the uneasy echo of Gustav's imploring remark. The child's death is firmly located in the past by a full fade to black; the somber music concludes with an emphatic chord and the film moves out of the death scene by cutting to the optical sound situation of a light, transparent frame, an on-location shot of the scarred surface of the building facade from which Willi fell. We hear the sound of a detonation, the building collapses, and dust, slowly filling the screen and continuing fluidly out of frame, creates a hollow space that visually translates the void or silence engulfing the dead of the Second World War, the overall "taboo of remembering and mourning."[33] Seconds later, the dust gives way to a children's chalk drawing on a leftover wall; that is where the future lies, and from here the film quickly ties up the remainder of the narrative to move without further ado toward the final transformative staging of Iller. Affirming the notion that postwar masculinity cannot be restored around men who struggle with their war experience, the film concludes with a final triumphant scene in which the recuperated paternal figure is pushed forward into a linear course of constructive action and progressive history. A dramatic low angle shot shows how the transformed antifascist citizen, literally positioned on top of a pile of rubble and surrounded by a group of children, begins to engage with the future by rebuilding a new postwar society.

It is in the discursive and visual rearrangements performed by early DEFA (rubble) film, that an elusive presence of death continued to be palpable. The cinematic specters left behind by blocked (not absent) practices of sadness and sorrow reveal the contours of an unsettled elegiac postwar memory. Not only can we say with hindsight that the psychic numbness, or neutralization of distress, was both the minimal and also ultimate sign of grief and devastation in postwar Germany,[34] but, seen through a perspective that emphasizes the productive aspects of melancholic mourning as a persistent and open-ended process, it is precisely those "hollow spaces of emotions" that allow us today to gain new insights into the Germans' difficulty in coming to terms with the past.[35] As we attend to these impasses from a *reparative* historical perspective, that is, with empathy and ethical renewal in mind, postwar rubble film emerges as an indispensable cultural archive including a range of mutable affective and representational responses to historical loss and trauma. This is not to ignore the historically specific experiences of perpetrators, victims, and bystanders but rather to open a trajectory toward a transnational comparison with other posttraumatic cinemas that will bring the preoccupation of German rubble film with overlapping modes of suffering and perpetration more sharply into view.[36]

Notes

Pinkert is the author of *Film and Memory in East Germany* (Bloomington, IN: Indiana University Press, 2008). The chapter in this volume is drawn from this book.

1. Alexander and Margarete Mitscherlich, *Die Unfähigkeit zu trauern* (München, Zürich: Piper, 1977), pp.36–37.

2. W. G. Sebald, *Luftkrieg und Literatur* (München: Carl Hanser Verlag, 1999), pp.19, 37.
3. Jörg Friedrich, *Der Brand. Deutschland im Bombenkrieg* (München: Prophyläen, 2002). For different positions with respect to the discussions of the air war and German victimization, see Lothar Kettenacker, ed., *Ein Volk von Opfern. Die Debatte um den Bombenkrieg 1940–45* (Berlin: Rowohlt, 2003).
4. For a theoretical elaboration of this approach to historical understanding, see Dominic LaCapra, *Writing History, Writing Trauma* (Baltimore, MD: Johns Hopkins University Press, 2001), pp.40–42.
5. Ann Cvechovitch, *An Archive of Feelings: Trauma, Sexuality, and Lesbian Culture* (Durham, NC and London: Duke University Press, 2003), p.7.
6. Julia Kristeva, *Black Sun: Depression and Melancholia* (New York: Columbia University Press, 1989) p.226.
7. Michael Geyer, "The Place of the Second World War in German Memory and History," *New German Critique* 71 (Spring/Summer 1997): 19.
8. L. M., "Im Dschungel der zertrümmerten Stadt: Der neue DEFA-Film 'Irgendwo in Berlin' uraufgeführt," *Volksblatt* (December 20, 1946).
9. Jaimey Fisher, "Who's Watching the Rubble-Kids? Youth, Pedagogy, and Politics in Early DEFA Films," *New German Critique* 82 (Winter 2001): 91–125, esp. pp.108–112.
10. Elisabeth Domansky, "Lost War: World War II in Postwar German Memory," in *Thinking About the Holocaust: After Half a Century*, ed. Alvin H. Rosenfeld (Bloomington, IN: Indiana University Press, 1997), p.243. For the privatization of mourning after 1945, see John Bornemann, "Gottesvater, Landesvater, Familienvater: Identification and Authority in Germany," in *Death of the Father: An Anthropology of the End in Political Authority*, ed. John Bornemann (New York: Berghahn, 2004), p.66.
11. Barnouw, *Germany 1945: Views of War and Violence* (Bloomington, IN: Indiana University Press, 1996), pp.173–181. I borrow the term "perceptual paralysis" (*Wahrnehmungsstarre*) from Louis A. Sass, *Madness and Modernism: Insanity in the Light of Modern Art, Literature, and Thought* (New York: Basic Books, 1992), p.44.
12. Adolf Busemann, "Psychologische Untersuchungen an Hirnverletzten," in *Nervenarzt* 18.8 (1947): 337–349. W. Lindenberg, "Ärztliche und soziale Betreuung des Hirnverletzten," *Deutsches Gesundheitswesen* 3.5 (1948): 145–147.
13. For the connection between melancholia, mourning, and the figure of the pantomime in Benjamin, see Judith Butler, "Afterword: After Loss, What then?" in *Loss: The Politics of Mourning*, ed. David L. Eng, David Kazanjian (Berkeley, CA: University of California Press, 2003), p.470.
14. Gl, "Der Dritte Spielfilm der DEFA. Festaufführung von 'Irgendwo in Berlin,'" *Nacht Express*, (December 19, 1946).
15. W. Lindenberg, "Fehlbeurteilung Hirnverletzter," *Deutsches Gesundheitswesen* 2.7 (1947): 225–228.
16. For the war newsreel produced in the Third Reich, see Christiane Mückenberger, Günter Jordan, *Sie sehen selbst, Sie hören selbst: Die DEFA von ihren Anfängen bis 1949* (Marburg: Hitzeroth, 1994), p.32.
17. George Mosse, *Fallen Soldiers: Reshaping the Memory of the World Wars* (New York: Oxford University Press, 1990), p.202; Konrad Hugo Jarausch

and Michael Geyer, *Shattered Past: Reconstructing German Histories* (Princeton, NJ: Princeton University Press, 2003), p.331.

18. Klaus Latzel, *Deutsche Soldaten—Nationalsozialistischer Krieg?: Kriegserlebnis, Kriegserfahrung 1939–1945* (Paderborn: Schöningh, 1996), pp.228–283, esp. pp.275–283.

19. For the semantics of *fallen*/to fall in relation to trauma, see Cathy Caruth, *Unclaimed Experience: Trauma, Narrative, and History* (Baltimore, MD: Johns Hopkins University Press, 1996), pp.73–91.

20. Latzel, *Deutsche Soldaten*, pp.233–235.

21. The film rejects here the shift from family rituals to modern hospital death that took place between 1930 and 1950 (Phillipe Ariès, *Western Attitudes Toward Death: From the Middle Ages to the Present* [London: Marion Boyars, 1976], pp.88–87).

22. For Christian iconography in commemorative practices in the West, see Meinhold Lurz, *Kriegerdenkmäler*, vol. 6 (Heidelberg: Esprit Verlag, 1987), pp.215–227, also pp.170–172.

23. Robert R. Shandley, *Rubble Films: German Cinema in the Shadow of the Third Reich* (Philadelphia: Temple University Press, 2001), p.125.

24. A.M.U., "Irgendwo in Berlin," *Leipziger Volkszeitung* (January 1, 1947); Friedrich Luft "'Irgendwo in Berlin' eine DEFA Uraufführung," *Tagesspiegel* (December 20, 1946).

25. Mückenberger, *Sie Sehen Selbst*, p.68.

26. David Bathrick, "From UFA to DEFA: Past as Present in Early GDR Films," in *Contentious Memories: Looking Back at the GDR*, ed. Jost Hermand and Marc Silberman (New York: Peter Lang, 1998) pp.169–188.

27. Sabine Behrenbeck, *Der Kult um die Toten Helden: Nationalsozialistische Mythen, Riten und Symbole 1923 bis 1945* (Vierow: SH Verlag, 1996), pp.494–528; See also Geyer, "The Place," pp.17–18; Rudy Koshar, *Germany's Transient Pasts: Preservation and National Memory in the Twentieth Century* (Chapel Hill, NC: University of North Carolina Press, 1998), pp.95–99; Latzel, *Deutsche Soldaten*, p.278.

28. Domansky, "Lost War," p.243; Barnouw, *Germany in 1945*, p.168; Mosse, *Fallen Soldiers*, pp.212–220.

29. Lurz, *Kriegerdenkmäler*, pp.138, 148.

30. Benedict Anderson, *Imagined Communities: Reflections on the Origins and Spread of Nationalism* (London: Verso 1991), p.9 (notes 1 and 2).

31. Gilles Deleuze, *Cinema 2: The Time-Image*, trans. Hugh Tomlinson and Robert Galeta (Minneapolis, MN: University of Minnesota, 1986), p.21.

32. Geyer, "The Place," p.19.

33. Domansky, "Lost War," p.237.

34. For the connection between psychic numbness and grief, see Kristeva, *Black Sun*, p.228.

35. Julia Hell borrows this phrase from Anna Seghers (Julia Hell, *Postfascist Fantasies: Psychoanalysis, History, and the Literature of East Germany* [London and Durham, NC: Duke University Press, 1997], p.101).

36. Ann E. Kaplan and Ban Wang, *Trauma and Cinema: Cross-Cultural Explorations* (Aberdeen, UK: Hong Kong University Press, 2004).

CHAPTER FIVE

THE STONES BEGIN TO SPEAK:
THE LABORING SUBJECT IN EARLY
DEFA DOCUMENTARIES

Brad Prager

Fritz Lang's *Metropolis* (1927) is well known for its depiction of laborers being subdued by machines. More than once in that film, workers risk becoming part of the very machinery that has been manufactured to serve them. In one sequence a laborer—as though he were bound like Prometheus to his rock—attempts to control a machine's moving parts. Lang's cinematic subject seems to transfigure himself; he becomes one with an enormous mechanized apparatus. The film ultimately offers a humanitarian vision of class struggle, though one that was not incompatible with capitalism. Its famous moral tells us that between labor, or the hands that do the work, and capital, the head that administrates, there must always be a mediating heart. Despite the overall tenor of Lang's most iconic sequences—images that portend the domination of machines over mankind—industrial labor is not presented on its own as problematic. It appears in the film as something inevitable, a necessity accompanied by the risk that laborers will find themselves inside the belly of an industrial Moloch.

It was not long after *Metropolis*—less than two decades later—that Germany was compelled to begin its postwar reconstruction. In the occupied Soviet zone, German filmmakers involved in the founding of the DEFA attempted to depict the labors of the rebuilding process without characterizing the laboring subjects as dehumanized; they attempted to depict labor without its accompanying alienation. This type of idealization of labor, however, rings false insofar as mass production in the minds of most is unthinkable as something disjoined from the threatening jaws of manmade machines. Marx's promise, the one that the Soviet zone aimed to fulfill, was that Socialism would take the dehumanized fragment known as "man"—or the cog that the laborer necessarily becomes in the industrial machine—and transform that fragment into a whole. The society in which this goal would be achieved was, of course, not at hand. It was merely a promise, itself the fuel for a repressive and industrial state. Marx's vision was future oriented, and the state's short-term goal consisted of convincing laborers to be content in their role as fragments, or as individual planks on a bridge to the future. Unless socialism was to be called a permanent state of affairs—as it was years later, when East Germany finally ceased referring to it as a "transitional phase"—its laborers would have to be satisfied to serve as the bridge's struts and pylons.

German cinemas rapidly reopened following the capitulation, and films were a refuge from the rubble outside. Audiences in the Soviet zone even went to see films about Lenin and the Russian revolution.[1] The first films produced by the DEFA in the period immediately following the war marketed the project of rebuilding Germany directly to the German people. This new state-supported filmmaking structure was not unfamiliar to Germans because it functioned in some ways as did the Ufa both prior to and during the war. Sponsored by the state and overseen by the Soviet occupation, DEFA films were meant to encourage the rebuilding of a nation that was in transition. Some of the early films from this transitional phase can themselves be described as transitional films insofar as they were located formally and temporally between the DEFA's first newsreels (the *Augenzeuge* films, starting in 1946) and its well-known first features, including *Die Mörder sind unter uns* (The Murderers Are among Us; 1946) and *Irgendwo in Berlin* (Somewhere in Berlin; 1946), films that appeared later in that year.

These transitional films, those made prior to *Die Mörder sind unter uns*, merit scrutiny not only because they mark the movement from newsreel to narrative, but also because they depict Germany in the midst of its reconstruction. Labor in these films, the project of rebuilding the recently berubbled nation, is provided with an ideological ground, though the subjects that perform the labor seem to vanish or lose their particularity, much as the laborers in Lang's film were nearly swallowed by an enormous machine. These films that document the rebuilding of Germany and its emerging industry, generally referred to as the *Aufbau* films, depict Germany's reconstruction as an already successful enterprise. They capture in quasi-narrative form the revitalization of German cities, and as such they are documents of progress and sources of affirmation. They not only represent a transition to the subsequent feature films in a formal sense, but they also seek to construct a viewing public that can itself be described as transitional. Kurt Maetzig's *Berlin im Aufbau, Potsdam baut auf* by Adolf Fischer and Hans (Joop) Huisken, and Richard Groschopp's *Dresden* were each ostensibly aids in moving Germans out of the recent wartime past and into a new state of affairs, one that was exclusively oriented toward the future. This new state of affairs was meant to be internationally welcoming, at least in Soviet terms, and it was to be one in which Germans were meant to feel fulfilled through the labor of rebuilding. The films were intended to encourage the construction of literal and metaphoric bridges out of the rubble, bridges that would lead to better times.

The situation of the German psyche in 1946 has been described as delicate. As W. G. Sebald noted in his well-known lectures on the air war and its consequences, the intense push to rebuild—a push "forward"— was accompanied, perhaps out of necessity, by a prohibition "on any look backward."[2] In Sebald's psychologically inflected lectures, postwar Germans appear as anxious automata, directing their gaze on the future rather than on the past. Seen in general terms, his observations apply as much to the East (which did not properly recognize itself as East Germany until 1949) as they apply to the West. He writes that the admirable reconstruction of Germany following the devastation wrought by its wartime enemies prohibited scrutiny of the past "through the sheer amount of labor required" to rebuild, and through "the creation of a new, faceless reality, pointing the population exclusively towards the future and enjoining on it silence about the past."[3] Sebald's argument may be described as psychological insofar as the energy Germany drew upon to rebuild, was, according to him, predicated on an act of repression. He offers a psychological explanation of the source of Germany's energy, one that borrows from the Freudian concept of sublimation. Writing in 1999 he argued that the "stream of psychic energy" that served as the motor of the nation's productivity had yet to dry up, even five decades later.[4] He adds that this energy finds its source "in the well-kept secret of the corpses built into the foundation of our state, a secret that bound all Germans together in the postwar years, and indeed still binds them, more closely than any positive goal such as the realization of democracy ever could."[5] While his comment is significant for the way it engages with the question of how a nation obscures historical violence—that the very act of rebuilding is in this way transformed into an act of paving over the past—this same comment also implies a skepticism about the power of future-oriented ideologies, or the author's doubts that a vision of a positive goal would drive labor capacities nearly as much as repression. People may not be inclined to transform themselves into bridges to a new future or to lose themselves in the throng of rebuilding simply because they are offered a promise such as the realization of democracy. In Sebald's argument, the real sources of such energy are to be found elsewhere, in collective repression more than in collective reason.

Assessments of the postwar German condition, however, should not treat the drive to rebuild exclusively as an effect of psychological mechanisms. There were evident material causes of the German desire to rid themselves of the rubble and recreate Germany, including hunger, the lack of proper medical care, the lack of heat in winter, and numerous other afflictions associated with postwar poverty. Pervasive suffering in the Allied occupied zones was documented by the British-born journalist Victor Gollancz, who appealed to the former Allies to provide more aid for Germany and wondered if those Allies were not letting Germans suffer unnecessarily owing to their acknowledged or unacknowledged desire for retribution.[6] In the Soviet zone reconstruction moved even more slowly than it did in the West, in part due to the reparations that the Soviet Union continued to collect. There were, therefore, more than merely psychological needs being met by the postwar Germans who contributed to the progress. Yet at the same time, images of productivity had to be marketed to a dispirited populace; Germans had to be presented with the image of a greater good, one that merited their sacrifices.

Neither newsreels nor entertaining features, the *Aufbau* films can be understood as an apparatus of conversion, films made to produce forward-looking subjects. *Berlin im Aufbau*, *Potsdam baut auf*, and *Dresden* share this common structure and also offer a common view of the past. In these three films the Nazi years unsurprisingly appear as though they were imposed upon the victimized population of Germany. The treatment of recent history as an era of foreign occupation was consistent with what ultimately became the standard East German narrative of that time: Crises in capitalism produced the Second World War and these had now been abolished. The enemy was no longer among the Germans, and there was, therefore, no need to reexamine recent events. The films do not take up the challenge of pointing an accusatory finger at their German audiences, but rather assert that someone other than them did an awful thing to their homes and land. For the most part consistent with Sebald's conjecture—although his was predominantly an argument about the economic miracle in the West—these films relentlessly assert that there is nowhere to look but forward.

If the Germans became identified with the project of rebuilding, and therefore one with the rubble itself, then these films are less about Germans than they are about leveled cities, ones that call out for hands to reassemble them from the ruins. At the very onset of Maetzig's *Berlin im Aufbau* the letters that form the title, the words "Berlin im Aufbau," crumble backward; from a pile of rubble the text is made to appear legible. The words can be said to uncrumble, to rebuild themselves, as does a phoenix from the ashes. On the one hand, this text, a slogan appearing out of the ruins, depicts time moving backward or a clock being reset; it depicts the wishful thought that what had happened had never happened. This wish that time would move backward, however, should not be mistaken for a look backward, or a willingness to scrutinize the past. The undoing of time is a symptom of a film that does not look for causes, but one that simply wants the past to have never occurred. At one and the same time, however, the text that emerges from the rubble could also be understood as a city rebuilding itself without the help of its residents. There is no individual—no single ego—at the heart of the progress, but there is instead a city that rebuilds itself, a whole that is seamlessly composed of invisible parts.

Labor is depicted as the means to create a better future, but a typical staple of this type of utopian promise is that it evinces no trace of the labor that brought it into being. In *The Human Condition*, Hannah Arendt illustrates this point with reference to the labors of Hercules. She notes that included among Hercules's tasks was the cleaning of the Augean stables, but that this mythic labor cannot be understood as a paradigm for human labor because once it was completed, the task needed never be performed again. Using the cleaning of the stables as a point of contrast, Arendt draws attention to the way human labor never frees itself from labor; it must always be done. Arendt writes:

> The daily fight in which the human body is engaged to keep the world clean and prevent its decay bears little resemblance to heroic deeds; the endurance it needs to repair every day anew the waste of yesterday is not courage, and what makes the effort painful is not danger but its relentless repetition. The Herculean 'labors' share with all great deeds that they are unique; but unfortunately it is only the mythological Augean stable that will remain clean once the effort is made and the task achieved.[7]

To draw upon Arendt's understanding, our handiwork can be made to disappear in an idealized, utopian vision of a life without labor. But, especially as concerns the *Aufbau* films in question, one is compelled to ask whether the laborer himself or herself can be made to vanish. The disappearance of the laboring subject only takes place when his or her labor is done in the name of another, or in the service of a greater good. Arendt elaborates on this point: "Division of labor is based on the fact that two men can put their labor power together and 'behave toward each other as though they were one.'" She adds:

> this one-ness is the exact opposite of co-operation, it indicates the unity of the species with regard to which every single member is the same and

exchangeable [...] The inexhaustibility of this labor force corresponds exactly to the deathlessness of the species, whose life process as a whole is not interrupted by the individual births and deaths of its members.[8]

In this way the laborer vanishes from the *Aufbau* films, much as the laborer vanished into the machine in *Metropolis*. These postwar films are predicated on the transformation of the social body as a whole more than on the transformation of any individual. They convey a promise of prosperity that has been made to a species, the promise that it will transform itself through its labors. The *Aufbau* films attempt to convince viewers by way of appealing to their commitment to the whole. Such an appeal to the superego—speaking in the interest of the state—works to construct a short circuit, bypassing the ego and speaking directly to the id, the energies of which have been channeled for the sake of the greater good.

While the depiction of Germans working in solidarity to rebuild their occupied nation is particular to these films, one should not have the impression that the form of *Berlin im Aufbau* and the other *Aufbau* films is wholly unique. *Berlin im Aufbau* to some extent employed extant newsreel footage, footage that had already been put to use in the *Augenzeuge* films, coupled with new material. The scenes that comprise these films, depicting Germans in the midst of daily labors, were typical of other, similar American and European "documentaries" from the period, ones that meant to provide an overview of life as it is lived in a metropolis. Everyone in the cities depicted in these films (in Berlin, Potsdam, and Dresden) is presented as a productive member of an urban society. Though there are images of zoos, art museums, and horse races, the predominant theme is labor. The people of Berlin contribute through their work, not only in factories, but in educating one another, in gardening, and in performing a host of other, everyday tasks.

Berlin im Aufbau begins with a short course in German history as do the other *Aufbau* films. It presents a narrative through which the disorderly past can be ordered. As Christiane Mückenberger and Günter Jordan note, the *Aufbau* films "are connected through their basic structure and the unity of their cinematic form. In the expository part, each evokes a specter of militarism that is said to have dominated since the age of Friedrich. Following this exposition, the people—'hardy men and women taking the lead'—head off to the construction site."[9] Maetzig's film launches itself with one such abbreviated reference to history. It begins by going back to 1895, to what it describes as "the roots of our misfortune." The historical sketch then quickly propels viewers forward—in a matter of seconds rather than minutes—through World War I, to 1933, and finally to 1945. Maetzig's gloss on history rapidly dissolves into familiar images of World

War II and of the fires from Nazi torches that "set Europe ablaze," and to which "our city fell victim." This introductory part of the narration, all of which was written by Maetzig's wife, Marion Keller, concludes with Germany's final "liberation from the murderous swastika."[10] This view of totalitarianism and its historical antecedents offers little specific information about the coming of the new democracy. Particularly because the East was occupied, the *Aufbau* films' specific promises for the future had to remain vague.

Unlike Lang's portrait of a laborer beneath the surface of the city struggling against a machine in the very moment it attempts to subsume him, the postwar DEFA films, and in particular the *Aufbau* films, never present viewers with a hint of labor's dehumanizing character. They contain endless depictions of Germans working together, building a better Germany, sanguine in their solidarity. Portions of Lang's film, by contrast, can be taken to typify the attitude toward labor described by Arendt, who critiques all disavowals of labor's inherent violence, a disavowal that one finds both in Marx and Marxism where laboring is made apparently equivalent to living. Such a reading of Marx at first appears counterintuitive: Marx is generally taken to be more than other thinkers aware of and sensitive to the burden that industrial society places on the laborer. In Arendt's view, however, Marx places labor at the center of all things and promises liberation from labor through labor. One finds this same promise in the foreground of the optimistic *Aufbau* films. Arendt acknowledges that the idea that we will be liberated from the bonds of necessity—from our apparently endless imprisonment by labor—is a wish that is as old as recorded history. Such a promise of emancipation was, in the end, a promise made by the ideologues of industrial production both in the East and West. In Arendt's narrative, Marxism, which held out the promise of breaking the chains of labor, was, owing to its own glorification of labor, every bit as accountable for purveying these false idealizations as its capitalist counterpart.

Particularly in the period immediately following the war, both Eastern and Western ideologies spoke empty promises: they would each be the bridge to a laborless future. The concept of labor itself appears as a bridge in Marx's thought, connecting the animal and the human. Arendt points out that it is not thinking that differentiates the two from one another for Marx, but laboring, or the fact that the animal, in the process of becoming human, begins to produce its own sustenance.[11] While labor is that ground upon which the transition from the animal to the human is built, socialism is likewise taken to represent a conduit from one stage of human history to the next. It enables the transition from exploited laborer to fulfilled communist. Seen from this perspective, labor is itself the bridge precisely to those higher and more meaningful activities. In terms of the DEFA's *Aufbau* films, it is through labor that one awakens from a state of war into a peaceful new day.

Maetzig's film includes a bounty of images of Berliners in the process of building their future. There are multiple sequences in which bricks are moved, technical plans are drawn, and unions are founded. Ultimately, we are informed, it is the transportation system that will function as an opening onto better times. It is made plain that the rebuilding of the transportation system is the key, because as long as there is transit there is production, and if there is production there can be a future for Germany. The Berliners in the film are, at the end, seen building bridges over the Spree River, and even the film's soundtrack participates in connecting the whole of the community: the film ends with Bertolt Brecht and Hanns Eisler's anthem of solidarity, the "Solidaritätslied," and in its final montage, as the workers' hammers fall, and nails are driven in, individual faces are intercut with lines of people marching in the name of peace and freedom. The lyrics enjoin not only Germans, but proletarians of all nations, to unite and be free (*Proletarier aller Länder, einigt euch und ihr seid frei*). Socialism, one must be reminded, is international, not nationalist, and here again, individual Germans, the many faces, one after the next, can be said to vanish in the orchestration of postwar reconstruction.

Slightly different from Maetzig's film, Fischer and Huisken's *Potsdam baut auf* devotes more attention to the role of city leaders in the project of rebuilding. Mückenberger und Jordan note that the film "utilizes the inauguration of the Potsdam city council to outline all that has yet to be done in the bombed-out city."[12] At the end of the meeting, the mayor concludes, "Gentlemen, our task is clear. Let's go to work!" As pointed out by Mückenberger and Jordan, the citizens of Potsdam then head toward the rubble to the sounds of Beethoven's Leonore Overture. Using this overture, through its association with *Fidelio*, underscores the overarching theme: the rubble is the last trace of the Germans' political imprisonment. One also notes that *Potsdam baut auf* contains a significant number of images of women working as seamstresses, bottlers, and at other tasks. They look serious in their work, but to think with Arendt, or to watch the film from the perspective that labor is by nature difficult, it becomes unclear how one would recognize that one is not seeing forced labor. The film is devoid of testimonials that might explain the value of labor in the lives of these Germans, and it is only from the overall thrust of the narrative that viewers may understand what they are witnessing as a voluntary contribution to progress. The voices of the women weaving at the looms and elsewhere is not to be heard.

Of the three, Groschopp's *Dresden* is most like a conventional feature film. It begins with a dramatization, and in that it gestures toward the stylistic devices of feature films, one might suggest that it more than the others marks a transition from the newsreels to the DEFA's subsequent features. At the onset, following a long remark about Dresden's splendid yet undemocratically inspired architectural past, the viewer is told that "the voice of truth" was held prisoner in Germany for too long under the Nazis. In his lonely cell, the personification of Truth professes, "in this country everything became a lie. Germany has no conscience anymore, no upstanding people anymore. Everyone is silent." Groschopp's film then offers the following unattributed maxim: "When the people are silent, the stones begin to speak." Groschopp now shows us images of the rubble, and one has to ask whether the film means to suggest that the stones spoke during the war in the moment they collapsed under the assaults of Allied bombs, or if we are meant to understand that they are speaking now, insofar as they demand to be rebuilt? Furthermore, one wonders where the voices of the Germans are in this, amid the speaking stones. Is it only the rubble that calls to be repaired? Mückenberger and Jordan point to the subsequent series of questions raised by the film: "Is the will to survive strong enough? Can it clear the path? Is this rubble ever to be swept away?" and they note that these questions are answered with a single banality on the part of the mayor of Dresden who says simply, "Above all, we must get started" (*Vor allem müssen wir anfangen*). Mückenberger and Jordan observe: "The mayor of Dresden appears with a team of men, makes himself visible to the film crew in the rubble and with the single sentence, 'Above all, we must get started,' he erases all reservations about the impending troubles. The sentence is not just simple, as is the one in Huisken's film; it is banal."[13] Once again, as depicted in these films, the reconstruction of Germany is predicated on a promise. These largely voiceless figures transform into the stones that would rebuild themselves from the rubble. *Dresden* exhibits far more interest in moving forward than in taking time to reflect. The mayor's comment, "above all, we must get started," comes in response to the suggestion that there is "much to consider" (*viel zu bedenken*) before the people of Dresden can start their projects. The mayor reveals himself to be a man of action, and this bit of dialogue is suggestive with regard to Sebald's observation about the overall antipathy toward reflection in the postwar period. In the unreflective period immediately following the war, pace Sebald, there was no time or energy for looking back.

Groschopp's film resembles the features that appeared later in that year. Jordan notes that Groschopp was a cinematographer for Leni Riefenstahl and worked on the *Olympia* films, and that this may account for the film's tone, one that is at times more histrionic than the "sober" tone carried through by Keller's narration, written for *Berlin im Aufbau*.[14] In *Dresden*, a young man is offered the opportunity to earn money through the black market, but he declines when he notices demonstrating workers, a line of men and women, passing by. His sense of duty is aroused, and he finds himself inspired to make his own contribution to the rebuilding of Germany. When it is asserted that there really is little alternative for him but the black market, he enthusiastically responds that there is indeed something different out there for him, and that is "labor" (*Arbeit*). Maetzig's *Berlin im Aufbau* is at times similarly moralizing in that it contains an admonishment not to turn to prostitution. Here, *Dresden*, in its feature-film style, echoes some of the themes of Roberto Rosselini's *Germania Anno Zero* (Germany Year Zero; 1948), a film which similarly excoriated Germans for profiting from the black market while others rebuilt. In Groschopp's film, the hard-working folk are each meant as positive role models, heroes of the reconstruction.

In principle, Arendt rejects all attempts of this sort to promote industrial labor to the workforce, and she rejects as well the implicitly and explicitly expressed suggestion that laborers should find labor in itself fulfilling. Labor is not supposed to be enjoyed, and Arendt views attempts to convince people—mass publics, readers, or postwar Germans—that labor is a source of pleasure as merely an act of salesmanship on the parts of both Eastern and Western ideologies of productivity and on the parts of their deputies. For Arendt it should be taken as a fact that no one enjoys labor, least of all those who actually perform it. She details four ways in which endless labor can be marketed to a public—the various myths by means of which it can be idealized. She enumerates: the Catholics take labor as a means to attain a higher end; labor can be viewed as "an act of shaping in which 'a given structure is transformed into another, higher structure'"; labor can be made to appear as "pure pleasure" or something "fully as satisfying as leisure-time activities"; and, finally, labor can be understood as "man's confirmation of himself against nature, which is brought under his domination through labor."[15] The position of the DEFA—as evinced in the *Aufbau* films—is linked most closely to the second of these forms: labor is presented to Germans of the Soviet zone as "an act of shaping" in order to give something a "higher structure." Along these lines, the East attempted to absorb the laborer into their labor, or Germany into its rubble. These, the earliest of the DEFA films, seek to dedifferentiate Germans from the berubbled core of those cities to which they were bound.

As with *Berlin im Aufbau*, the construction of a bridge is central to *Dresden*.[16] The film ultimately concludes with the building of the "Bridge of Unity" (the *Brücke der Einheit*, known today as the *Albertbrücke*). The bridge's fabrication is not only literal but also stands for the bridge built between the Eastern Socialist Party (the *Ost*-SPD) and the Communist Party (the KPD), which was one of the key accomplishments of the party in 1946.[17] For Maetzig, the bridge metaphor is extremely important, and in this regard, one comment he made subsequently is telling. Mückenburger and Jordan note that Maetzig was particularly savvy in assessing the prospects for rebuilding, and that he took care not to overstrain the emotional tolerance of the German public. In a contribution to the journal *Sonntag* in 1947, the director compared postwar Germans to a bridge, writing:

> I like to compare the soul and the character of our contemporary German public with a bridge in which some of the struts have been destroyed. It can no longer handle the load it should, but it has to take on more traffic in order to bring nourishment to a starving country. Of course it would be easier, but would also be less responsible, to take only lighter loads over the bridge. Artists like us, however, have the task of driving the heaviest possible loads over this bridge, and until the "engineers of the soul" succeed in fixing the damaged struts and pylons, we must work hard to assess its load-bearing capacity.[18]

If the Germans were not already meant to function as planks on the bridge to the future, these films meant to construct bridges out of them. To think in film historical terms, with respect to the development of the DEFA, the *Aufbau* films connected the first newsreels to the features. They contain the seeds of the works produced by the DEFA later in that year, including *Die Mörder sind unter uns* and *Irgendwo in Berlin*. One certainly sees a resonance between the short, coarsely drawn narratives of the *Aufbau* films and the DEFA features that succeeded them. These features, like their shorter predecessors, assert that Germans have to get to work. As with the earlier films, however, one has to ask who is the German at the films' center. Postwar Germans emerge from out of the rubble, but they are by no means whole; they are physically and psychically broken fragments, pieces of stone each searching for a voice, and only gradually do they find themselves on the road to becoming whole.

The history of *Die Mörder sind unter uns* has been taken up elsewhere,[19] but I turn to it here in order to briefly explore how its depiction of labor follows directly from the *Aufbau* films. In this feature film, Dr. Hans Mertens has come back from the war a damaged man. Like the protagonist of Wolfgang Borchert's play *Draußen vor der Tür* (1947)—and in this respect the postwar work of Eastern and Western authors can be said to converge—Hans Mertens is a veteran who returns bitter and misanthropic. He is psychologically scarred, but according to the narrative of the film, he will function again one day. Hans need only find a place in society, a society that he perceives as unwilling to make room for him, and the film intends to have him accomplish this with the help of Susanne, the kind woman who was a political prisoner of the Nazis until the war's end. Susanne cleans up the apartment that the two find themselves sharing. She is always hard at work, and her devotion to maintaining the apartment comes to stand for her commitment to rebuilding her city. Susanne paints signs with positive messages such as "save the children," and all of her movement forward—her willingness to do the labor of sign painting, of maintaining their residence, and of patiently helping Hans heal his wounds through learning to help other, suffering Germans—implies that she will move ahead and not look back.

Adopting Susanne's disposition as its model, the film does not look back. Its villain, an industrialist who was responsible for atrocities he ordered committed during the war, one who has now come to capitalize on the reconstruction, meets with justice in the form of the laws of the new Germany. The film, however, sees no need to take up the details of his trial, nor does it concern itself with Susanne's own concentration camp experiences. In its most ideological moment the couple moves through the rubble arm in arm toward a new day. The two build a dwelling space together, and this space does not call for a look backward. They become feature film versions of their *Aufbau* film counterparts, positive heroes committed to the project of rebuilding.

Similarly, *Irgendwo in Berlin* takes up the relation between labor and the construction of a place where one could dwell. The film could certainly serve as a feature film analogue to *Berlin im Aufbau*. Its very title means to suggest that the city, prior to its reconstruction was an anarchic, disorderly space. It is a film in which, as Robert Shandley notes, the enemy "is the rubble itself."[20] The destroyed city is depicted not as a home but as its antithesis. It is a labyrinth, and it could hardly be mapped, hence the "somewhere" (*irgendwo*) in its title. At the film's onset, children are depicted as creatures of the rubble. They have access to fireworks and are more than idle enough to be a danger to themselves. The risks implied by this idleness are symbolized in the film's narrative of a boy who has so little to do and is so in need of structure, so to speak, that he climbs to the top of an unstable ruin and falls to his death. In the name of this boy, of this martyr, the film mandates that Berlin move forward. In its positive ending, the entire community bands together to build. The sequence, in which women and children work to reconstruct their city brick by brick, could have been pulled directly from the footage of the *Aufbau* films. Labor appears here in an idealized form. This is not to say that *Irgendwo in Berlin* or *Die Mörder sind unter uns* do not have merits or that they are lacking in their own particular beauty. It is instead to account for the fact that these films are an outgrowth of the logic of the *Aufbau* films; they present worlds in which persons emerge from the rubble as fragments in order that they may rebuild in the name of the greater good. Years later, other types of depictions of labor and of the construction of East Germany found their way into DEFA films. Subsequent features regularly reversed the terms: The East German was no longer subordinate to an ideology of labor in the name of a better future, but, as the vessel of that ideology, they often found themselves superior to their own state, one that could hardly make good on its own policies. After another two decades, the laborer was more frequently depicted as a whole, and the state was that which was a fragment of what it hoped to be. The terms were thereby reversed such that they threatened the very hegemony that meant to subordinate the laborer to his or her future. If one does not labor for the sake of the species, or if that labor refuses to yield the expected progress, then the new question is "why labor?" It becomes possible that the principles for which one labors do not justify or merit the labor that is at stake. Ultimately in Frank Beyer's *Spur der Steine* (Trace of the Stones; 1966), the reversal is complete: Not the laborer, but Socialism itself has become the collapsing bridge over which the laborer must walk. The film features the disillusioned hero, Balla, and his construction crew, a crew that does not have the tools they need to complete their projects. Balla is an epic hero, and can hardly be described as a fragment of a man.

As has been pointed out by Karen Ruoff Kramer, Balla and his striking coworkers are depicted as more committed to the nation than the bureaucrats for whom they work. She writes that the laborers in *Spur der Steine*, "strike because there are no raw materials. In effect, they are striking not against but for socialism, against system-immanent inhibitions. Ironically, they are commanded back to work by party functionaries who drive onto the scene—though of course they cannot go back to work without the delivery of the wood whose failure to arrive had sparked the strike."[21] Such a reading, one that is apparently consistent with Beyer's intentions, offers one possible take on the film's title. The "trace of the stones" has all but vanished. Germany has been rebuilt and it is the citizens themselves rather than the stones, or the ruins, or the rubble, who have begun to speak. It is little wonder that *Spur der Steine* was quickly banned following its release. According to the official line, it was banned because it was seen as a film that did not understand the Socialist worker's mentality and depicted workers without an inkling of what their society expected from them.[22]

Despite the film's censorship, the reversal of the accusatory finger, which was now directed at the Party by its people, continued. The difference between the people and their Party became the source of continued conflict. One sees it depicted in another form as late as *Die*

Architekten (The Architects; 1990), which was still a DEFA film, though one that was released following the fall of the Berlin Wall. It is a film in which the will to build a better Germany is there, but on the part of individuals rather than on the part of the overly bureaucratic state. Viewed through the lens of labor, from a perspective that asks where one's labor stands in relation to the state for which one works, one finds a means of reading these films next to one another, films that were among the very first and very last in East German history. To suggest that labor was, right from the start, marketed to the public is thus a hermeneutic assertion, not an indictment of Maetzig, Marx, or the DEFA. It is meant as a means of negotiating the difference between the speaking and the laboring subjects in East German films.

Notes

1. Noted by Rolf Steininger, *Deutsche Geschichte 1945–1961. Darstellung und Dokumente in zwei Bänden*, vol. 1 (Frankfurt am Main: Fischer, 1983), p.145.
2. W.G. Sebald, *On the Natural History of Destruction*, trans. Anthea Bell (New York: Random House, 2003), p.7.
3. Ibid.
4. Ibid., p.13.
5. Ibid.
6. See Victor Gollancz, *In Darkest Germany* (Hinsdale, IL: H. Regnery, 1947). Gollancz is also discussed by Dagmar Barnouw in *Germany 1945. Views of War and Violence* (Bloomington, IN: Indiana University Press, 1996), pp.149–150.
7. Hannah Arendt, *The Human Condition* (Chicago: University of Chicago Press, 1958), p.101.
8. Ibid., pp.123–124.
9. Christiane Mückenberger and Günter Jordan, '*Sie sehen selbst, Sie hören selbst…*': *Eine Geschichte der DEFA von ihren Anfängen bis 1949* (Marburg: Hitzeroth, 1994), p.250. The translation of this quote and others is my own, except where a published translation has been cited.
10. With respect to the violence of the recent past, one should note that the film by and large remains silent. Apart from a figure singled out in the first moments of the film as "a Jewish carpenter" (*ein jüdischer Zimmermann*), Jews are hardly mentioned. Similarly, the fact that these films occasionally linger long on images of industrial ovens carries its own eerie resonance. Although one must acknowledge that at this point there was much that still needed to be uncovered about the connection between the ovens and the death camps, these images today seem like symptoms of a film that wishes to assert that German ovens have in fact other uses.
11. Arendt points to a statement of Marx, one that he later deleted from *The German Ideology*: "Der erste geschichtliche Akt dieser Individuen, wodurch sie sich von den Tieren unterscheiden, ist nicht, dass die denken, sondern dass

sie anfangen ihre Lebensmittel zu produzieren." See Arendt, *The Human Condition*, p.86 n.14.

12. Mückenberger and Jordan, p.252.
13. Ibid., p.253.
14. Pointed out by Günter Jordan in "Die frühen Jahre." 1946 bis 1952," in *Schwarzweiß und Farbe. DEFA Dokumentarfilme 1946—92*, ed. Günter Jordan and Ralf Schenk (Berlin: Jovis, 2000), pp.19–20.
15. Arendt, p.127 n.75.
16. The construction of a bridge is a metaphor that plays a central role in Gustav Fröhlich's *Wege im Zwielicht* as well. This latter film is not a DEFA film, but the parallel here is striking. See Jaimey Fisher's "Planes, Trains, and the Occasional Car: The Rubble Film as Demobilization Film," in this volume.
17. Albert Wilkening explains: "Die kommunistiche Partei war in diesen Tagen die einzige Organisation, die ein klares Programm entwickelte. Um dieses Programm in Angriff nehmen zu können, war die Schaffung einer einheitlichen Massenbasis Voraussetzung. Daher sah die kommunistische Partei als erste Aufgabe die Überwindung der Spaltung der Arbeiterklasse. Als praktisches Ziel stand die Vereinigung der KPD mit der SPD." See Albert Wilkening, *Geschichte der DEFA von 1945–1950* (Potsdam-Babelsburg: VEB DEFA Studio für Spielfilme, 1981), p.40. In 1946 Maetzig also made a short documentary film entirely devoted to the uniting of the two Parties entitled *Einheit SPD-KPD*.
18. Kurt Maetzig, "Für den neuen deutschen Film," *Sonntag* Berlin 2.27 (July 6, 1947), p.12. Also quoted in Mückenburger and Jordan, *Sie sehen selbst, Sie hören selbst*, pp.248–249. The term "engineers of the soul" likely refers to writers under Stalin's regime. The phrase is sometimes attributed to Maxim Gorky.
19. See Robert R. Shandley, *Rubble Films: German Cinema in the Shadow of the Third Reich* (Philadelphia: Temple University Press), esp. Chapter 2.
20. Ibid., p.124.
21. Karen Ruoff Kramer, "Representations of Work in the Forbidden DEFA Films of 1965," in *DEFA: East German Cinema, 1946–1992*, ed. Seán Allan and John Sandford (New York and Oxford: Berghahn Books, 1999), p.138.
22. See Hans Konrad, "Spuren der Steine? Zu einem Film von Frank Beyer," *Neues Deutschland* (July 6, 1966), p.4. Reproduced in *Filmland DDR: Ein Reader zu Geschichte, Funktion und Wirkung der DEFA*, ed. Harry Blunk and Dirk Jungnickel (Cologne, Germany: Verlag Wissenschaft und Politik, 1990), p.22.

CHAPTER SIX

WHAT'S NEW? ALLEGORICAL
REPRESENTATIONS OF RENEWAL
IN DEFA'S YOUTH FILMS, 1946–1949

Marc Silberman

This essay investigates a small corpus of early DEFA films, "rubble film" productions about contemporary youth. Set among urban ruins, they focus on typical postwar dilemmas of young people: absent or war-traumatized fathers, broken families, child impoverishment, and the temptation of petty criminality to survive. *Trümmerfilme* are transitional films in a temporal and thematic sense. They address topical issues of stabilizing the demoralized German survivors in a country whose infrastructure had been destroyed by aerial bombing and whose political institutions had been discredited. They articulate anxieties about endings and new beginnings, about losses and the unknown future. Visually these anxieties are sometimes expressed in striking camera work or editing, but more frequently they can be found woven into the narrative sediment of conflict between and among generations. Rubble films have been regarded both as documentary evidence of Germany's postwar misery as well as allegories where the ruins are the external sign of internal desolation, a metaphor of Germany's spiritual devastation.[1] In the DEFA features under consideration here the notion of youth as a transitional time of self-realization and search is inscribed into the adventures that animate the young people. Moreover, the fact that the stories usually take place in the summer (sometimes explicitly identified as Summer 1945), when young people are not in school and hence unsupervised, becomes an analogue for the more general status of an unstable, transitional social environment. Finally, the narratives are transitional too in the sense that they offer recuperative resolutions and compromises to characters' conflicts, no matter how unreal(istic) or dramaturgically unmotivated they might be. DEFA's rubble films about young people—addressed to adult as well as young audiences—expose ambiguities, tensions, and contradictions in the attempt to mold identification with the project of social(ist) renewal. These are the subject of this essay, in particular as they are pressed into genre conventions that were already familiar in the cinema of the Third Reich.

While the DEFA rubble films feature young people from prepubescent juveniles to university students, they all tell stories from the perspective of the young protagonists about generational conflict, abandonment, loss of confidence, and the need to establish a moral compass independently of the compromised adult generation. Hence, in contrast to the youth films of the Third Reich, these early postwar features, while not ignoring punishment, pedagogical disciplinary measures, and paternalistic moral values, tend to frame them within stories that make social structures and ruptures transparent.[2] In contrast to rubble films produced in the Western occupation zones, where youthful figures usually are integrated into the narrative as the young female companion or lover of a much older war returnee and/or in the conflictual figure of the returnee's son, the DEFA features stress the way common interests of young people emerge and can be channeled toward social renewal.[3] Set against the transition from war devastation to reconstruction and often filmed against backdrops of architectural ruins, the narratives reveal the physical and psychological wounds of the adults as well as the energy and enthusiasm of young people who are thrown together into gangs or groups motivated by survival and solidarity.

Five films constitute the corpus of DEFA rubble films about young people that concern us here: Lamprecht's *Irgendwo in Berlin* (opened on December 12, 1946), Hans Müller's *1–2-3 Corona* (began production exactly one year later and opened on September 17, 1948), and three additional films that went into production during the first half of 1948, Gustav von Wangenheim's *Und wieder 48!* (opened November 5, 1948), Wolfgang Schleif's *Und wenn's nur einer wär* (opened on March 18, 1949), and Hans Deppe's *Die Kuckucks* (opened on April 8, 1949).[4] These stories of personal transformation show how, despite the social collapse, new communities of trust emerge among young people, providing a model for the war-weary, impoverished, and displaced populations in the cities. And consistent with conversion narratives, the resolutions are filled with visual, musical, and verbal pathos to suggest that the new beginning or spiritual rebirth carries the promise to erase physical destruction (ruins) and material shortages (hunger).

As one of the first post-1945 German films, *Irgendwo in Berlin* is the best known of these rubble films and introduced many of the formal qualities that would come to typify them. Director Gerhard Lamprecht, who was responsible for the most popular youth film of the Weimar Republic, *Emil und die Detektive* (Emil and the Detectives, 1931, based on Erich Kästner's 1928 best-selling novel), could be regarded as a symptomatic choice for DEFA's early attempt to connect to the progressive tradition of youth film entertainment that was established during the late Weimar Republic. Indeed, he reworked in this early postwar rubble film Kästner's basic idea about children defending themselves against injustice and thereby providing demoralized or cynical adults a pragmatic model of solidarity and self-help. In addition, Lamprecht reprised from his 1931 genre thriller visual effects (the climactic scene of a gate opening to reveal the crowd of children), character types (the petty thief and some of the children), and even the actor Fritz Rasp who played the thief in 1931 as well as the pickpocket in 1946. In contrast to the earlier film, however, which consistently holds to the perspective of the children, *Irgendwo in Berlin* includes a spectrum of adult figures as well as a series of narrative threads only tenuously related to the trials and tribulations of the young protagonists.

The constellation of adult figures represents the postcollapse transitional society and as such the point of departure for social renewal. The adults comprise two groups that structure and comment upon the dramatic conflicts: the well-meaning, who are emotionally or psychologically damaged by war but searching for a new orientation, and the opportunists, who exploit the current state of social disintegration for selfish ends. The first group consists of two "couples." Anxious and overworked Frau Iller struggles to survive while waiting for her husband to return from the war, and the absent Iller, who indeed returns about one-third into the narrative, is the classical traumatized POW who has lost his bearings and will to live. Frau Steidel is an older woman who had lost her husband 30 years earlier in WWI (a reminder of the historical dimension to the current catastrophe) and now nurses her son, who returned from the recent war mentally disturbed. Paired with her is the painter Eckmann, a grandfatherly figure who advises and commiserates with her while he works in his atelier on a large painting showing in the background the ruins of the city and in the foreground a large, broken tree trunk that is beginning to sprout new branches and leaves. Also belonging to the group of the kind-hearted is Kalle, the Illers' close family friend who lost his own son in the war (and apparently his wife too, since she never is mentioned) and now has found new meaning in life through his work restoring damaged furniture. He will also become the deus ex machina who can translate his experience into an inspiring message for the child protagonist that will lead to the happy ending. The opportunists also comprise two "couples" flanked by a single male. One "couple" consists of Birke, a black market dealer who provides the children with fireworks in exchange for stolen food items he resells, and Frau Schelp, who sublets to Birke a room behind her small shop and gladly accepts his illegal foodstuffs for protecting his operation. The other couple consists of Herr and Frau Timmel, owners of a questionable club where Herr Timmel sells Birke's illegal cigars and Frau Timmel teaches the girls' chorus line the song "Rejoice, Make Merry," corresponding inversely to Eckmann's allegorical painting: "... happiness smiles at those who know how to grab it." Flanking these two couples is Waldemar, a petty thief and magician who, like Birke, knows how to exploit the children's innocence.

The parallel group of children is visually much larger (swarms of kids between the ages of 5 and 12 engage in "war games" by exploding fireworks in the rubble), and yet for dramatic efficiency the group is restricted to only four active characters. Gustav is the child protagonist, the Illers' young son who yearns for nothing more than for his father to return but fails to recognize the starved, exhausted man when he finally arrives. Unlike the adults, he has an intact sense of generosity: he brings home the pickpocket Waldemar to have his mother mend a torn jacket and also invites home the unrecognized father for a meal, thus inadvertently reconstituting the kernel of the nuclear family. Willi, in contrast, is an orphan, his parents having been killed in a bombing raid, and he has now found a home of sorts with Frau Schelp (who has lost her own children) and Birke, whom he helps in organizing the black market operation. The two boys are paired dramaturgically as best friends, and against his mother's admonition that Willi is not good company Gustav must defend him repeatedly with an emphatic statement of unconditional trust: "Willi ist mein Freund." Willi returns this trust by stealing from Birke's (stolen) goods to make a gift to Gustav for his hungry father. When Birke discovers the "crime," Willi must flee and he finds protective refuge and sympathy with Eckmann. Kapitän is the third, clearly asocial boy and catalyst for the film's catastrophe: he breaks the children's pledge to Eckmann not to play with explosives after one of their rockets crashes through his atelier window and destroys his painting on the easel, and later the ringleader Kapitän calls Willi a coward, a challenge that leads to the latter's foolish and ultimately deadly feat of climbing the remaining, unsteady wall of a destroyed building. Kapitän is also the only boy who does not participate in the triumphant resolution brought about by Gustav's plan to have all the children help his father rebuild his destroyed automotive repair shop.

The final, fragile vision of restoration and renewal, which rechannels the children's anarchic energy from dangerous war games to the practical task of clearing rubble, has its price: dramaturgically the orphan Willi is eliminated, a victim associated with false hubris and isolation (his childhood memory of crawling into the doghouse while his family searched for him); similarly Kapitän opts out by disappearing with Waldemar into the ruins just before the triumphant restorative scene, undoubtedly to pursue a life of petty crime. Finally, the fourth "child" is Frau Steidel's 32-year old son whose madness marks him as less than an adult. A blinded soldier-survivor and, as such, a contrast figure for returnee Iller, Hansotto is visually associated with Willi as cross-cuts show him following the boy's fatal climb and then standing watch over his sick bed. Like Willi, he is a victim who has internalized the scars of war that erupt in his battle flashbacks and verbal comments and, like Willi, he is excluded from the final resolution. All these figures, the adults and the children, constitute Lamprecht's imagined transitional society, both the negative and positive aspects. In this case the children's powerlessness and emotionalism represent for the adults in the film story as well as in the cinema audience a threat, but one with which they can identify. Such is the conventional moral construction of the child as hero, who mirrors adult potential and represents adult loss.

The symmetry of dramatic characters is not, however, adequate for holding together the film's centrifugal plot strands, which apparently confused contemporary audiences and critics who also registered the film's slow pace and episodic quality. This overladen plot may account for Lamprecht's heavy-handed use of explicit symbolism, a means not only to connect the diffuse plot elements but also to guarantee that no viewer would miss the film's upbeat message: Eckmann's allegorical painting of rebirth destroyed by the children's war games, Iller angrily crushing Gustav's toy tank under his foot, the pathos-laden sequence of Frau Iller clutching her husband's shoes worn out by the trek home, and the kitsch staging of Willi's death, all underscored by dramatic orchestral music, expressive lighting, and close-ups. Dialogues too are often preachy or redundant, explaining motivations or actions better conveyed by the images themselves: the various exchanges among adults about contemporary youth, Eckmann's lectures to the children about proper behavior, Iller's complaints to Karl about his depressive state of mind, and Karl's paternalistic advice to Gustav that leads to the resolution. Contemporary critics and later film historians did appreciate the dramatic topography of ruins dominating the film's visual images: low angle shots of collapsed arches and walls, high angle shots of mountains of rubble, and traveling shots of streets lined with debris. Nonetheless, there is also evidence that contemporary viewers criticized the film, as they would later rubble films as well, complaining that they did not need movies to show them ruins and neglected children, demanding instead reprises of old UFA films.[5]

If Lamprecht's film is an uneasy mix of crime thriller (black market plot), adventure film (children's war games), and conversion tale (restoration of the pater familias), Hans Müller's *1-2-3 Corona* extends the popular circus genre into the postwar landscape of rubble while maintaining many of the same thematic elements of the prior narrative. The German cinema has a long tradition of circus films going back at least to the remarkable 1925 Expressionist feature *Variété* by E. A. Dupont, a triangle love story starring the Mexican trapeze artists "The Codonas." During the Third Reich a series of circus film releases developed the classic story elements constructed around the daring and danger of trapeze artists and the exoticism of circus animals. Not only do acrobats lend themselves to dramatic situations in which a beautiful woman depends on the timing and strength and just as often on the love of her male partner(s), but they also provide appealing opportunities for erotically charged images of bodies in revealing costumes. Thus, Hans Zerlett's 1936 *Truxa* presented a triangle story featuring a trapeze artist and a circus dancer, filmed on location in the Berlin Wintergarten; A. M. Rabenalt's 1940 *Die drei Codonas* reprised the tragic story of the Mexican trapeze stars; and Wolfgang Staudte's first feature film, *Akrobat schö-ö-ön* (1943), focused on a failed trapeze artist who becomes a clown. Hans Müller, who was assistant director for the 1940 *Die drei Codonas*, adapted many of these plot elements in his postwar film about young gang members in Berlin who discover the meaning of life when the circus comes to town. Doubtlessly the title *1-2-3 Corona* resonated with recent audience memories of such genre entertainment and, as the subtitle suggests (*eine kleine romantische Geschichte aus nicht lange vergangenen Tagen*) presented an upbeat twist to the cinematic model of "The Codonas."

The film opens with one of the young actors introducing, like a circus director, the film credits projected on a screen behind him and explaining how much fun it was to participate in the production, followed by young actors stepping forward and announcing their names. This framing gesture of entertainment, just as the subtitle, were signals to the audience that DEFA was trying to broaden its reputation from that of a producer of propaganda, antifascist dramas, and contemporary social problem films. And indeed, situation comedy, visual humor, and circus spectacle are integrated into the rubble film's basic conversion narrative that shows how two rival youth gangs in Summer 1945 with no parental oversight become the protectors of the young, maltreated trapeze artiste Corona, who has lost her parents in the war. Typical for the humor are two episodes in the expository sequences. The school director, an inveterate smoker, encounters one of his pupils in the middle of a black market deal, who offers the embarrassed and disapproving mentor a cigarette with the comment: "Every man for himself!" The pupil, Gerhard, is the ringleader of a youth gang whose immediate goal is to steal some heating coal for a new deal. Their well-organized ambush of a delivery truck brings on an attack by the rival youth gang, which leads to a free-for-all during which the adult onlookers quickly help themselves to the kids' stolen coal. When the dust clears, the kids are outraged that someone has stolen "their" booty. Like in Lamprecht's film, the intergenerational relations represent the young people, here mainly marginalized and delinquent adolescents, as a mirror of larger social issues (black market operations, stealing), but in the course of the narrative their pragmatic skills in stealing are rechanneled into an impressive circus performance that models for the adults how enthusiasm and trust can bring about a new order.

The narrative establishes a symmetrical triangle of characters: Gerhard and Dietrich, both war orphans living in the ruins, are gang leaders who displace their internecine squabbles over black market operations onto their competition for the attention of Corona. Their adult counterparts consist first of Frau Schmittchen, a small-time black market operator who needs the young people to procure stolen goods for her lucrative trade but then pretends self-righteous, moral outrage about imputed sexual goings-on when the boys' attentions for the injured Corona displaces their interest in her black market deals. Dr. Waldner, a graying physician, is the sympathetic but stern father figure who helps the young people in their effort to care for Corona because he recognizes they can be socialized only when they learn to take responsibility for their actions. His rival is the school director who has no confidence in his pupils' maturity and yearns for the time when the schools will reopen and he can reassert his institutional authority. After the traveling circus occupies the empty lot that happens to be the gangs' territory and the youth discover that the beautiful, young Corona is being victimized by the ornery circus director, they concoct a plan to disrupt the circus performance by shooting spit balls at the performers. Unaware that the director is Corona's trapeze partner, they aim at him just as he is to catch her in midair, causing her fall. The circus leaves town without the injured Corona, providing the narrative motivation for the boys to focus all their attention on caring for her and keeping up her spirits.

As was the case in Lamprecht's film, dialogue functions to introduce or reinforce messages that can not otherwise be generated by genre conventions. This happens at three junctures in *1–2-3 Corona*. When Dr. Waldner comes the next day to check on Corona, he quizzes Gerhard and Dietrich about what happened, and they all take responsibility for the accident

("We were all guilty...All of us."). The subtle insinuation of collective guilt—a topic familiar enough to German viewers after the Nuremberg trials of 1945–1946—elicits from Waldner an expression of outrage mixed with an admonition: "And now you think you can redeem your guilt. Atonement, that's easy." This challenge plants the seed that the young people can make good their "mistake." Shortly thereafter Waldner and the school director discuss the boys' project of caring for the incapacitated Corona. Waldner defends them against his rivals distrust:

> *Director*: Do you know how demoralized they are?
> *Waldner*: The best thing for that is a responsible task.
> *Director*: That's why I wanted to start a tutoring group.
> *Waldner*: I think groups the young people initiate themselves are better...Where is trust supposed to come from if we don't have it.
> *Director*: We should let the boys and girls do as they please? That would work?
> *Waldner*: Yes, I think so.

The rest of the narrative elaborates the youth's creativity and sometimes reckless enthusiasm in learning circus acts but also their ability to learn from mistakes. Waldner's pedagogical confidence in the young people nurtures their superior wisdom that in turn reveals to the adults the consequences of their own absurd and harsh prejudices. Later Waldner invites circus director Barlay, demoralized and ready to throw in the towel, to the dress rehearsal of the kids' make-shift circus. In the ensuing dialogue, he assures Waldner: "I wanted to give up, but I won't now. I know once again that the circus has a future. Now I have a task." The circus becomes an allegory and model of the new society, while Barlay becomes the deus ex machina: he hires Corona for a new trapeze act, invites all the boys to her performance under the big top and then to an elegant dinner out of gratitude for their inspiring enthusiasm, and finally resolves the emotional conflict between Gerhard and Dietrich by suggesting that they both become part of Corona's new act, the eponymous "1-2-3 Corona" performance.

Müller's circus feature, which was advertised as "A film *with* young people" (not "for" young people), works efficiently with a series of displacements. First, rubble and ruins are shifted to the visual margins, vaguely surrounding the empty lot where most of the film is shot or seen in the far background during the long conversation between Dr. Waldner and the school director as they walk along a canal. Only two sequences are actually staged in the ruins, when Gerhard and Dietrich confess to each other in a bombed-out cellar that they have both lost their families in the war and later when they compete on a makeshift trapeze strung up in the ruins. In both cases the physical ruins visually suggest the psychological burden of the past that must be left behind in order to survive. Second, the infighting among the youths is displaced onto a generational conflict, first vis-à-vis the circus owner who mistreats Corona and then more generally vis-à-vis a society that makes no allowance for young people's initiatives. Third, the ubiquitous black market activities, a cinematic index for social misery prior to the currency reform in Summer 1948, is transformed into the kids' circus performance, punctually illustrated when a panhandler begins collecting and pocketing "donations" for their free rehearsal. From the narrative logic Frau Schmittchen must also be punished, and indeed she is arrested for her illegal transactions prior to the happy ending. Finally, the erotic subplot of the classical triangle between Gerhard, Dietrich, and Corona is displaced into the career opportunity they choose as professional partners and sealed by the final sequence of the trapeze artists performing under the big top in typically revealing body stockings. Ten years after it opened in GDR cinemas, *1–2-3 Corona* was withdrawn from circulation because precisely these displacements were identified as its bourgeois tendency: "young people left to themselves and allowed to develop and implement their own interests, tasks etc. does not contribute appropriately to guiding and improving youth."[6]

Gustav von Wangenheim's *Und wieder 48!* follows least closely the paradigm of the rubble film under examination here. For one, it is in large part a historical film whose plot involves the production of a film about Germany's failed 1848 Revolution, yet at the same time the contemporaneous discussion surrounding the film production within the film clearly locates it as a conversion narrative in which history serves as an object lesson for topical issues regarding German unity. Second, although the film is about students, and the film critics explicitly perceived these students as young people,[7] the main protagonists in fact are clearly returning adult students. As flashbacks indicate, Else Weber lost her husband and child in a bombing raid, while Heinz Althaus—his family name (old house) marks him as conservative and bound by tradition—was a soldier on the Eastern Front. Moreover, at the time of production Inge von Wangenheim (the director's wife), who played Else, was 36 years old, and Ernst Wilhelm Borchert in the role of Heinz was 41; and both of them look their ages! While other students seem to fit the more typical age group of students in their twenties, Else's motherly role is only emphasized by caring for her sick sister's 8-year old son, whom she explicitly sees as the hope for the future ("He is also the best investment."). Yet the sister and her son fade out of the narrative about a quarter of the way into the plot, never to reappear.

Wangenheim, who had a successful acting career in Weimar theater, cabaret, and cinema, was a leftist radical involved as well in Communist

Party agitprop theater. In exile in the Soviet Union he directed one of the few German exile films (*Borzy*, 1936) and was a member of the exile communist group (Nationalkomitee Freies Deutschland) sent back by Soviet authorities in 1945 to spearhead the recovery and reeducation effort. The structurally imbricated film and cabaret sequences suggest self-reflexive distancing elements that gesture to late Weimar experiments of disrupting normal viewing conventions, while long, slow-paced dialogues and declamatory speeches as well as the generally static camera suggest a film maker who thinks like an agitprop theater director. The plot develops around a group of students at the (East) Berlin Humboldt University who are earning pocket money as extras in the filming of a historical farce about the 1848 Revolution. Quickly two opposed groups emerge who argue whether the failed revolution was indeed just a farce. Else, who is studying to become a history teacher, is the dynamic and attractive spokeswoman of the Marxist students, while the articulate medical student Althaus is pushed forward by his conservative friends (former military comrades) to become their spokesperson. Heinz, however, is struck from the beginning by Else's self-confidence and follows her example of reading historical literature that slowly brings his views into alignment with hers. Else, meanwhile, recognizes in Heinz a suitable challenge for her pedagogical skills and then increasingly for her romantic desire. After numerous political debates and intrigues that retard the romantic pairing, they fall into one another's arms at the location shoot of the historical film's last scene at the Wartburg, where the (film's) revolutionaries played by the student extras swear to defend German unity. While not exactly conforming to the enthusiastic and innocent youthful protagonists of other rubble films, the trope of the youth-as-savior is capacious enough for Else and Heinz as representatives of the renewal invested in the younger generation.

The discourse of German unity focuses on the historical example of the failed revolution and the contemporary politics of 1948, when the cold-war standoff was becoming ever more palpable in daily life (the film opened after the currency reform and during the Berlin Airlift, which anticipated the founding of the two German states in Fall 1949). The satirical cabaret scenes Else organizes for the student ball make explicit the danger implied in the title's iteration of "48." The first song ("German unity can only come from freed people"), a typical chorus line arrangement, warns that the 1848 Revolution did not succeed because the common people failed to organize themselves. The second song ("A German passport") contrasts the consequences of German disunity under the princes in 1848 and the occupation in 1948 with a quick set change from painted scrims with a Prussian garden to a landscape of urban ruins. The witty but stagy citation of Berlin's rubble is duplicated much more impressively in the film's location shooting in the city's historical center. In fact, more than any of the films under discussion, *Und wieder 48!* integrates striking images of rubble and ruins not only as metaphor or atmospheric backdrop but as a visual element of the narrative. The crumbled buildings along the Spree that come into view during the film shoot, the damaged facade of the Humboldt University where the students congregate, and most spectacularly the ruins of the Berlin Palace (dynamited by the GDR government in 1950) are visual reminders of Germany's recent catastrophic failure that Else mobilizes in her discussions with Heinz. They walk by the bombed-out imperial palace, for example, while discussing the nature of personal memory and historical interpretation; they visit the Friedrichshain Cemetery where she points out the commemorative monument to the dead of the 1848 and 1918 revolutions; and later Else and Heinz attentively listen to a tourist guide in the interior of the destroyed palace who makes explicit for a group of German-American tourists the historical connection between 1848 and the bombed-out ruins surrounding them. The weight of a hundred years of history substitutes in *Und wieder 48!* for the generational antagonisms found in other rubble films so that the narrative and ideological conflicts become an issue among the students, while benevolent teachers and advisors guide their process of discovery and self-transformation.

In the next rubble film, which went into production right after the first cut of Wangenheim's film was completed, Wolfgang Schleif returns to the implacable authoritarian and antihumanistic attitudes of the older generation and thus reasserts the conflict model of the previous films. *Und wenn's nur einer wär* confronts representatives of a traditional pedagogical approach based on discipline and obedience with an idealistic youth counselor who develops a successful experiment of self-administration for the delinquent boys in the detention camp he supervises. Other differences in respect to Wangenheim's film also may be considered symptomatic of the rapidly evolving social and political environment in 1948/49. The presence of ruins and rubble is reduced to a minimum: during a bicycle ride in Berlin a clumsily executed back projection shows vague urban ruins. Otherwise, there is only one verbal reference to rubble when a passerby gives directions to the work camp ("over the bridge, through the rubble..."). Rubble has shifted entirely into the allegorical, represented by the ruined families and desperate misery that have made delinquents of these kids and by the remnants of Nazi attitudes that must be cleared away for a better future to emerge.

Another difference is registered in the physical division of Berlin. What was only hinted at in the second cabaret song of *Und wieder 48!,* in which the checkpoints between Berlin's four sectors are compared to the earlier borders between Germany's many states, now provides the resolution and happy ending. The narrative action is clearly located in the western part of Berlin.[8] After Jochen Denecke, the youth counselor, is dismissed from his supervisory position, the new guardian introduces barbed wire, guard dogs, and a rigid disciplinary regime based on denunciations. Dressed in riding pants and high black boots, it is no surprise that he is ultimately exposed as a former SS-guard working under a false name and identity. Meanwhile, Denecke has become supervisor of a new detention camp in the "democratic sector" (i.e., in Berlin's Soviet sector), and with the help of a sympathetic policeman from the east five boys are able to escape their prison-like camp and join Denecke in his new camp, where swarms of happy, active kids have just completed building a new well and greet the five "refugees" with clear, cool water, life's elixir. Cold-war patterns underlie the narrative resolution: the restoration of old habits and methods, those that specifically led to Nazi barbarism, is identified with the west, while in the east, in the "democratic sector," the seeds of a new spirit of self-governance and humanism are being nurtured.

Schleif, who trained in the theater and began his cinema career in the mid-thirties, among other things as an assistant to Veit Harlan (for this reason he was unemployable in the West for several years after 1945), seems to have been influenced more by the likes of Luis Trenker or Gustav Fröhlich in the way he constructs suspense in this nascent adventure film. The quick editing of the noirish, thriller-like exposition rapidly presents the criminal acts and sentencing of young delinquents who will surface later at the detention camp, changing pace unexpectedly then to the cabaret performance of "The song of the delinquent kids." Here Denecke meets the underemployed actress Bettina Rupprecht and afterward protests that she knows nothing of the delinquents about whom she sings with such cynicism. She turns out, however, to share Denecke's idealism and accepts his invitation to visit the camp, working with his charges on a theater performance and ultimately arranging for the boys' escape to the new camp. The remainder of the film presents everyday life in the youth camp, showing how Denecke's charges learn responsible behavior: they democratically choose their own leaders, punish wrongdoings, and negotiate conflicts with the camp administrators. Like the earlier rubble films, this one too presents a spectrum of adult attitudes toward young people, ranging from well-meaning but skeptical tolerance to institutional inflexibility to outright resistance with the goal of undermining any innovative idea, culminating in the acceptance of concentration camp methods to discipline the youth. The astonishingly positive portrayal of youth self-governance and democracy landed an audience hit for DEFA.[9]

The film was screened regularly for youth groups, school classes, social workers, and even at youth detention centers, eliciting enthusiastic reviews and audience responses because its vision of the future was grounded in real anxieties and yearnings.[10] *Und wenn's nur einer wär*, however, was rarely shown after 1952 and is hardly mentioned in DEFA film histories, probably because the pedagogical methods and self-governance shown in such a positive light had mutated into the authoritarian practices of a Stalinist regime.

The last film in this series, Deppe's *Die Kuckucks*, resembles *1–2-3 Corona* in the genre expectations of light entertainment but also marks the exhaustion of the rubble film paradigm in youth-oriented films. Although it started production two months before Schleif's feature (in May 1948), because of repeated difficulties in finding a director willing to carry through the project, it was completed and licensed for distribution only several months after *Und wenn's nur einer wär*.[11] The comedic elements derive from the fairy-tale genre film, suggested by the diminutive in the subtitle—"a small story from a large city"—and including the infantile cartoon drawings and graffiti-like printing in the credits sequence, peppy background music or a magical lullaby to sing the children asleep, and trick photography used to convey the children's extravagant visions of transforming a ruined villa into a livable abode. The narrative too is constructed around the traditional fairy-tale plot of abandoned children pursued by mean-spirited adults and saved by a prince charming. Like in *1–2-3 Corona*, the resourceful and invariably cheerful young people are confronted by a range of adult figures, from petty neighbors and selfish landladies to unresponsive bureaucrats and social workers to criminals who prey on the innocent young people. But they are flanked too by pragmatic adults like Rolf's boss, who helps the eldest brother construct a cooking oven, or Inge's boss, who gives the older sister and family matriarch furniture and sympathetic advice. Meanwhile, the war ruins play a minimal role, visible only in two sequences, vaguely in the background when the children walk to what they hope will become their new home and more emphatically when they scavenge for usable construction material in the rubble piles. In contrast, the bombed-out villa and its overgrown garden, where the plot unfolds, suggest a romantic refuge rather than the stark ruins of the earlier rubble films.

As in the previous films the narrative concerns a group of children whose self-help allow them to overcome the harsh reality—especially housing shortages—in postwar Berlin. Yet this group differs from the gangs and organized youth in the earlier features in a symptomatic way: it consists of a family of 5 children between the ages of 4 and 18 whose mother is dead and whose father is still missing. Corresponding to the reduction of rubble, then, the focus on family cohesion and creating a comfortable nest for the siblings (the title's reference to cuckoos echoes their family name Kuckert) marks a retreat from the public to the private. The family finds itself pushed from one inadequate, makeshift sublet to another until the two younger boys, Max and Moritz, discover the abandoned villa. Like a messenger from heaven, a young Herr Krüger appears, dressed in a white suit, claims he is the owner/heir, and gives them permission to move in. The children set about renovating several rooms in the villa with the help of young apprentices in practical occupations like carpentry and plumbing, who spontaneously pitch in their expertise. Gersdorf, the young neighbor living in the garden house next door, turns out to be an angel in disguise. A journalist, he "amplifies" their energy and enthusiasm by writing a witty series of columns about their trials and tribulations, but he also uses his contacts to find Krüger after a threatening Herr Schultz arrives to claim ownership of the house and empty their nest. Krüger in turn recognizes Schultz as the culprit who stole his dead parents' antique furniture (i.e., his inheritance) in the confusion of the bombing raids, and the happy ending is finally sealed with a kiss between Gersdorf and Inge, the mother-like sister who will now presumably marry him to complete the family idyll.

   Die Kuckucks was an audience success when it opened in April 1949, probably because it responded to their expectations for light entertainment. In December 1952 its license was provisionally renewed—despite ideological doubts—because of the notable lack of humorous features being produced by DEFA in the early 1950s, and in 1956 it was withdrawn completely from distribution.[12] This, of course, says more about the direction in which the political winds were blowing in the GDR than about Deppe's film, although it does substantiate a fundamental change in official attitudes toward youth. After the founding of the German Democratic Republic in September 1949, a partisan, orthodox view of childrearing and education came to dominate, which rejected the ideal of individual self-realization as bourgeois ideology. On the contrary, the socialist personality could be planned and "produced" by means of normative guidelines. Thus, unlike the rubble films, narratives about and for young people were no longer to be "transitional" in any sense of the word. Popular fairy-tale films like *Das kalte Herz* (Paul Verhoeven, 1950) and *Die Geschichte vom kleinen Muck* (Wolfgang Staudte, 1953) as well as the productions by the DEFA studio for children's film established in 1954 were to represent youth as the guarantor of progress and symbols of the triumph over old ways.[13] From the beginning DEFA's youth films were understood to be a vehicle of moral concepts and ideological (re)orientation and as such subject to the broader political dictates of educating young people. In general they were seen as specially structured fictions aimed at socializing youth by showing people to be capable of learning new ways and by producing acceptable heroes as models. At the same time the five films discussed above suggest that prior to the founding of the German Democratic Republic in Fall 1949, it was still possible—at least in films for and about young people—to imagine spontaneous, self-directed organizational forms developing against the ineptitude and incompetence of authority figures. It would take years before DEFA was once again able to thematize this kind of politically sensitive social issue, and even then it was not without suspicion and reprisals.

Notes

1. Robert R. Shandley, *Rubble Films: German Cinema in the Shadow of the Third Reich* (Philadelphia: Temple University Press, 2001), p.2.
2. Jaimey Fisher argues for the pivotal role of children and generational conflict in postwar films in "Who's Watching the Rubble-Kids? Youth, Pedagogy, and Politics in Early DEFA Films," *New German Critique* 82 (Winter, 2001): 91–125. See also his earlier "Deleuze in a Ruinous Context: German Rubble-Film and Italian Neorealism," *iris* 23 (Spring, 1997): 53–74.
3. On young people in the rubble films from the west, see Jaimey Fisher, "Kinder der Sterne: Jugend und Wiederaufbau in frühen westdeutschen Nachkriegsfilmen," *Zeitschrift für Germanistik* NF 14.1 (2004): 83–101.
4. Other early DEFA youth films that do not feature rubble are A. M. Rabenalt's *Das Mädchen Christine* (1949, a historical film set in the Thirty Years' War whose protagonist is a cross-dressing 17-year old girl hiding from marauding soldiers), Artur Pohl's *Die Jungen von Kranichsee* (1950, about a school teacher and his pupils in a rural village), and Wolfgang Schleif's *Saure Wochen—frohe Feste* (1950, about a theater competition between older and younger workers in an electricity generating plant in the provinces).
5. See, for example, the review in the *Leipziger Zeitung* (April 1, 1947, signed A.M.U.). For a sample of reviews, see Christiane Mückenberger, ed., *Zur DEFA-Geschichte. Spielfilme 1946–1949* (Potsdam: Hochschule für Film, 1976), pp.110–131.
6. See the licensing record of the Ministry of Culture dated August 4, 1959, BA-FA [= Bundesfilmarchiv Berlin] DR1 MfK-HV686 (microfiche). Five years later, on December 7, 1964, *1–2-3 Corona* was reviewed again and licensed for screening in art cinemas only with the evaluation: "some sentimental tendencies, but full of vigor, movement, and optimism."
7. A typical review in *Neues Deutschland* after the premiere (November 9, 1948, signed by Melis) comments that this film about young students shows "how a young man [Althaus] from a bourgeois background comes step by step to a progressive point of view." A letter written by the student Horst Schotzki to *Deutschlands Stimme* (November 28, 1948) argues that "it is about the self-development of young students," indicating correctly the lack of generational conflict in this narrative. For a sample of reviews, see Christiane

Mückenberger, ed., *Zur DEFA-Geschichte. Spielfilme 1946–1949* [Folge II], *Filmwissenschaftliche Beiträge* (Sonderband 1/1981): 216–227.

8. An alternative production title was "The Boys Gang from Wannsee." The location shooting was in Schmöckwitz, a suburban community in the East Berlin lake district; the script was adapted by Schleif and Wolfgang Weyrauch from the documentary novel *Verwahrlost* by Sia Scazziga, Swiss education expert and director of a youth theater.

9. Comparable attendance figures indicate, for example, that *Irgendwo in Berlin* had reached almost 4 million by 1950, *Und wenn's nur einer wär* over 3 million and *Und wieder 48!* only 1.5 million (these latter figures are listed as "until 1976," but both films were withdrawn from circulation in the early 1950s). See the unpaginated foldout tables in Mückenberger, ed., *Zur DEFA-Geschichte. Spielfilme 1946–1949.* Folge II: 274–291 also contains a selection of contemporary reviews of Schleif's film.

10. See BArch [= Bundesarchiv Berlin] DR 117 / 21858 (unpaginated), containing a Ministry of Culture file (Büro Schwab) with long reports concerning screenings in Schwerin, Treuenbrietzen, Stollberg, and Erfurt.

11. BArch DR 117 / Vorl. S 416 (unpaginated) contains a confidential report from the DEFA management (signed Fischer) that summarizes the contract carrousel in May/June 1948 among directors R.A. Stemmle (who also wrote the script), Hans Heinrich, Alfred Braun, and finally Deppe, all of them from West Berlin or the western zones. On DEFA's practice of hiring directors and technicians from the West, see Marc Silberman, "Introduction: Cold-War German Cinema," *Film History* 18.1 (2006): 3–5. Also the location shooting at the ruined villa and grounds ("the cuckoos' nest") was in Grunewald in West Berlin (Auerbacherstr. 13/15), after the Berlin crisis commenced on June 24, 1948, when the Soviets sealed off transportation routes between the city and the Western zones that led to the Berlin Airlift, lasting almost a year.

12. See the licensing records, BA-FA DR1 MfK-HV690 (microfiche). Three reasons were given for withdrawing the film in 1956: the bourgeois perspective; the lack of working-class figures; and the fact that the father was repeatedly characterized as "missing" (anti-Soviet propaganda). *Die Kuckucks* was relicensed for screening in art cinemas only in 1969 and then withdrawn once again in 1984.

13. On these early DEFA fairy-tale films, see Marc Silberman, "The First DEFA Fairy-Tale Films: Cold-War Fantasies of the 1950s," in *Take Two: Fifties Cinema in Divided Germany* (New York and Oxford: Berghahn Books, 2007), pp.106–119.

CHAPTER SEVEN

IN THE RUINS OF BERLIN:
A FOREIGN AFFAIR

Gerd Gemünden

We wondered where we should go now that the war was over. None of us—I mean the émigrés—really knew where we stood. Should we go home? Where was home?

—Billy Wilder[1]

Sightseeing in Berlin

Early into *A Foreign Affair*, the delegates of the U.S. Congress in Berlin on a fact-finding mission are treated to a tour of the city by Colonel Plummer. In an open sedan, the colonel takes them by landmarks such as the Brandenburg Gate, the Reichstag, Pariser Platz, Unter den Linden, and the Tiergarten. While documentary footage of heavily damaged buildings rolls by in rear projection, the Colonel explains to the visitors—and the viewers—what they're seeing, combining brief factual accounts with his own ironic commentary about the ruins. Thus, a pile of rubble is identified as the Adlon Hotel, "just after the 8th Air Force checked in for the weekend," while the Reich's Chancellery is labeled Hitler's "duplex." "As it turned out," Plummer explains,

> one part got to be a great big padded cell, and the other a mortuary. Underneath it is a concrete basement. That's where he married Eva Braun, and that's where they killed themselves. A lot of people say it was the perfect honeymoon. And there's the balcony where he promised that his Reich would last a thousand years—that's the one that broke the bookies' hearts.

On a narrative level, the sequence is marked by factual snippets infused with the snide remarks of victorious Army personnel, making the film waver between an educational program, an overwrought history lesson, and a comedy of very dark humor. This generic ambiguity is underscored on the visual level: documentary footage is spliced into the studio photography of the Congress delegation in a limousine obviously kept in motion by the illusion of an outside passing by, and by invisible studio hands gently rocking the vehicle. To these contrasts in genre and tone, soon a political tension is added. Just as Plummer is telling the group about the Zoo bunkers in the Tiergarten, the only female member of the delegation, Miss Frost, begins to detect signs of American fraternization with German women, and nondiegetic, upbeat music sets in. Soon thereafter, while Plummer lectures the Congressmen about the SS, a flabbergasted Frost records in her little book the consequences of such rapprochement—a German woman pushing a baby carriage with two American flags attached to it while upbeat music flares up. If Frost is shocked by such miscegenation, for Plummer the close tie that has evolved between Germans and Americans is a positive sign for the future. Baseball, Plummer believes, will help the youth unlearn blind obedience and turn them into true democrats ("If they steal now, it'll be second base"), and the fact that a German baby has been christened DiMaggio Schulz is for him a clear sign that reeducation is working.

The political and aesthetic tensions that mark this sequence are indicative not only of the overall structure of *A Foreign Affair* but are also reflective of the historical factors and discursive strategies that shaped the making and reception of the film. Conceived in 1945, set in the spring of 1946, filmed in 1947 (with some documentary footage from 1945), and released in 1948, *A Foreign Affair* both takes stock of and intervenes in the role of the United States in immediate postwar Germany. The film's central concern is the future of Germany and what America has to do with it. This task includes assessing the legacy of the Third Reich and the question of collective guilt; searching for native traditions untainted by Nazi rule; and outlining the scope and purpose of U.S. occupation, denazification, and re-education. To make matters even more complicated, the film chooses to address these political concerns by way of a sexual comedy (which makes for the double entendre of the title). Made by an erstwhile refugee from Hitler's Germany at the precise point as he is contemplating a return, it is informed by multiple and contradictory perspectives that defy easy political categorization, with its mixed messages a clear indication of the conflicted and overdetermined position of exile cinema.

In what follows, I want to explore the political questions the film raises and their translation on the visual and narrative level, along three distinct axes of inquiry: the political function of film in postwar Germany and Wilder's role in it; the film's curious mix of styles and genres that shows an indebtedness to various Hollywood traditions as well as a search for German cinematic traditions appropriate for post-Nazi filmmaking; and Wilder's use of stars as gendered allegories of nation.

Selling a Few Ideological Items

Commenting on the issue of reemigration, Wilder's fellow exile Theodor W. Adorno wrote: "It is an ancient tradition that those who are arbitrarily and blindly driven out of their homeland by tyranny return after its down-fall."[2] For the antiassimilationist Adorno it was a foregone conclusion that he would return to Germany as soon as possible, but the defeat of Nazi Germany also occasioned many successful film professionals to consider a return to Europe. Thus Fritz Lang, Robert Siodmak, Douglas Sirk, William Dieterle, and Peter Lorre would return to Germany for shorter or extended stays where they met with very mixed professional success. Among the very few emigrants to actually set foot in Berlin in 1945 were the German-Jewish writer Curt Riess, who arrived in the capital in July, the actress Marlene Dietrich, who was reunited with her mother in Tempelhof airfield in September, and Billy Wilder, who arrived there in August, after already having flown over the city with a cameraman earlier that summer. All three were naturalized Americans returning to Germany in uniform and with various assignments. Riess was reporting for the American press, Dietrich was performing for the American troops at the Titania Palast, and Wilder had an appointment as a colonel in the U.S. Army's Division of Psychological Warfare. While Wilder and Dietrich would end up collaborating on *A Foreign Affair*, Riess's vignettes and portraits of the city, which he collected in *Berlin Berlin*, capture much of the immediate postwar reality that also informs the film.[3]

As a former employee in the pre-Nazi German film industry and now acclaimed writer-director in Hollywood, Wilder was to assist the military in its task to reconstruct the film industry in occupied Germany. The U.S. military government considered film an instrument not only for confronting Germans with the atrocities they committed, but also for providing Germans relief from the horrible conditions in postwar Germany. Film was thus to serve an educational, democratizing, and escapist purpose. As Wilder recalled, Germans would receive ration cards only if they were willing to sit through documentaries that detailed the atrocities of the Nazis and that challenged its viewers to face moral and political responsibilities many were eager to forget.[4] At the same time, American-produced feature films were to provide German viewers with a diversion from the wretched conditions under which they lived while subtly instilling them with the democratic virtues the heroes of these films embodied. As it turned out, Wilder became involved in both tasks.

While Wilder was enlisted for the so-called denazification interviews that were to establish who would be allowed to work again he also worked on editing *Die Todesmühlen* (Death Mills), a documentary about concentration camps, directed by Hanus Burger and using footage taken by the Allies when they liberated the camps.[5] This was a particularly demanding task for Wilder since at that point he was still searching for clues whether his mother and grandmother had survived the Holocaust. At any moment, the images in front of him could be of his family, but Wilder did not see them. Only later a letter from the Red Cross confirmed their deaths in Auschwitz.[6]

While Wilder was eager to have *Todesmühlen* screened in front of German audiences, he also realized that the long-lasting educational effect of atrocity films was limited.[7] He was equally skeptical of the apolitical diversion provided by standard American entertainment films that were later to flood the American zone. Wilder thus postponed his actual task in Germany, which was to write a report on the state of the production facilities and personnel available for use in the industry, and instead pitched his own idea about film to the Office of Military Government in Germany/ United States (OMGUS). The so-called Wilder Memorandum contains the director's credo about the politics of feature films made for postwar German audiences:

> *Cover Girl* [1944, starring Gene Kelly and Rita Hayworth] is a fine film. [...] It has a love story, it has music and it is in technicolor. However, it does not particularly help us in our program of re-educating the German people. Now *if* there was an entertainment film with Rita Hayworth or Ingrid Bergman or Gary Cooper, in Technicolor if you wish, and with a love story—only with a very special love story, cleverly devised to sell us a few ideological items—such a film would provide us with a superior piece of propaganda; they would stand in long lines to buy, and once they bought it, it would stick. Unfortunately, no such film exists yet. It must be made. I want to make it.[8]

What the "Memorandum" does not state is that Wilder's original role as observer and consultant for OMGUS was actually in conflict with his professional interest as director and writer at Paramount. His evaluation in the memo that "no production of German pictures is possible in the near future" clearly served his argument that Americans needed to make movies for Germans, but it neglects to consider the feasibility of a German film industry. Thus Wilder made no mention of the fact that the film studios at Geiselgasteig near Munich had survived the war in good condition, or that in the Soviet Sector the centralized DEFA film studios were already beginning to produce German films. Wilder's memorandum exudes the commercialism typical of the U.S. film industry, which after 1945 was looking to be rewarded for its wartime support of Washington, even though that support had already spelled revenue at the home box office. With Germany no longer sealed off from the outside and its film industry in shambles, a substantial new foreign market was opening up, even if that market would not yet yield any significant revenue. Wilder's pitch for a love story with high production values promoted a product for which there would not only be high demand but one which Germany's rudimentary film industry could not yet provide.

A Foreign Affair would be Wilder's most daring attempt yet to use entertainment in order to "sell a few ideological items," yet what precisely those items were was far from predictable. If one compares Wilder's brief story outline from 1945 with the 1947 script and the actual film, one notices that in the latter the moral ambiguity of his characters has been dramatically increased, an indication that in the two-year span Wilder had become doubtful about the mission of the Allied occupation. Originally, the film was to focus on a German *Trümmerfrau* who sees no meaning in living in a defeated country and is ready to commit suicide as soon as the Americans have turned on the gas again. Through her encounter with Occupation forces, she will slowly regain a modicum of hope and a certain degree of self-esteem. As for the GI, he was not to be "a flag waving hero," but a man not "too sure of what the hell this [i.e., the war and occupation] was all about." The character as played by John Lund, however, has no qualms about enjoying the spoils of the victor, bartering at the black market, and even hiding the incriminating file of his German mistress for sexual favors. The Dietrich character is even further away from Wilder's original figure. While she may live in a bombed-out apartment, she is no brick shoveling rubble woman, but a glamorous nightclub singer who knows how to survive in a starving city. She defies being a victim and defends her opportunism by pointing to the moral corruption of those empowered to judge her. Through the introduction of the delegation from Congress, the focus shifts from an assessment of the German state of mind ca. 1946 to one of America's position on Germany, ultimately questioning American hypocrisy more than the legacy of Nazism.

Made by an émigré who returns as ranking officer in the occupying army to the city that he loved and from which he had to flee, the film is saturated with ambiguity—with a nostalgia seeking to recover a better past so as to forge a better future, but also with the urge to take the Germans to task for the atrocities of Nazi rule, thereby disallowing historical amnesia and a simple plea for innocence. Americans, in turn, are being confronted with a less than flattering image of their occupying force, and with a portrayal of Berlin that celebrates the city's resilience, wit, and irreverence. Planned as a glossy studio production suitable for export to Germany, the film's main predicament was that it needed to communicate certain "ideological items" to very different audiences. As it turned out, *A Foreign Affair* was a commercial success, but American critics had mixed reactions; Congress attacked it, and OMGUS considered the film inappropriate for the German public. Ironically, it was Wilder's successor as film officer, veteran producer Erich Pommer, who would eventually approve the film for distribution in Germany, but it would not be premiered until May 1977, when the state-run TV station ARD showed it.

Screening the Rubble

The multiple perspectives of *A Foreign Affair* not only stem from the contradictory conceptions of the film, but also from the way in which the film consciously situates itself vis-à-vis two distinct, though interrelated film histories, namely, the styles and genres of 1930s and 1940s Hollywood as well as German film of the Weimar, Nazi, and postwar eras. *A Foreign Affair* could indeed be seen as a synthesis of Wilder's American sexual comedies such as *Ninotchka* (which was actually premiered in Germany in December, 1948), *Midnight,* and *The Major and the Minor* and the classic Weimar cinema of the 1930s, stressing its affinity to the latter to such an extent that one reviewer wondered where the UFA trademark was.[9] At the same time, it alludes to German Expressionism of the 1920s and film noir of early 1940s at the very moment when these styles get rearticulated by various American, German, and Italian films of the immediate postwar years.

To unravel the generic layering of *A Foreign Affair,* let us consider its stunning opening. If Billy Wilder's 1945 trip to Berlin provides the biographical seed for *A Foreign Affair,* a visit also sets its plot in motion. The first shot of the film, over which the opening credits roll, shows us a plane traversing the clouds while the soundtrack plays a medley of Erika von Schlütow's songs. Suddenly the music turns from upbeat to ominous as we glimpse the ruins of Berlin from high above. Inside the plane, a delegation from the U.S. congress is on its way to inspect the troops in Berlin, and the view of bombed-out Berlin prompts the various congressmen to debate what to do with the destroyed city and its inhabitants. While the representative from Texas suggests planting grass and "moving in the longhorns," echoing the Morgenthau plan to turn the defeated Germany into an agrarian society, his colleague from the Midwest urges to "get the industry going" and "feed the people." "But let 'em know where it's coming from," the Texan adds, a clear indication of the importance to implant in the Germans a sense of gratitude to their American liberators for future political developments. This approach is quickly criticized by the only Leftist in the group (presumably a New Deal democrat), representing the Bronx, who earlier lauded the Soviet efforts in the conquest of Berlin and now comments: "If you send a hungry man a loaf of bread it's democracy; if you leave the wrapper on it's imperialism."

The witty one-liners the congressmen shoot at each other quickly identify the film as a comedy. From the outset, there is a fundamental ambiguity regarding the appropriateness of humor in light of the seriousness of the topic, namely, the laborious replacement of one regime by another. Even though Congresswoman Frost is quick to point out to her colleagues that the charge of the committee is merely to investigate the morale of American occupation forces, the opening exchange indicates that an underlying concern of the Congressmen is what to do with the Germans now that the war is over.

The shots of an airplane descending through the clouds recall the opening of another film intended to "sell a few ideological items," Leni Riefenstahl's famous documentary *Triumph of the Will* made in 1935. In that film it is Adolf Hitler who, to Wagner's music, swoops down God-like from high above onto the medieval town of Nuremberg, to be greeted by its enthusiastic burghers and NSDAP party members gathering for the annual Reichsparteitag. Wilder's comic reworking of the scene replaces the Führer's dogmatic message with the pluralistic vision of the six quarreling U.S. representatives, and the welcoming committee, composed of a half-size military band and a weary Colonel Plummer reminding his troupes to behave, is a far cry from the jubilant Nazi supporters of Nuremberg. For the Berliners, however, the power descending from the sky is just another version of political rule to which one needs to adapt, as it is made poignantly clear when Erika von Schlütow salutes Captain John Pringle as her *new* Führer: "Heil Johnny."[10]

Spoofing Riefenstahl's film certainly indicates which traditions will *not* serve as a model for postwar German filmmaking, but the question which film traditions will actually provide a foundation is far more complex. The films that are involved in finding an adequate postwar aesthetics all do so by linking the question of realism to the representation of rubble and most of them do so by combining studio sets and location photography of the devastated Germany. The American films of this period that use extensive location photography include Jacques Tourneur's *Berlin Express* (1948), a noirish espionage thriller written by Curt Siodmak and shot mostly in Frankfurt; Fred Zinnemann's neorealist influenced *The Search* (1948), about a young Czech boy, a survivor of Auschwitz, and his mother's search for him in refugee camps all over Germany; and George Seaton's *The Big Lift* (1950) about two Air Force sergeants during the 1948 Berlin airlift. These films share *A Foreign Affair*'s ambition to ground and authenticate the narratives by situating them in a clearly defined historical and geographical space, but they differ significantly in how they employ the ruins for aesthetic and moral purposes.[11]

The first—and ultimately only— new film genre to emerge in Germany after the war was the rubble film (*Trümmerfilm*), for which the ruins became more than just a location. While they would often provide a dramatic backdrop for the storyline, they are more importantly a metaphor for the traumatized German psyche in the immediate aftermath of the war. The narratives of films in this genre usually revolve around building a new country or community amid the physical destruction and the shadows of the past. They also often portray the hardship of Germans who returned from the front trying to recover—often without success—a sense of home amid the debris. Focusing on German suffering, these films often evade the question to what degree Germans themselves are responsible for the destruction of their cities, and very few of them addressed the Holocaust.

The very first German film to be shot and premiered after the war became also one of the most significant of the genre—Wolfgang Staudte's 1946 *Die Mörder sind unter uns* (The Murderers Are among Us), produced by the newly founded DEFA film studios in the Soviet Occupation zone. Along with Roberto Rossellini's neorealist *Germania Anno Zero* (Germany, Year Zero) from 1947 (though not released in Germany until 1952), it became the most widely acknowledged portrait of immediate postwar Berlin. Made within one year of each other and produced by the same studio, the two films make remarkably different use of Berlin's ruins, even though both actually mix studio photography with location shooting. Rossellini's film, cowritten by Wilder's longtime friend Max Colpet and much admired by Wilder and Dietrich, is a filmic testimony to Berlin and the Germans of 1945 and revolves around a destitute family, among them a boy who prefers death to life.[12] For Rossellini, the purpose of realism was, in its most reduced definition, finding images that convey the experience of suffering so as to avoid its perpetuation or repetition. *Germania Anno Zero*'s sights of a dead, ghostly city with its disconnected streets, piles of detritus, and a landscape of ruins resemble an abstract portrait, turning it into a symbol not only of Germany's fall but also of a world destroyed by ambition. A cruel and unsentimental film that avoids any optimism, it resonates with *A Foreign Affair*'s sober look at Berlin two years later.[13]

Die Mörder sind unter uns taps into different traditions of (anti)realism to convey its sense of postwar Berlin, most strongly German Expressionist cinema. Staudte's use of chiaroscuro lighting, distorted camera work, shadows, and dramatic backdrops that look like cutouts visually capture the inner torment of the film's male protagonist much like *The Cabinet of Dr. Caligari* did two-and-a-half decades earlier. Relying on ruins rebuilt in the studio for heightened dramatic effect, the film uses location shots to render interiority visible.[14] Apart from the locations, *Die Mörder sind unter uns* and *A Foreign Affair* have little in common. Where Staudte's film raises the question of how the German nation can heal, only to answer it in humanist rather than political terms, Wilder's film understands denazification as an American, not a German, task, without however putting too much faith in their efforts. *A Foreign Affair* portrays the Germans as having the lessons of Nazism too deeply ingrained in them to promise betterment in the near future. The boy who compulsively draws swastikas is a long, long way from being a good democrat, and his distant cousin, the heel-clicking Schlemmer of Wilder's *One, Two, Three* will still embody authoritarian traits more than a decade later.

Allegories of the Nation

A Foreign Affair is indebted to the cinematic traditions that first shaped Wilder's own development as a writer, both at UFA and Paramount, and it is precisely by consciously alluding to these traditions that the film contributes most to the discourse on postwar German reeducation and cinema. These traditions are most strongly conveyed by the two female protagonists as well as the stars who played them, Jean Arthur and Marlene Dietrich. Before doing so, however, a few general remarks are in order on how the film anchors itself in both German and American films of the 1930s.

The most direct allusion is of course to *Der blaue Engel* (The Blue Angel, Josef von Sternberg, 1930), which not only launched Marlene Dietrich's international stardom but also underscored UFA's standings as artistically innovative and commercially successful studio, including its star producer Erich Pommer. The look and feel of this film informs virtually every frame of *A Foreign Affair*, no matter whether Dietrich is present or not. Friedrich Hollaender, who also happens to play the piano at the Lorelei nightclub, composed the songs for both films.[15] Performing with him are the Syncopators, whose members were backup musicians in *The Blue Angel*, while the bass drum advertises the Hotel Eden, a famous Berlin establishment of the 1920s. The presence of Hollaender and Dietrich as fellow émigrés recuperates a film culture that has apparently survived the Third Reich unscathed. But unlike the Expressionism conjured up by *Die Mörder sind unter uns*, this is a decidedly cosmopolitan (and Jewish) Weimar culture, created partly by foreign talent and celebrating the wit, decadence, and sexual freedom that was soon to become the target of Nazi *völkisch* cultural politics.

The 1930s were the decade that saw both Jean Arthur and Marlene Dietrich rise to stardom in Hollywood, both beginning their acting career during the silent era.[16] While Dietrich's image as seductress was shaped in a series of highly stylized Paramount productions directed by Josef von Sternberg, Arthur developed a flair for farcical comedy in films by John Ford and Frank Capra, most notably *Mr. Deeds Goes to Town* (1936) and *Mr. Smith Goes to Washington* (1939), in which she costarred with Gary Cooper and James Stewart, respectively. In the former, she plays a famous journalist who has to cover the doings of a millionaire heir for her paper, while in the latter she is a hardworking, Washington-savvy secretary to freshman senator Smith. In both films she plays an independent, smart, yet down-to-earth woman who rescues a besieged hero and becomes a heroine of sorts herself. Persuaded by Brackett and Wilder to come out of retirement, she was cast against character in *A Foreign Affair* as a prissy, puritanical, and uptight Congresswoman from Iowa who is the butt of many jokes. (Dietrich, for example, comments on her looks by saying: "What a curious way to do your hair—or rather not to do it.") Although one year her senior, Arthur's wide-eyed and innocent Frost comes across as much younger than Dietrich's "used" glamorous-hard appearance. At the beginning of the film, the two women are introduced as direct opposites, with Frost's naiveté emphasized by the film's narration, as the audience finds out about Pringle's corruption long before she does. The alluring and experienced von Schlütow, in contrast, knows about everything, from how to survive in difficult times (be it in Hitler's Germany or the ruins of Berlin) to how to change the line of her eye brows. (Dietrich herself changed her eye line as part of von Sternberg's makeover of her.) Ironically, Dietrich functions as a role model for Arthur, enlightening her about men and about how to be a woman, corrupting Arthur's moral superiority in the process, thereby making her more attractive to Captain Pringle. It is even possible to argue that Frost is more drawn to von Schlütow than Pringle, making Dietrich and not John Lund the center of the love triangle that structures the film. She not only affects Frost's character reversal, but also seems to be the true object of Frost's desire. When von Schlütow's analytically seductive songs melt Frost's defense layers, thereby awakening Frost's own sexuality, Frost's eyes are fixated on her.[17] Building on the Dietrich of the Weimar cabaret and early von Sternberg films at Paramount, when the star flaunted her attraction to women, Dietrich's von Schlütow unsettles gender roles, just as she questions the line between what is typically German and what is American.

The two women are obvious symbols for the state of mind of the respective countries they come from, and were used as such in the advertising campaign for the film. As one Paramount cartoon had it: "Jean Arthur: The People's Choice in IOWA. Marlene Dietrich: The Army's Choice in BERLIN." The German is a femme fatale with a past, only that in this tale that past has not only sexual but also political connotations. Dietrich is cast in the mid-1930s Sternbergian glamour chiaroscuro, an ironic comment on her old image with an undercurrent of self-parody. Arthur's face, in contrast, is mostly shown from the front and in full light, giving it the scrubbed look Dietrich ridicules. The morally upright but sexually repressed American with the telling name—Frost—is a symbol for stability and steadfastness, including puritan virtues and political incorruptibility, but also simplemindedness, provincialism, and naiveté, while the worldly but cynical von Schlütow represents a defeated yet resilient urban culture where, as Brecht knew, food comes before morals. Yet not only does Miss Frost undergo a character change that will bring her closer to Dietrich's allure (including bartering at the black market and singing at the Lorelei) but from the outset the line that divides these two distinct representations of national identity is more blurred than the stereotypes suggest.

Contemporary German audiences will have seen more in Phoebe Frost than an American, and more in Marlene Dietrich than a former Nazi. Frost's rhetoric about Berlin being "infected by moral malaria" that needs to be "fumigated with all insecticides at our disposal" resonates not only with official political discourse of U.S. wartime and postwar intelligence but also quotes almost verbatim Nazi rhetoric of defending the purity of the German soul. (Incidentally, the Nazis too considered Berlin a decadent city in need of fumigation.) Frost's straw-blond hair in tight braids, her wholesome features, and her upright posture make her look like the girls in the *Bund deutscher Mädchen* (Confederation of German Girls), and Joseph Goebbels would have been pleased with her restrained sexuality and overall concern with duty to the fatherland. Life in conservative and virtually crime-free Iowa, where 62% support the Republicans, was certainly not that different from life in the German provinces during the Third Reich. And while the Nazis did not favor women in the role of political leadership, they would have approved of Phoebe Frost's sense of (initial) restraint and incorruptibility. No wonder, then, that when the two women first confront each other in the film, Dietrich expresses her surprise about Arthur's looks. To Pringle's question whether Dietrich realizes to whom she is speaking, Dietrich replies: "An American woman. And I'm a little disappointed, to tell you the truth. We apparently have a false idea about the chic American woman. Oh, I suppose that's publicity from Hollywood."

The film further underscores Arthur's resemblance to German women by the fact that Frost is actually twice able to pass for a German woman—first as *Gretchen Gesundheit* with the American GIs, and then with the German police after being picked up during a raid at the Lorelei. Afterward, at her apartment, von Schlütow comments on Frost's lack of honesty vis-à-vis the German police, "Now you're one of us." When Frost leaves that apartment, in the one moment the film bestows true dignity on her after finding out about Pringle's feelings for von Schlütow, she walks alone among the dark ruins, the looming shadows of the destroyed buildings now also an appropriate metaphor for the state of mind of an *American*.

Just as Arthur's Frost is more than just an American woman, Dietrich plays a German who for many contemporary viewers must have looked very un-German. A native Berliner, Dietrich had left Germany in 1930 with von Sternberg after her success in *The Blue Angel* and under his direction became a major star at Paramount. Her role as Erika von Schlütow thus not only goes back to Lola Lola, but also to her American roles of Amy Jollie, Blonde Venus, Shanghai Lily, and Concha Perez. As Gaylyn Studlar shows, Dietrich was carefully Americanized by Paramount studios, a process that ironically occurred at the hands of such European directors as von Sternberg and Ernst Lubitsch (and later Wilder). Hers was the kind of image of womanhood the Nazis derided, and one that in the immediate postwar years would be associated with the alleged "decadence" of American society propagated by the Nazis. (Many Germans in fact considered Dietrich a traitor, and her 1960 tour through Germany was picketed with signs that read "Marlene, go home!") Yet, even though Goebbels discredited the parts Dietrich played in Hollywood, he repeatedly extended to her generous offers to rejoin the German film industry under his command, which she steadfastly refused. Having become a U.S. citizen in 1939, she entertained American troops during the war for extended periods in North Africa and Italy. By wearing her own dress from the USO shows in the Lorelei scenes, Dietrich underscores the continuity between her on-screen and offscreen incarnations. That she now performs in a Berlin nightclub creates the illusion of a permanent return to her native city (even if, as noted earlier, all her scenes were shot on the Paramount lot.) Seen in this light, the title of Wilder's film may have suggested to Berliners that Dietrich's liaison with America, *her* foreign affair, was now over.

There are thus multiple ironies in casting the steadfast opponent to Hitler as the former concubine of a high-ranking Nazi. Because of Dietrich's performances for the USO, a widely publicized and carefully integrated part of her star image, her von Schlütow is a complex and contradictory figure. Dietrich's appearance in the film conjures up the memory not only of all of her previous roles but also her offscreen and public persona, turning the figure of the Nazi sympathizer into a politically much more layered and ultimately sympathetic character. After all, von Schlütow continues what Marlene had been doing during the war, namely, "taking care of the boys." When at the end of the film von Schlütow gets sent off to a labor camp under the escort of first two, then four, and finally five GIs (each assigned to watch the others watch von Schlütow) the audience registers with relief that she will in all likelihood avoid harsh punishment. Marlene's exit as unrepentant and unpunished German provides a strong contrast to the highly conventional (and improbable) melodramatic climax that finds the two Americans united and going home together—a conclusion obviously meant to placate the Production Code Administration that remains too unconvincing to be taken seriously.

Before the Curtain Fell

Nine months before the capitulation of the German Wehrmacht, Theodor W. Adorno reflected in Los Angeles on the issue of justice in a future Germany.

> To the question what is to be done with the defeated Germany, I could say only two things in reply. Firstly: at no price, on no conditions, would I wish to be an executioner or to supply legitimations for executioners. Secondly: I should not wish, least of all with legal machinery, to stay the hand of anyone who was avenging past misdeeds. This is a thoroughly unsatisfactory, contradictory answer, one that makes a mockery of both principle and practice. But perhaps the fault lies in the question and not only in me.[18]

Billy Wilder's *A Foreign Affair* offers a similarly unsatisfactory answer to the question Adorno raises. His mixed messages about good and bad Germans, about sincere reeducation and American simplemindedness, cultural hypocrisy, and sexual repression, embody the paradoxical situation of the exile contemplating a possible return to the land that chased him out.

As Wilder told Cameron Crowe, *A Foreign Affair* is (in hindsight) his most personal film (he originally even intended to make the Pringle character a Jew). It is indeed an extended homage to a culture and a city that served as his training ground before abruptly being forced out. The film suggests that the period before 1933 becomes for Germans the only possible orientation for rebuilding, a time warp Wilder deftly captures in the shots of Hollaender at the Lorelei, which create the impression that he's been sitting at that same piano for the last fifteen years. Dietrich's lack of sentimentalism, her worldliness, and her resilience are the guarantee that, as she sings, "they won't return/the phantoms of the past." Unlike any other film of that period, the Germans are portrayed not only as perpetrators but also victims. Dietrich is allowed to tell her story of air raids and the threat of being raped by the conquering Russians, which clearly makes an impression on Congresswoman Frost. (She would play similar ambassador roles in Wilder's *Witness for the Prosecution* and Stanley Kramer's *Judgment at Nuremberg*, where as the widow of a high-ranking German officer she explains to the judge of a war tribunal [Spencer Tracy]: "I have a mission with the Americans—to convince you that we're not all monsters.") The Berlin of 1945/48 is indeed a city where the return to the time before the descent into barbarism seems possible, a site of unprecedented exchange, openness, and experimentation. A truly international city that united not only the four victorious powers, but also German Jews coming out of hiding as well as refugees and displaced people from all over Eastern Europe. There was much life in the ruins of Berlin.

Yet there is also something profoundly nostalgic in Wilder's defense of a culture irrevocably lost, for it overlooks the fact that this culture not only had run its course prior to Hitler's rise to power but that it also offered little to stand in his way. Accessing it now in 1945/47, as if it had been preserved in a "time capsule left untouched all those years," as the historian Wolfgang Schivelbusch calls it, is certainly more naïve than Miss Frost's unawareness of what occupation is all about.[19] But perhaps Wilder's real audience are not the people in the ruins of Berlin, but in the American heartland to whom he wants to tell a tale about a culture that shaped him, that disappeared, only to reappear for a brief moment before the Berlin airlift and the onset of the Cold War that put Berlin into a 40-year deep freeze. And perhaps it is an appropriate gesture that at Potsdamer Platz, the onetime wasteland that separated East and West Berlin until 1989, today a bistro called "Billy Wilder's" celebrates the director's faith in the city's ability for rejuvenation and rebirth.

Notes

1. Quoted in Ed Sikov, *On Sunset Boulevard: The Life and Times of Billy Wilder* (New York: Hyperion, 1998), p.236.
2. Theodor W. Adorno, "On the Question: 'What is German?'" trans. Thomas Y. Levin, *New German Critique* 36 (1985): 125.
3. See Curt Riess, *Berlin Berlin: 1945–1953* (Berlin: Mittag & Co, 1953).
4. In a very detailed account of the production history of *Todesmühlen*, Brewster S. Chamberlain has shown that the U.S. Information Control Division did *not* want to force Germans to watch atrocity films, but rather hoped that Germans

would want to see them on their own accord. However, certain local military governments did make it a policy to stamp food ration cards of those who had set through a screening of *Todesmühlen*. See Brewster S. Chamberlain, "*Todesmühlen*: Ein früher Versuch zur Massen-'Umerziehung' im besetzten Deutschland 1945–1946," *Vierteljahrshefte für Zeitgeschichte* 3 (1981): 420–436.

5. In interviews, Wilder has given conflicting accounts to what degree he was involved in the editing of this film. According to Chamberlain, it is rather unclear what Wilder's role really was. Chamberlain concludes that the reception of *Todesmühlen* by German audiences showed the Americans that documentary film was not successful as a tool of reeducation, which is also what Wilder states in his memorandum (discussed below) to the Information Control Division.

6. On *Todesmühlen* see also: Jeanpaul Goergen, "Aufnahmen beglaubigter Kameraleute: *Die Todesmühlen*" *Filmblatt* 7.19/20 (2002): pp.25–31.

7. In his memoirs, Czech director Hanus Burger claims that Wilder from the beginning disliked the concept of hitting the audience over the head with something they are unwilling to see. Wilder also claims to have been instructed by Washington officials "not to antagonize our logical allies of tomorrow." (Quoted in: Thomas Brandlmeier, "Von Hitler zu Adenauer: Deutsche Trümmerfilme," in *Zwischen Gestern und Morgen: Westdeutscher Nachkriegsfilm 1946–1962*, ed. Hilmar Hoffmann and Walter Schobert [Frankfurt am Main: Deutsches Filmmuseum Frankfurt am Main, 1989] pp.32–59; here p.44.) Wilder trimmed *Todesmühlen* from 86 to 22 minutes. The film was released in 1946 and widely shown, but pulled from distribution before the end of the year.

8. "The Wilder Memorandum," reprinted in: Ralph Willett, *The Americanization of Germany, 1945–1949* (London and New York: Routledge, 1989), pp.40–44; here p.40.

9. Stuart Schulberg, "A Communication: A Letter about Billy Wilder," in *The Quarterly of Film, Radio and Television* 7.1 (1952): 434–436; here p.435.

10. *Todesmühlen* uses scenes of jubilating Nazi supporters from *Triumph of the Will* to intercut with shots of German civilians forcibly marched through liberated concentration camps by the Allies, a contrast set up to question the lack of knowledge Germans claimed to have had about the evil of Nazism and the dimension of the Holocaust.

11. Max Colpet, Wilder's longtime friend, remarks in his memoir that Rossellini would mark with chalk the ruins he used for location photography so as not to use the same location shots taken by Paramount for *A Foreign Affair* and RKO for *Berlin Express*. (*Sag mir, wo die Jahre sind*, p.186.)

12. Dietrich was so impressed with Rossellini's *Roma, Città Aperta* (1945) and *Paisà* (1946) that she offered to translate his treatment of *Germania Anno Zero* into English. See Werner Sudendorf, *Marlene Dietrich* (Munich: Deutscher Taschenbuch Verlag, 2001), p.143.

13. Reviewing *A Foreign Affair, Le Nouvel Observateur* wrote: "C'est Rossellini en version ironique."

14. For a perceptive analysis of this film and the genre of the *Trümmerfilm* in general see: Robert Shandley, *Rubble Films: German Cinema in the Shadow*

of the Third Reich (Philadelphia: Temple University Press, 2001). See also Enno Patalas, "The German Waste Land," *Sight and Sound* 23.25 [1953–56]: 24–27.

15. According to Dietrich's biographer Steven Bach, Hollaender wrote the songs not for the film but for his failed Hollywood cabaret, "Tingeltangel." "They are dark, corrosive, mockingly romantic. Their voice is that of a survivor not sure survival is all it's cracked up to be." See Steven Bach, *Marlene Dietrich: Life and Legend* (New York: Morrow, 1992), p.332.

16. The careers of Jean Arthur (1900–1991) and Marlene Dietrich (1901–1992) offer some striking parallels. Both had their beginnings in the silent age, but did not find success until the sound era. Both actresses tried to hide their age, and both were often paired with younger men, as they were in *A Foreign Affair*.

17. See Alice Kuzniar, "'It's Not Often That I Want a Man': Reading for a Queer Marlene," forthcoming in Gerd Gemünden and Mary Desjardins, eds., *Dietrich Icon* (Durham, NC: Duke University Press, 2007).

18. Theodor W. Adorno, *Minima Moralia: Reflections From Damaged Life*, trans. E.F.N. Jephcott (London and New York: Verso, 1978), p.56.

19. Wolfgang Schivelbusch, *In a Cold Crater: Cultural and Intellectual Life in Berlin, 1945–1948*, trans. Kelly Barry (Berkeley, CA: University of California Press, 1998), p.14.

CHAPTER EIGHT

RUBBLE NOIR

Jennifer Fay

> *Spatial structures are the dreams of a society. Whenever the hieroglyph of any such spatial structure is decoded, the foundation of the social reality is revealed.*
>
> —Siegfried Kracauer[1]

It is perhaps appropriate that the first German feature film made in the American zone of occupation, *Zwischen Gestern und Morgen* (1947), was a criminal thriller, a noir of sorts, shot in what remained of Munich's Regina Palast Hotel. The plot, fragmented through a series of flashbacks, shuttles between the immediate postwar era and the Nazi period as various characters recount the events surrounding the tragic fate of one of the hotel's late guests, the Jewish stage actress, Nelly Dreyfuss (Sybille Schmitz). In the 1930s, Nelly furtively breaks the Nuremberg laws when she checks into the Regina so that she may experience, one last time, the luxury of her cosmopolitan Weimar life. When the Nazi secret police ("disguised" in trench coats and fedoras) pursue her through the hotel's dark corridors, Nelly takes her own life by throwing herself from the banister of the interior grand staircase. Now, in 1946, one of her acquaintances, Michael Rott (Viktor de Kowa), has returned to the Regina from his exile in Switzerland. He comes in search of another woman he loved only to find himself accused of having stolen Nelly's jewels before he himself fled the Nazis. To clear his name, these jewels must be recovered from the rubble that is already in the process of being removed.

Director Harald Braun recalled that the idea for this film came to him when he first beheld the Regina in its half-intact state.[2] In a building where total destruction was only a wall away from the eerily preserved splendor of plush accommodations, action could be filmed, and shifts in temporality signaled, by simply moving the camera and crew from the structure that survived the war to the spaces that succumbed. Thus filmed images of the hotel signify both palimpsestically and spatially: for, in every scene that takes place in the prewar period, postwar rubble lies only a few meters away, and the rubble, suffused with the traces of the hotel's luminous past, is in the shadow of the still-intact half structure. In tribute to his architectural muse, Braun initially called the film *Palast Hotel*. The title on which he finally settled, however, *Between Yesterday and Tomorrow*, is a rather awkward ode not to the hotel as the palace it once was, but to the oscillating temporality that encompasses its rise and ruin.[3]

As *Zwischen* circulated in Germany from 1947 through 1949, Hollywood noirs brought to the American zone captured a U.S. metropolis intact and untouched by war, but in the process of disappearing. As Edward Dimendberg writes of *Naked City* (1948), *Lost Weekend* (1945), and the film discussed below, *Call Northside 777* (1948)—all of which were shown in occupied Germany—film noir was drawn to "urban topoi on the verge of destruction."[4] These films' investigation of ethnic neighborhoods and working-class slums brings to attention the hidden places that would soon fall prey to urban redevelopment. Other "educational" documentaries about the U.S. city shown in the occupied territory, such as *A Better Tomorrow* (1944) and *Zehn Minuten in Amerika* (Ten Minutes in America, 1949), showcase postwar urban planning that proposes to demolish ghettos, clear the debris, and create in city centers the built environments that would become the housing projects of the 1950s and 1960s. Hollywood noirs share with *Zwischen* a complicated relationship to the buildings that both hide and protect the ethnic variety and criminal history that made the prewar city so exciting and alluring, and perhaps worth forgetting.[5]

In the spirit of the epigraph above, this essay aims to decode the imagistic and spatial affinities between *Zwischen* and the American films brought to and shot in U.S.-occupied Germany including *Call Northside*, *Berlin Express* (1948), and *A Foreign Affair* (1948) for what they reveal about social reality of postwar urbanism. These films all have subplots in which a character searches for a person or thing in a metropolitan area that is so fragile, impermanent, and on the cusp of complete demolition that the evidence and history it contains threaten to vanish forever. Dimendberg argues that the "historical content" of film noir is the American city of the 1940s and 1950s, a space "increasingly bereft of its former glories, a site of social and technological alienation, the domain of the older "invisible city" now increasingly overtaken by expanding rings of centerless suburbs."[6] Noir registers the experience of late modernity as the experience of dwelling in the ruins of man's grandest ambitions. *Zwischen* is particularly interesting in this regard, and not only because it uses Regina's ruin in temporally significant ways. Symptomatic of film's architectural melancholia, the plot enacts how we get from the urban grandeur of the Weimar era to the enrubbled present by destroying those spaces that remain. In the final shot from the last flashback sequence the camera lingers in the "1930s" hotel lobby where Nelly's husband (Willy Birgel), mourning her death and his own moral weakness against Nazism, passively sits in an armchair as the ceiling gives way to the Allied bombs from above. To represent the violence of the past, Braun had to reenact this cycle of destruction in the present. *Zwischen*, then, literalizes modernity's ravaging force and questions its progress narrative in a way that American noirs could at best inadvertently signal. But Braun's film also traces something more: as a noir made under the conditions of military defeat and foreign occupation it encrypts the provisionality and temporality of life in catastrophe's wake. More than its American film counterparts, *Zwischen* participates in a materialist historical reckoning that is concerned with the erasure of history and the ends of a corrupt social order whose remnants are everywhere.

* * *

Zwischen has been largely overlooked as an important and inventive film about postwar Germany in large measure because, at the time of its release, German critics lambasted Braun for trivializing Nazi treachery through the tired conventions of a thriller.[7] These reviews, like Braun's film, bear the signs and stress of occupation film culture. Writing for the *Süddeutsche Zeitung*, Gunther Groll lamented:

> From the first postwar film in this zone we had hoped for not the familiar and well-tried, but for new directions. New insights. New people. At least (and with this alone we would be satisfied) we would like to detect a few new profiles, new ideas, a few points of departure.[...] It is great that the Nazi tendency has been replaced, but it is not all that useful when in other respects, stylistically and substantially, everything old remains.[8]

Berlin's *Tägliche Rundschau* summarily dismissed the film, derisively retitling it, *Between the Day before Yesterday and Some Other Time*—a mock title that, not incidentally, bespeaks *Zwischen's* unstable temporality.[9] Most damning of all was the review in the Berlin *Tribüne* that attacked Braun for promoting a counterfactual fantasy of Germany during the war. "It is difficult," the writer concedes, "to see the world of yesterday through the eyes of today as it really was and not as we would like it to have been."

But in the yesterday of this film there are so many anti-Nazis all living in this hotel, "that the average viewer, confirming his good opinion of himself, will abandon his high consciousness in the movie theater and think, 'we were all against it.'" Apostrophizing those self-satisfied spectators, the critic concludes the review with this incriminating corrective: "But you were not against it, Herr Professor, nor you Herr Actor, nor you Herr Businessman, and all you others."[10]

U.S. military censorship required that German films demonstrably reorient viewers away from Nazism by dramatizing the devastating toll of Hitler's reign on civil society and by emphasizing the average German's complicity with genocide.[11] As one film officer explained: "The central problem in reorientation is to convince the individual German that he was *responsible* for National Socialism, not a helpless *victim* of it."[12] On the other hand, no film would be approved for screening that the U.S. authorities perceived as glorifying "the ideology of Fascism, Nazism, or racial distinction," idealizing "war or militarism," "politically subvert[ing] or pervert[ing] German history" or that was "in any way derisive of the Allied peoples, their governments, their political or national leaders."[13] Which is to say, German directors were expected to take up the problem of German history, Nazism, and the postwar conditions without presenting this history in a way that could be interpreted as sympathetic to German collaboration or equivocal about the complexities of Nazi citizenship. The American Film Control Branch vetted and often rejected scripts because filmmakers had failed to interpret these directives according to American wishes.[14] At the same time, these occupation films were expected to be both commercially popular with audiences in Germany and to serve as hard-currency-generating exports abroad, even as Hollywood dominated the American zone and was aggressively reclaiming European markets.[15] German critics took up the mantel of reeducation by pressuring directors to develop a new postwar aesthetic that was politically responsible, historically sensitive, and aesthetically inventive. Public opinion polls conducted by the U.S. Military Government in 1946, however, indicated that German filmgoers were eager to see entertainment films that could help them to forget the miseries of the past and of reconstruction. "In general," the survey concluded "purely escapist fare would on the whole be most welcome, provided it's the German type of glamour."[16] Braun's contemporary, director Helmut Käutner, expressed his disappointment with audiences who, he believed, were unwilling to watch anything but the most conventional dramas. In 1947, while film attendance in Germany reached record numbers, postwar German productions were barely breaking even.[17] Käutner could only conclude: "The audience wants suspense and conflict instead of problems. They want external action instead of experience."[18] Germans, he surmised, wanted to see images of the interwar period; they want to go back to the time before Hitler.

Caught between the rubble-fatigued public and the political mandate of historical accountability, Braun's film may have satisfied the vagaries of U.S. military censorship, but it disappointed its opposing German constituencies. I am not concerned here to redeem the plot of *Zwischen Gestern und Morgen* as a complex indictment of Nazi anti-Semitism. Rather as an artifact of war and occupation, *Zwischen* commands our attention less for the particular story about the past that it tells, and more for the destructive and cyclical history of urban ruin and catastrophe it both realizes and forecasts.

* * *

Like so many rubble films, *Zwischen*'s visual style is marked by the privations that follow in the wake of total war and unconditional surrender. Most interior scenes Braun shot at night because there was insufficient electricity during the day, and day scenes he illuminated primarily with natural light. Even as the film attempts to transport us from 1946 back to the more plentiful Nazi era, these flashback sequences bare the poverty of the occupation: characters in this film conspicuously drink, occasionally smoke, but *never* eat, because in these postwar hunger years, food, like electricity, is in dangerously short supply.[19] In some ways, *Zwischen*'s credit sequence, shot against what we are to take as Regina's once-revolving door, recalls a similar shot from Murnau's *Der Letzte Mann* (The Last Laugh, 1924). As a homage to UFA's past, this shot announces that the days of Weimar cinema—and the era of "German glamour"—are over. UFA's Berlin studio is now under Soviet jurisdiction, and the Munich studio, which in 1945 served as a temporary displaced person camp, is, in 1947, occupied with the dubbing of American and British films and the production of "reeducational" documentaries for Germany.[20] Thus Braun not only shot, but lived with his actors on location in the bombed-out Munich hotel.[21] In a strange reversal of architectural determinism, the occupation turns movie studios into temporary housing and half-destroyed hotels into temporary studios.

It is in comparison to other American films shot (but not shown) in the occupied territory, however, that *Zwischen*'s impoverished style, political tone, and relationship to history become distinct signifiers of defeat. For example, Jacques Tourneur's *Berlin Express* is a noir thriller that shuttles its characters from Paris to Frankfurt to the American sector of Berlin on the U.S. military train *Berlin Two*, a locomotive the film describes as a "traveling grand hotel." As the train approaches the city, a voiceover introduces viewers to Frankfurt as "a ghost town, a community of hollow shells chipped and battered by Allied bombings according to a methodical plan." As we watch the unpeopled ruins flit by through the window, our narrator explains that the "methodical plan" was to "cancel out the city as a tough enemy center and still retain some choice spots" for occupation authority. In the next scene, the camera is mounted on top of the bus the Express passengers take to the military base. As if narrating a travelogue, the voiceover directs our gaze to what the film refers to as the "modern touches" of Frankfurt's rerubbled architecture. The film jokingly coins the aesthetic of the ruins' "new lines" and "new shapes" as an example of "early twentieth century modern warfare." "So universal is the destruction" our narrator remarks "that it blends into one continuous pattern." The *New York Times* was especially impressed with the film's "realistic, awesome, and impressive vista" of the German city: "it is the panoramic and close view of life amid the 'new architecture' of Frankfurt and Berlin[...]which gives the adventure the authentic impact of a documentary."[22]

Or consider the opening sequence from Billy Wilder's comedy noir *A Foreign Affair*, shot on location in 1947 but banned in Germany until 1977.[23] Flying over postwar Berlin, U.S. representatives from Congress approvingly behold, and even film, the destructive power of American tax dollars, as their plane casts a shadow on the Allies-made destruction below. Wilder's opening sequence pays ironic homage to Leni Riefenstahl's *Triumph des Willens* (Triumph of the Will, 1935) that similarly begins with Hitler's extraterrestrial descent into Nuremberg. Hitler's plane also casts a shadow, this time over the dazzling orchestration of parades below in which individuals are subsumed into geometric forms, their design so vast that it can only be captured from the air. In quoting *Triumph*, Wilder not only compares Nazi and American triumphalism, he invites us to consider how the abstracting logic of the former has given way to otherworldly ruin of the latter. In Wilder's film too, the politicians view the rubble at such a physical and emotional remove that they may entertain its formal imagistic properties. One of the group exclaims of Berlin: "Look at it! Like packrats been gnawin' at a hunk of old moldy Roquefort cheese." These American films are shot through the mobile, congressional gaze that masters the cityscape as a panoramic and touristic view of a conquered territory, and they do so through the technology that just a few years earlier rendered it a target.

Zwischen, by contrast, is bound by a terrene, quite literally, pedestrian vision. In the first scene, Braun's camera perambulates with Rott from the train station to the Regina hotel, as he slowly takes in Munich's catastrophic scene and the seemingly *random* effects of air war where a destroyed apartment building is just a stone's throw from an intact church. Darting across the frame are bedraggled survivors of this "cancelled out" city who push carts of rubble and salvageable goods down roads banked with debris. Once Rott finds the Regina, the camera, stationed just outside the hotel entrance, shows us a portion of what appears to be the Regina miraculously preserved. Coming in through the hotel atrium however, Rott once again finds himself outside. The hotel's ceiling has collapsed, taking with it half of the stairwell. The lobby now opens up onto a field of exposed rubble where the café once thrived. Though Braun's camera often gazes up at the ruins from below—that is, from Rott's perspective—it never gains purchase on Munich's ruin from above, except when Rott, opening the door to what once was his lover's fifth-floor hotel room, shockingly discovers in its place a vertiginous vista of Munich's disintegrated rooftops. Compared to the aerial optics of American and Nazi films, in this shot, the only one of its kind in the film, the camera constructs an acrophobic point of view that frames the rubblescape as an eruptive site of intimate loss. We assume, as does Rott at this moment, that the lover he seeks has suffered the same fate as her room. Where Rott, above all, sees a woman's absence, we register the enormity of war's destructive power. But this is not the abstracting view of an erased city from afar; it is a vision and space that is particularized, personalized, and historically grounded. Seeing at eye level, Braun shows us Rott's encounter with Regina's disappeared spaces through the no less defamiliarizing proximity of what Kracauer aptly describes as "the abyss of nearness."[24]

* * *

As an abyssal space, Regina's foyer uncannily exposes and fully materializes the void, the "vis-á-vis de rien" that Kracauer famously argued was architecturally aestheticized in Weimar's grand hotel lobby.[25] His critique of the hotel lobby as a space of idle distraction merits brief elaboration insofar as it reaches its apotheosis in Braun's film. Kracauer likened the hotel lobby of the 1920s to an "inverted church," because both spaces, through different means and toward different ends, deindividuate those who visit. Equality in the congregation, Kracauer explains, is achieved through each member's relationship to God; their differences are erased in spiritual transcendence, or, what Kracauer calls "the question of the provisional."[26] But the hotel lobby is a space of "relaxation and indifference." It convenes guests who share no higher purpose, who come to meet no one, and who achieve an equality not in relationship to God, but to "the nothing" of fragmented modernity.[27] The hotel lobby "signifies only its own emptiness."[28] The cold rationalism of secular reason that, as Kracauer sees it, levels all things to abstract concepts, all individuals to anonymous members of society, and that posits historical events as "progress in one-dimensional time," is the same abstracting logic that governs the estrangement of the hotel's disintegrated sociality. For this reason, the hotel lobby is the exemplary setting for the detective novel, a fiction that assembles the elements of fragmented culture into an aesthetic totality rendering the state of affairs legible.

> Just as the detective discovers the secret that people have concealed, the detective novel discloses in the aesthetic medium the secret of a society bereft of reality, as well as the secret of its insubstantial marionettes. The composition of the detective novel transforms an ungraspable life into a translatable analogue of actual reality.[29]

If the lobby of the 1920s hides the reality of an unreal world, Braun's lobby, with its gaping holes and berubbled architecture reveals ungraspable life of a new order. Regina's lobby lays bare the deastheticized and disenchanted catastrophe that was always enshrouded in the 1920s space. The hotel's secular guests are now all too aware of their provisional life and the cyclical, multidimensional nature of history. Here in the Regina, the abstracting and violent logic of *Ratio* has been actualized not in the restitution of genuine reason, but in warfare, strategic bombing, and mass annihilation.

Against this postwar backdrop, the drama of detection—the search for a necklace—may be a trivialization of the past. But the incommensurability between story and setting speaks to the challenge of any diegesis set in the rubble to contain or explain the surfeit of catastrophic detail. Put differently, *because* he uses the conventions of the thriller, Braun unmasks what Kracauer called the "disguised quality of lived existence" in the world of yesterday's hotel lobbies and detective novels, and Braun does so through a medium that, by its very nature, elucidates rather than effaces this incommensurability. Where the hotel of the 1920s "conceals from its guests the real events which could put an end to the false aesthetic situation shrouding that nothing," there is no concealing the real events of Regina's past and current state that far exceed the plot circumscribing Rott's departure and return.[30] And the hermeticism of the detective story in which all clues and details are subsumed into a tidy cause and effect chain of action is ill-equipped to demystify the "strange mysteries" of warfare, guilt, and genocide that underwrite Regina's rubble in 1947.

* * *

Zwischen registers the shock of destruction from the perspective of one who returns to find neither home nor homeland, but their traces. For German audiences who walked through the rubble to see a film shot in the rubble, the representation of Germany's destruction hardly registered. To rephrase an observation from the critic above: it is difficult to see the world of today through the eyes of today as it really is. But the fate of German cities did stand out once images of postwar America were projected on German screens. In 1947, the same year of *Zwischen's* release, *The Best Years of Our Lives* (1946), itself a homecoming film, premiered in German theaters. One sequence in particular announces that the differing toll of war on these two countries could not have been more pronounced. Three returning veterans hitch a ride to Boon City in a B-17, the "Flying Fortress" made famous for its bombing missions over Germany. Sitting in the nose of the low-flying plane at the bombardier's station, the three marvel at the familiar, unaffected topography below. "The old hometown hasn't changed very much, has it?" remarks Sgt. Derry (Dana Andrews) with just a touch of disappointment. "There's the golf course. People playing golf like just as if nothing had ever happened."[31] In contrast to Munich's uncanny ruins that externalize the horrors of war, the life-as-usual American city refuses the eventfulness of the last six years—that is, until the plane turns toward the new airport and we survey the sublime scene of the B-17 graveyard, this plane's final destination. From this aerial perspective the bombers, grounded in formation, are patterned like the lackluster suburban development that would soon be forming on the outskirts of this city. At the end of the film, Derry finally secures work constructing prefabricated houses from the metal of these very planes. Where Germans live in the wake of the Allied bombers, Boon City's veterans will take up residency in their discarded hulls. The "tomorrow" of *Best Years's* soon-to-be-built suburb is thus already marked as refuse by the building materials that, like these characters, have given their best years to the war. The synthetic track housing intimates that despite America's being spared the bombs, here, as in Europe, in Theodor Adorno's words, "the house is past."[32] Writing from his American exile, and having taken up intellectual residence in what Georg Lukács called the "Grand Hotel Abyss," Adorno observed that "the bombing of European cities, as well as the labor and concentration camps, merely proceed as executors, with what the immanent development of technology has long decided was to be the fate of houses. They are now good only to be thrown away like old food cans."[33]

As a counterpoint to *Best Years'* bleak prognosis for Boon City residents, the first episode of *Zehn Minuten in Amerika* (Ten Minutes in America), a ten-part series on American life and culture produced for German audiences in 1949 by the U.S. High Commissioner for Germany, provided evidence of America's cold-war optimism.[34] The first segment "A City District Gets a New Look" takes us down into the streets of New York, to Harlem's dilapidated prewar tenement flats. We are told that these buildings, left behind by the city's urban development, will be razed and replaced by new, modern apartments.[35] This is no sooner declared, then we see a demolition ball lay waste to a brick exterior. In a wider shot, skeletons of new construction loom over the rubble of old Harlem, and suddenly postwar New York looks much like postwar Munich. It is only as these structures take shape as modern apartment buildings, however, that the narrator invites the comparison to Germany, which, he understates, is also seeing improved construction of this proportion. In just a few minutes, much of the complex is complete. A tracking shot shows us treeless block after block of uniform, functional, high-rise apartment buildings, and it becomes clear that modern seriality has replaced the eccentric shabbiness of Harlem's nineteenth-century dwellings. A montage sequence introduces us to the new building's residents by showing them first in their work place and then at home. The African-American machinist, the white female copyist, the Buick engineer, the automotive mechanic all live in uncluttered, white-walled, standardized quarters akin to their standardizing jobs, an arrangement that evinces urban democracy through a mass architectural technology of deindividuation. While this film was made chiefly to debunk Soviet anti-American propaganda in Germany, particularly Soviet critiques of America's treatment of its underprivileged and minority citizens, this segment suggests that Kracauer's hotel lobby for the rich has found an abyssal rejoinder in the apartment complexes for the poor.[36] Coincident with this documentary's German exhibition, Hollywood noirs played in Germany that were shot on location in America's vanishing neighborhoods, films that show us the secret life of America's unreconstructed underclass.

*   *   *

Call Northside 777 was shot on location in Chicago's decrepit South Wabash and South State slums, as well as inside the Criminal Courts Building and the state penitentiary in Joliet, Illinois. Like *Zwischen*, *Call Northside*, unearths the crimes of the 1930s by seeking out their traces in the 1940s.[37] Unlike *Zwischen*, however, *Northside* abides by a progress narrative by which cities are always born again and improved through destruction. This story, based on true events, begins with a recreated panorama of Chicago in 1871 engulfed by the flames of the Great Fire, an image evoking Munich, Dresden, and Berlin in the wake of fire bombing. As the image track dissolves into a bird's eye view of the 1930s skyline, a voiceover introduces the geographic and historical contours of this "new Chicago" that rose "out of the ashes of that catastrophe." This city "of brick and brawn, concrete and guts" has its own "short history of violence beating in its pulse." That short epoch is not the fire, but the prohibition era, inaugurated in 1932 with a record 365 murders. Newsreel and stock footage of liquor raids, bootlegging, and scenes of Chicago's legendary windy streets establish the milieu of the film's crime scene: Wanda Skutnik's speakeasy on South Ashland Avenue, a tiny storefront in the heart of Chicago's Polish district. Here in 1932 a police officer was brutally murdered, and due to the corruption of those days, Frank Wiecek (Richard Conte) was wrongly found guilty and sentenced to life in prison. Now in 1943, newspaper man P. J. McNeal (Jimmy Stewart) investigates the case by digging up new evidence that exonerates Wiecek and sets him free from his eleven-year stay at the penitentiary. In search of clues, McNeal takes to the bars and back alleys that abut Chicago's stockyard and slaughter houses. His investigation leads him to Wanda and reveals a real Chicago district rundown by years of depression and a belt-tightening war economy, a district that even in the 1940s, is destined to get a "new look."

To impress upon Germans the film's democratic lesson, the U.S. Military Government arranged a special screening of *Northside* for members of the Bavarian press and film circles in 1948.[38] From this film they would learn that despite the gross miscarriage of justice in Chicago history, thanks to investigative journalism, the state reverses the judgment against Wiecek and sets the record straight. "It's a big thing," McNeal explains to Wiecek in the film's final scene, "when a sovereign state admits an error. Remember this: there aren't many governments in the world that would do it." But what impressed the German film reviewers was not the story of juridical process and justice so much as the film's real, gritty location: "The director captures genuine life in the streets of Chicago made possible through the camera's mobility which is missing in most films of this kind. It presents truth and passion without falling into the incredible."[39] The *Rheinische Post* announced that the film's "perfect Realism," "prosaic and everyday," heralds a new *Neue Sachlichkeit*.[40] Indeed, when McNeal visits Wanda at night, we see the details of her ramshackle, dimly lit tenement apartment, filthy from the soot of passing trains and crumbling from decades of neglect, a mise-en-scéne that resembles those Weimar studio films associated with the *Neue Sachlichkeit* such as G. W. Pabst's *Die Liebe der Jenny Ney* (The Loves of Jenny Ney, 1928) or Karl Grune's *Die Straße* (The Street, 1923). Variously translated as the "New Objectivity" or "New Sobriety," the *Neue Sachlichkeit* was coined by Gustav Hartlaub to describe the vision of 1920s German artists who "in the midst of the catastrophe have begun to ponder what is most immediate, certain, and durable: truth and craft."[41] In the context of postwar America, the Weimar use of *Sachlichkeit* collided with another translation, "functionality," that described the fate of these neighborhoods. Chicago's postwar urban designs proposed not to restore the rough world in which Wanda Skutnik lives—to lay it bare for the truths about poverty and immigrant life it contains—but to replace it with buildings that realize the Chicago School of skyscraper modernism, an architectural movement that developed in the wake of the Great Fire.[42] That is, planners looked back to the architectural promises of the nineteenth century in order to envision a more utopic future free of the ghettos and debris amassed in the failure of Chicago's first attempt at systematic urban planning. The 1950s witnessed the mass demolition of Chicago's prewar buildings (most of which housed the poor immigrants and working-class African Americans) that would be replaced by structures and people city planners believed to be more true to the vision of the "Chicago School."[43] In this respect, the opening scene of the Great Fire, an event that matters not in the least to the film's plot, gestures to the cyclical ruin of the twentieth-century city and the displacement of its poor and disenfranchised in the name of progress. This is a cycle of total destruction the film knows but does not quite speak of or worry about.

The only sign of Chicago's new architecture in *Call Northside*, significantly, is neither the public housing of *Zehn Minuten*, nor the Mise van der Rohe structures of the new city, but rather the modern State Penitentiary in Joliet. We first see the building from a faux aerial perspective of its model on display in the visitor's lobby, a lobby that looks more like the entrance to a fashionable apartment building than prison. Indeed, with its clean lines, white smooth surfaces, bright illumination, and well-ordered visual and sonic environment, the prison is, ironically, a vast improvement over the stockyard ghetto, and resembles an upscale version of the public housing in New York. In fact, the prison incarcerates innocent ethnics and a few miscreants who, in this film, once called the stockyard ghetto "home." But once we visit the prisoners, we see the panoptic tower that presides over the five-story block of cells. In the buildings of this future there are no mysteries to solve, or people to seek, because there is nowhere to hide.

*   *   *

Dimendberg writes that film noir is saturated with a "nostalgia and long-ing for older urban forms combined with a fear of new alienating urban realities" such as the "loss of public space" and "the homogenization of everyday life." The heroes of noir "appear cursed by an inability to dwell comfortably anywhere."[44] Where American noirs nostalgically juxtapose decrepit old buildings against the new alienating structures, rubble films are paradoxically suspended between the past that is no longer and a future that has yet to be built. The hero of Braun's film, returning to what was already a temporary residence, can find no comfort in memories of 1930s. And Nelly Dreyfuss pays for her urban, Weimar longings with her life. To put it simply, there is no past to which these character may comfortably or safely return. By inviting us to tarry for a while in the ruins, *Zwischen* suggests, moreover, that uncomfortable dwelling has become not just a postwar truth of life in debris or the experience of a few individuals resistant to modern development; such dwelling is an ethical imperative in war's aftermath. Adorno cryptically mused from his exile: "It is part of morality not to be at home in one's home."[45] As Nico Israel argues, Adorno's aphorism attacks "the prefabricated, ready-made thought that could produce the concentration and death camps along with the single-family suburban house with garden."[46] Boon City's soon-to-be-built track housing and the new prison in *Northside* are not the opposite of the slums they replace, nor are they the antithesis of the concentration camp. They are merely new iterations of the same architectural logic.

Above all, then, rubble films, and *Zwischen* in particular, offer a critique of the change-as-progress narrative that American features discussed here ambivalently uphold. In *Berlin Express* and (perhaps ironically) in *A Foreign Affair*, Germany's ruin is evidence of American military and moral superiority; *Northside's* prison is a clean, new building of postwar order where justice prevails; even *Best Year's* Boon City beheld from the bomber is a testament to American endurance. Whatever war's cost, these films tell us that this country is worth it.[47] Filming in the aftermath of war and genocide, rubble films offer a more profound confrontation with history and disaster. In her analysis of Walter Benjamin's Arcades Project, Susan Buck-Morss writes that the "debris of industrial culture teaches us not the necessity of submitting to historical catastrophe, but the fragility of the social order that tells us this catastrophe is necessary. The crumbling of the monuments that were built to signify the immortality of civilization becomes proof, rather, of its transiency.[48] Rubble noir is a requiem for a social order and cataclysmic modernity to which postwar American noir nostalgically clings. Against the optimism of U.S. Cold War renewal that demolishes the ghettos along with the visible signs of democratic neglect (only to reproduce these ghettos and neglect in the coming decades), rubble films, in confronting us with the overwhelming details of destruction, remind us that while we must remove the debris in order to live, we clear our conscience of its dismal history at the peril of abetting that history's return.

Notes

1. Quoted in Thomas Y. Levin, "Introduction" to Siegfried Kracauer, *The Mass Ornament: Weimar Essays*, trans. Thomas Y. Levin (Cambridge, MA: Harvard University Press, 1995), p.29.
2. "Ruinen, Ruinen und nochmals Ruinen," *Süddeutsche Zeitung* (Munich) (April 7, 1997), *Zwischen Gestern und Morgen*, press clippings (*ZGM*, hereafter), Siftung Deutsche Kinemathek, Berlin (SDK, hereafter)
3. Ibid.

4. Edward Dimendberg, *Film Noir and the Spaces of Modernity* (Cambridge, MA: Harvard University Press, 2004), p.64.

5. In a recently published essay, Tim Bergfelder argues that there is little continuity between American and postwar German noir, in part, because the key milieu of noir—the city—is simply absent in postwar Germany, obliterated by strategic bombing. The "literal or metaphorical absence of the city in postwar German cinema" is, in turn, the "foundation on which other cinematic absences" such as the missing femme fatale also rest. My essay argues that the city and its destruction are precisely what connect the rubble films to American noir (quite apart from the question of influence). Both "genres" were, in U.S. controlled Germany at least, anchored in the culture of occupation, reeducation, and the "dialogue" between American and German films. "German Cinema and Film Noir," in *European Film Noir*, ed. Andrew Spicer (Manchester: Manchester University Press, 2007), pp.141–142.

6. Ibid., p.18.

7. One significant exception to the film's critical neglect is Robert E. Shandley, who argues on behalf of Braun's imaginative use of the detective story "as a formula for interrogating every character's moral complicity in the crimes of the Third Reich." *Rubble Films: German Cinema in the Shadow of the Third Reich* (Philadelphia: Temple University Press, 2001), p.69.

8. Gunter Groll, "Der erste Münchner Nachkriegsfilm: 'Zwischen Gestern und Morgen,'" *Süddeutsche Zeitung* December 16, 1947, *ZGM*, SDK.

9. "Zwischen vorvorgestern und irgenwann," *Tägliche Rundschau* (Berlin) March 23, 1948, *ZGM*, SDK.

10. "Zwischen gestern und morgen," *Tribüne* (Berlin) March 23, 1948, *ZGM*, SDK.

11. "Confidential Operational Priority" from HQ European Theater, USIS to McClure, Chief, Information Control Division. August 6, 1945. Papers of the Office of Military Government United States (OMGUS hereafter), folder 9, box 17–3, shipment 10, RG Z45F (microfiche) Bundesarchiv, Koblenz, Germany (BA hereafter).

12. Response to "Die Letzen Tagen," Robert Schmid, Chief Research Branch, Film, Theater, and Music Control to Chief, FTM. December 11, 1947. OMGUS, folder 4, box 16–3, shipment 10, RG Z45F, BA. Emphasis in the original.

13. This is only a partial list of forbidden themes as stated in U.S. Military Regulation 21–606, 21–606.1. Quoted in Peter Pleyer, *Deutscher Nachkriegsfilm, 1946–1948* (Munster: C.J. Fahle Verlag, 1966), p.26.

14. That German films should emphasize the average German's participation in Nazism is explicit in U.S. military government rejection of the proposed script *The Other Side*. "Response to 'The Other Side,'" From Film, Theater, and Music Branch to Eric Pommer. March 3, 1946. OMGUS, folder 14, box 16–3,shipment 10, RG Z45F, BA.

15. Mandate that German films be both pedagogical and commercial is made explicit in the "Press Release no. 74" Information Control Division, August 6, 1947. OMGUS, folder 14, box 16–3, shipment10, RG Z45F, BA.

16. "Film Situation in all zones of Germany," Motion Picture Branch Report, May 5, 1946, OMGUS, folder 1, box 11–3,shipment 10, RG Z45F, BA.

17. In 1946 film attendance in western zones of Germany was at 300 million. It rose to 459.6 million in 1947. In 1948, however, after the currency reform, attendance dipped to 443 million. Berkhard Dreher, *Filmförderung in der Bundesrepublik Deutschland* (Berlin: Duncker & Humblot, 1976), p.66.

18. Helmut Käutner, "Demontage der Traumfabrik," in *Käutner,* ed. Wolfgang Jacobsen and Hans Helmut Prinzler (Berlin: Schulz & Schulz GmbH, 1992), pp.113–114.

19. Dennis L. Bark and David R. Gress, *A History of West Germany: vol. 1, From Shadow to Substance, 1945–1963* (Oxford: Basil Blackwell, 1989), pp.130–131.

20. Memorandum "Report on the German Motion Picture Industry in the U.S. zone," from the Film, Theater, and Music Division, Information Control, May 22, 1947, OMGUS, folder 12, box 17–2, shipment 10, RG Z45F, BA.

21. "Es rührt sich was in Geiselgasteig," *Süddeutsche Zeitung* December 13, 1947, *ZGM, SDK.*

22. A.W. "Screen in Review," *New York Times.* May 21, 1948, p.19.

23. For a short discussion of the film's belated arrival in Germany see Brigitte Jeremias "Amerikaner in Berlin" *Frankfurter Allgemeine Zeitung,* September 9, 1977. *Eine besondere Affäre (A Foreign Affair)* press clippings, SDK.

24. Siegfried Kracauer, *Theory of Film: The Redemption of Physical Reality* (Princeton, NJ: Princeton University Press, 1997), p.55.

25. Kracauer, *Mass Ornament,* pp.176–177.

26. Ibid., p.184.

27. Ibid., p.179.

28. Ibid., p.177.

29. Ibid., p.175.

30. Ibid., p.184.

31. Though *Best Years* earned rave reviews from German critics, several commented on the stark contrast between the U.S. and German city. One wrote that *Best Years* reveals "another, a foreign world." "For those living in devastated Europe...the way back [home] has been reduced so that there is no 'back' to which one might return." "Wenn Männer heimkehren," *Berliner Zeitung* July 18, 1947; Another critic likewise praised *Best Years* as a great film accomplishment but noted: "we have yet to return home because we no longer have a home." "Die bester Jahre unseres Lebens," *Berlin am Mittag* July 22, 1947. Both from *Best Years* press clippings and SDK.

32. Theodor Adorno, *Minima Moralia: Reflections on a Damaged Life.* trans. E.F.N. Jephcott (London: Verso, 2005), p.39. In a way that speaks to the temporality of Braun's film, Nico Israel notes that this "enigmatic and hyperbolic" claim *Das Haus ist vergangen* means both "the house is gone" and "the house is [in the] past." *Outlandish: Writing between Exile and Diaspora* (Stanford: Stanford University Press, 2000), p.83.

33. Georg Lukács, *The Theory of the Novel.* trans. Anna Bostock (Cambridge, MA: MIT Press, 1971, 1983), p.22. The hotel abyss is the wonderful architectural metaphor Lukács uses to describe the community of German intellectual exiles in the United States who live in a "beautiful hotel, equipped with every comfort, on the edge of an abyss, or nothingness, of absurdity." This phrase has also come to characterize the spirit of Frankfurt School

criticism. Israel, *Outlandish*, pp.85–86, 200–201; Quote from Adorno, *Minima Moralia*, p.39.

34. The *Zeit im Film* series was created by the Motion Picture Branch division of the Office of Military Government in Germany. Henry P. Pilgert describes the series as "reveal[ing] the accomplishments of democratic governments and their peoples." *Zehn Minuten in Amerika* was the American portion of this series. Though no release date is listed, these films likely began in 1949. *Press, Radio and Film in West Germany*, 1945–1953 (n.p.: Historical Division of the Office of the Executive Secretary, Office of the U.S. High Commissioner for Germany, 1953), p.99. Only the first two episodes of this series are currently available at the National Archives, Motion Pictures, Sound and Video Unit, College Park, Maryland.

35. These, in fact, are the public housing projects built in Harlem with Title One funds under the 1949 Federal Housing Act. "City Plans Scored of Slum Projects," *New York Times* July 15, 1949, p.33.

36. For a discussion of the anti-American Soviet propaganda in occupied Germany see Norman M. Naimark, *The Russians in Germany: A History of the Soviet Zone of Occupation, 1945–1949*. (Cambridge, MA: Harvard University Press, 1995), pp.426–427.

37. For a discussion of *Northside's* production history and its use of on-location shooting see Steven N. Lipkin, "Real Emotional Logic: Persuasive Strategies in Docudrama," *Cinema Journal* 38.4 (Summer 1999): 68–85.

38. "Ein amerikanischer Pressefilm: 'Call Northside 777' lief in München," *Film-Information* (Wiesbaden) May 25, 1948. *Kenwort 777* press clippings, Archive, Deutsches Filmmuseum. Frankfurt am Main, Germany (DF hereafter).

39. Ibid.

40. "Neue Sachlichkeit im Film," *Rheinische Post* (Düsseldorf) December 10, 1950. *Kenwort 777* press clippings, DF.

41. Gustav Hartlaud, "Introduction to 'New Objectivity': German Painting Since Expressionism," in *The Weimar Republic Sourcebook*, ed. Anton Kaes, Martin Jay, and Edward Dimendberg (Berkley, CA: University of California Press, 1994), p.491.

42. Daniel Bluestone, "Preservation and Renewal in Post–World War II Chicago," *Journal of Architectural Education* 47.4 (May 1994): 212.

43. For example, in Chicago's South Side, more than 880 prewar buildings were destroyed to make room for new buildings designed in the spirit of the older Chicago School. Ibid., p.214.

44. Dimendberg, *Film Noir and the Spaces of Modernity*, p.7.

45. Adorno, *Minima Moralia*, p.39.

46. Israel, *Outlandish*, p.83.

47. In a similar vein, Dean MacCannell argues that film noir's putative critique of capitalism and democratic disenfranchisement stops short of genuine repudiation of American late modernity. Perniciously, noir may actually function as an inoculation against them. "Democracy's Turn: On Homeless Noir" in *Shades of Noir*, ed. Joan Copjec (London: Verso, 1993), p.283.

48. Susan Buck-Morss, *The Dialectics of Seeing: Walter Benjamin and the Arcades Project* (Cambridge, MA: MIT Press, 1999), p.170.

CHAPTER NINE

WHEN *LIEBE* WAS JUST A
FIVE-LETTER WORD: WOLFGANG
LIEBENEINER'S *LOVE 47*

Robert G. Moeller

A man comes to Germany.
And there he sees a quite fantastic film[…]. And when at the end he's standing
in the street again[…] he realizes that it was really a perfectly ordinary everyday
film[…] About a man who comes to Germany, one of the many. One of the
many who comes home—and then don't come home, because there's no home
there for them any more. And their home is outside the door.[1]

So begins Wolfgang Borchert's *Draussen vor der Tür* (The Man Outside),
a "play," the subtitle tells us, "no theatre will produce and no public will
want to see." Borchert completed *The Man Outside* only a little over a year
after the end of World War II. Produced as a radio play in early 1947, a
stage production followed, but Borchert never saw it. He died, a victim of
diseases contracted during the war. The play was a hit. Its protagonist is
Beckmann, a Wehrmacht soldier whose homecoming is delayed because of
an involuntary stay of "three years in Siberia" in a Soviet prisoner of war
camp. He is tortured by the knowledge that by following his orders, eleven
men detailed on a reconnaissance mission went to their deaths. But he has
also suffered. He explains: "We are murdered each day, and each day we
commit murder!" He plunges into the Elbe, but the river "spit[s] on [his]
suicide," forcing him to seek another way out.

Condemned to "limp through life" because the Russians "stole" his
kneecap, he faces other tragedies. He wears prescription glasses, fitted for
his gas mask. They are precariously held onto his head by gray bands that

give him a "sort of leaden robot's face," and they highlight his otherworldliness. His shorn head bespeaks his POW experience. His wife, believing him dead, has taken up with another man. The infant son he's never seen lies buried "under ten thousand stones," reduced to "human mud, bone mortar" by an Allied bomb. The Girl, who offers him food and shelter, clothes him in the suit of her husband, "missing since Stalingrad." But at least in Beckmann's imagination, her husband, named simply One Legged, reappears and thinking himself displaced, commits suicide, reappearing at the play's end to charge Beckmann with his murder. Beckmann is plagued by a recurring nightmare in which a "fat, bloodstained general" plays a xylophone made of bones. As he pounds out German martial music, an army of "Old Comrades" appears, the dead of all wars, all, the general tells him, Beckmann's responsibility, and they are joined by beseeching wives, children, parents, and lovers. His attempts to end the nightmare lead him to his former commanding officer, who dismisses him, believing that Beckmann means his story as comedy, not tragedy. He stumbles on to a cabaret producer, who finds Beckmann "too grey, too *naked*." Rhetorically, the producer asks: "Who wants to know anything about truth nowadays?" Next stop is his parents' apartment, now inhabited by a woman who tells him that his parents are dead. They had, she explains, "carried on a bit too much in the Third Reich," and his father "was a bit hot on the Jews." "When the Brown Age was over," they turned on the gas and "denazified themselves." He wants to know "*How* shall I live?" Neither the "God no one believes in now" nor Death, who's "put on a bit of weight this century [because] [b]usiness has been good" offer any guidance, and when the curtain falls, Beckmann has no answers.[2]

Borchert's drama joined other tales of returning POWs on the stage and airwaves in Germany in the late 1940s, but no other variation on the theme was so successful.[3] It has been revived countless times, and it became standard fare in school curricula. A mythologized Borchert was "forever young," the "prototype," historian Ulrike Weckel writes, "of the 'betrayed' or 'lost' youth," tortured by a responsibility that had been foisted upon it.[4]

Two years after the play premiered, Wolfgang Liebeneiner, the director who had brought it to the stage brought it into movie houses.[5] Working together with Kurt Joachim Fischer, he added to Beckmann's tale a parallel story in which the anonymous Girl of the play becomes a full-fledged character, Anna Gehrke, played by Hilde Krahl, Liebeneiner's wife. *Liebe 47* (Love *47)* was in many ways "a quite fantastic film," but it was not one the public wished to see. It flopped at the box office. Why? In 1949 German audiences did not explain their reasons for *not* going to see a big-budget new release, but by putting *Liebe 47* in its historical context and using contemporary film reviews as one measure of public opinion, it is possible to offer at least tentative answers. After considering how Liebeneiner's celluloid version diverged from Borchert's play, that is what this essay will attempt to accomplish.

First, what Liebeneiner changed: Borchert's play follows a linear chronology. Once the Elbe disgorges him, Beckman moves from one interlocutor to the next, ending with his unanswered anguished cry. Liebeneiner's film moves back and forth from present to past, allowing Beckmann's (Karl John) story to unfold in flashbacks. Although much of the dialogue remains true to the play, Liebeneiner adds dramatic touches. We see Beckmann's wedding, a simple civil ceremony at which the presiding official exhorts the happy couple to create soldiers and fill an expanding German *Lebensraum*. The son, already dead beneath the rubble in the play, comes into the world on screen, though by now, Beckmann has left wife and child for the front. When Beckmann returns, Liebeneiner gives us footage of the "field of rubble" of which Beckmann speaks in the play, and the camera pans over bombed-out buildings and the corrugated metal huts that provided temporary housing for millions of Germans after the war. And when he reaches his apartment, we follow his gaze up the mountain of ruins topped by a cross marking his son's grave. Beckmann performs his exaggerated martial music, more Brecht than cabaret, at a club called the Pompey—another city buried in ashes. Inside Beckmann is out of place amidst a well-dressed group of men, veterans who have clearly moved on with their lives. While Beckmann attempts to explain himself, in the forefront of the scene the woman in the group shows no interest, turning away to freshen her makeup. Liebeneiner also inserts a prewar memory in which Beckmann returns home after an evening of music making to his mother who has stayed up to fix his supper. This nurturing presence can be found in Borchert's short story, "The Kitchen Clock," and Liebeneiner borrows the figure for the film.[6] In the play, Borchert refers explicitly to the anti-Semitism of Beckmann's parents. In the movie, we still learn that his father was an enthusiastic Nazi, but Liebeneiner leaves his audience sympathetic to Beckmann's mother and eliminates all references to Jews. Beckmann's victim toll includes those killed in battle and also by cold, hunger, and bombs, and those expelled from their homes and carried off to do forced labor in the Soviet Union. In these generic categories, he makes no distinction between German victims and victims of Germans.[7]

But what really distinguishes the film version from the play is that the Girl now has a name, a personality, and a past. The opening credits are accompanied by the syrupy sweet music that signals the love in the film's title, an answer to Borchert's existential question, but Beckmann will grasp it only once he understands that he's not the only one with problems. Anna meets Beckmann by the Elbe, where she is also contemplating suicide. She jars him out of his self-absorbed ruminations, reminding him that because German men had to "go defend us in the Caucasus [mountains],"[8] German women were left alone. Her husband was in Russia too. Liebeneiner takes Anna back to happier times, a wedding ceremony that bespeaks upper-class affluence. Borchert's One Legged gets a name, Jürgen, a boyishly good-looking mountain-climbing enthusiast. But looking back to this past from the film's present, filled with cynicism and scorn, Anna knows that "we were betrayed, so horribly betrayed," not just—like Beckmann—by Hitler and his henchmen but also by men like her husband—and Beckmann—who were absent when the *Heimat* they claimed to defend was laid waste. When Beckmann explains that "it had to be like that, Fatherland, Langemarck, the flag . . . no one told us it was hell," she responds indignantly, "Hell? Hell is here, the here and now is hell," and it's a hell for which Beckmann is responsible. "Perhaps women worshipped Hitler, but men made the war. The world is ruled by men," an indictment that does not spare Beckmann.

Although Anna takes Beckmann back to her room, offering him a shirt and jacket that her husband once wore, whatever warmth he feels is not coming from Anna. When he undresses to change, Anna's landlady peeks in, scandalized by what she imagines, but as the camera lingers on Beckmann's bare back, the shot from Anna's perspective evokes pity, not desire. She consistently addresses Beckmann with the formal *Sie*. Anna resists becoming more familiar. Beckmann tells her that "he cannot [go on] any more." War and Siberia have left him impotent, and he bears all the symptoms—exhaustion, sleeplessness, anxiety, fears of persecution—that the postwar medical and psychiatric professions would pack under the global diagnosis of "dystrophy."[9] Anna's problem is different: she can, but she does not want to.

What's brought Anna to this point is played out in flashbacks that let the audience know that her hell has been created by the war and its aftermath. When she gives birth to a daughter—a scene to which Liebeneiner cuts from the birth of Beckmann's son—her husband has already abandoned her to "raise the flag in the Caucasus" mountains. He is absent when Allied bombs begin to fall. Anna confronts terror by falling into the arms of another man in uniform who helps her save her apartment from the flames. She blames herself "and the times that have brought [her] to this point," not the man, but she also bitterly observes that she is gradually learning what "the knights demand for their services." Fleeing the bombs for the East Prussian countryside, Anna runs into the Russians, and although they remain off camera, viewers in 1949 would know that for many German women, the arrival of the Red Army was accompanied by mass rapes. Anna is more fortunate. She's picked up by the roadside with her daughter and aunt by an aristocratic estate owner who takes them in. He explains that he will shoot himself rather than face the "masses, one face like the next," the fate that Hitler has brought to Germany, but he too will first claim his reward. When he deposits them at a train station for transport westward, Anna loses sight of her daughter in the crowd, frantically fleeing ahead of the Red Army's advance. Her daughter strays, and she's killed by an oncoming locomotive.

"We had already atoned enough in the war," she muses, but peace proves to be no better. She accepts assistance from a smooth operator who greases the right hand, securing her a room in Frau Puhlmann's apartment, but then demands that she spend the night with one of his business associates. She throws him out, but her options are limited. Work in a factory where she cans fish paste provides sisterly camaraderie, but the formula for something better offered by her mates is once again love reduced to the level of a commercial transaction—in the form of fraternization with a "Tommy," a soldier in the British forces of occupation, or someone with ties to the black market. In the winter of 1947—in popular memory, the "eighth winter of the war"[10]—Anna huddles beneath a mound of blankets in her unheated room. As she leafs through an American fashion magazine, she lingers over advertisements for "Angel Face Make-Up" and photo spreads of consumer visions that are "forever lost for us, and...we are sentenced to be beasts of burden." She's filmed through the bars of her bed frame, the prisoner of a war that has not ended. The next knight, Alfred, seems like a kinder alternative, but the police are on to Alfred's black-market dealings, and his wife is on to his relationship with Anna. Off camera, he takes his own life in a prison cell.

Only when we know Anna's story does Beckmann's really begin, but as part of a back and forth with Anna, it takes on a different set of meanings than the staged version in which the Girl's past is a pale shadow of Beckmann's. Borchert takes a particularly German story of the end of the war and translates it into an existential antiwar allegory; by making Anna part of the story, Liebeneiner locates Beckmann in a far more specific time and place, a Germany that in 1947 still bore the signs of a quite particular destructive war. Anna reminds viewers that the rubble Beckmann passes in search of his apartment building is the evidence that he failed to defend the home front. In their misery competition, his hell confronts hers, and she will not accept that his was worse. Beckmann has been lied to, but Anna lets him know that he too is a liar. And the sexuality that she chooses no longer to deploy contrasts with his impotence and childlike dependence on her. When Beckmann screams out the play's central question—why go on living?—Anna, both exhorting and berating, reminds him, "But you're a man! You can do something about it." Women, "hopelessly in excess"—a reference to the "surplus of women" in postwar Germany, a result of the high losses of adult male death at the front—have fewer chances. What they can do, the movie suggests, is help broken men restore their masculinity. "We want to change the world," muses Anna, "and in the process we forget about supper." As she races toward the kitchen and a domestic role she has yet to perform, the camera softens her features and the lighting gives her a glow that has been decidedly lacking up until now. Her future lies in taking care of a man, not expecting that a man will take care of her.

The restoration of masculinity and the rediscovery of femininity will begin in the kitchen, on the one hand, and in Beckmann's dreams on the other. Anna, now assisted by Frau Puhlmann who has finally understood that there's no sex involved, whips up supper while Beckmann drifts off into a troubled sleep. Beckmann's dream begins with a radiant Anna, her hair back to prewar length, her arm around him. She addresses him using the familiar form and professes her love. Stars fall in the foreground, and the opening romantic music plays. Anna is once again ready for desire. But this romantic idyll is shattered by the reappearance Anna's husband— One Legged from the play—who is accompanied by an army of similarly disabled veterans. Beckmann is tossed from a God who has no answers to Death who sweeps this "human waste" into a gutter. Reduced to Lilliputian dimensions, Beckmann looks up as a prosperous postwar society rushes by to a jazzy accompaniment. We see no faces, just legs in tailored pants or nylons, and a parade of lapdogs, signs of a postwar recovery that does not slow down for Beckmann. He's rescued by Anna—a gauzy vision of femininity—and they finally kiss. Once again it's One Legged who ruptures this resolution, and drives Beckmann into the Elbe, which spits him out—the scene that begins the play comes near the end of the movie.

Beckmann cries—as he does at the play's end—"Is there no answer?" Anna rushes in, and Beckmann calls out to her—"Anna, Anna Gehrke, Frau Gehrke"—retreating from the dream's familiarity, but the dream that includes Anna is one he will not forget. Anna knows what to do. Beckmann should give *her* the responsibility. Addressing him again in the formal, she is not ready for intimacy, but she's realized that they have each other. Her benediction: "Why do we need to make the world better? Let's begin with ourselves, I'll help you and you help me." And as Beckmann begins to eat, a first, not the last, supper, haltingly stepping out on the road to resurrection, Anna lights a candle and switches on the radio that plays the same romantic music we've heard before.

In a 1949 review of postwar German films, the weekly *Die Zeit*, proclaimed *Liebe 47* a "work of art." In a world densely populated with "rubble films," it required a director of Liebeneiner's ability to elevate the genre.[11] With its "unforgiving, uncompromising approach" and its unwillingness to stoop to a "happy-ending" of "erotic kitsch," commented Gertrud Runge, writing in the same paper, *Liebe 47* rejected the "factory of dreams," the cinema of escapism toward which postwar Germans were fleeing.[12] And in a Frankfurt daily, Willy H. Thiem pronounced it "the most honest, flawless, artistically convincing and sincere postwar German movie."[13]

"We'll have to wait and see," concluded another positive review, "whether moviegoers will pay the price of admission in order to ask themselves the questions that this film poses to us all." The reviewer did not have to wait long. *Liebe 47* quickly proved to be a financial disaster. Before suggesting why, it's worth pointing out that *not* on my list is the fact that Liebeneiner was well-known for his past in the Nazi film industry, UFA, of which he became production chief in April 1943, and for which he had made such well-known movies as *Ich klage an* (I Accuse, 1941), a melodramatic justification for euthanasia. Beginning in November 1944, when more and more Germans began to doubt Hitler's predictions that the Third Reich would triumph, Liebeneiner began work on "Life Goes On," a film, discussed in this volume by Erhard Schütz, which celebrated the resiliency of Berliners amidst falling Allied bombs. Krahl played in this film too.[14] I have located only one review from 1949, which found it remarkable that the "film professor of the Propaganda Ministry" should once again have the opportunity to make movies, paying no attention to the "thoughtlessness that was the origin of the catastrophe."[15] Some stories on *Liebe 47* reported that Liebeneiner's next big project was a film version of Goethe's *Faust*, but no one commented on the deal he made with the devil during the Third Reich.[16] Drowning out denunciations of Liebeneiner's brown past was the applause of critics who welcomed back "one of our most able directors," who could hold his own alongside the "most original French [filmmakers]."[17] Liebeneiner's Nazi ties were not incriminating enough to distress the postwar forces of occupation—and *Liebe 47* was produced only once the British had given their approval—and it apparently troubled very few Germans.[18]

No more disturbing to reviewers was the film's exclusive focus on what Germans had suffered because of the war and its complete silence about the suffering that Germans had brought to others. When Beckmann dreams of a field of war dead, the dead of *all* wars, their graves are marked with crosses, signs of a Christian past, and the responsibility he bears is for sending Germans in uniform on an impossible mission, not killing others. However, this preoccupation with what Germans had suffered was by no means the exclusive preserve of Liebeneiner's film. For the most part, well into the 1950s the psychological, spiritual, and physical legacies of the war that movies explored were exclusively German. Audiences did not shun *Liebe 47* because it shared this focus; they would have expected nothing else.[19]

So why did the public stay away? Let me briefly suggest three possible reasons: (1) The times, they had a' changed; (2) the film was plagued by genre confusion; (3) and it also suffered from gender trouble.

The Times, They Had A' Changed

Liebe 47, a film that depicted a world in ruins, was filmed in the Germany it described in 1947, but it was not released until March 1949. Much had happened in the meantime, and more and more Germans were eager to clear away the rubble, not dwell on it. By May 1947, a British-American "Bizone" had etched out the future form of a West Germany, separated from the East, and by early 1948, it was ruled by a shadow parliament, Germans elected by Germans. On June 20, every German citizen was entitled to exchange 50 Reich marks for 50 new *Deutsch* marks. Overnight, the black market—a set piece in Liebeneiner's drama—vanished, and in the formulation of Ludwig Erhard, the German politician most centrally involved in introducing a new currency, "The only ration card from here on in is the German mark." What Anna saw in the American fashion magazine was still missing, but with currency reform, shop windows filled, and dreams of a bountiful consumer future were permissible.[20]

Unlike the black market, returning POWs had not vanished from the social, political, and cultural landscape of 1949, and in 1950 Chancellor Konrad Adenauer claimed that as many as 1.5 million German soldiers were still held captive. The demand for the release of all POWs remained a staple of West German politics until the last 9,262 came back to Germany in 1955. For those whose homecoming was in the late 1940s, the Bundestag, the parliament of the new West German state, convening for the first time only six months after *Liebe 47* premiered, left no doubt that POWs would not be left "outside." Politicians answered Beckmann's question by instituting a range of policies to ease the reintegration of returnees, and former POWs organized to represent their interests. In West Germany, POWs were presented as "survivors of totalitarianism," courageous men who walked tall and had been able to withstand Soviet barbarism. These were not the POWs of the immediate postwar years, the broken, defeated, bedraggled specters, whom Beckmann represented.[21] And by the early 1950s, nightmares of a violent past were relegated to the intimate sphere of the family and the psychiatrist's office, private affairs for which there was no space in public discourse or movie theaters.[22]

POWs did not disappear from German movies, but in the early 1950s, West German films featured POWS who came home unbroken, ready to play their part in rebuilding Germany. A loving woman might have to smooth off rough edges, and it might take a child to remind the returnee that real masculinity began at home, but rehabilitation was a fairly rapid affair. And by the end of the decade, movies that portrayed the POW experience pursued them "behind the Urals," taking as their subject the "barbed wire university." Indeed, even Liebeneiner, best known in the mid-1950s for his venture into the genre of the *Heimatfilm* in *Waldwinter: Glocken der Heimat* (1956) and even more famously, *Die Trapp-Familie* (1956), also tried his hand at this variety of POW film. *Taiga*, which premiered nine years after *Liebe 47*, depicted a "camp for three hundred men, the forgotten of the war," and one woman, the German doctor detailed to tend their ills. Starring Ruth Leuwerik and a firm-jawed Hannes Messemer, the film offered a variant on the theme of romantic melodrama, this time behind barbed wire. Messemer *kann* and Leuwerik *will*.[23]

Beckmann of the *The Man Outside* survived into the 1950s in ways Beckmann of the movie could not because on stage, like a character in a medieval mystery play, he was a timeless everyman surrounded by a cast of characters more symbolic than real. In East German productions, he could figure as the opponent of the imperialist ambitions of the West. In the West, he could take on many guises, opposing heightened fears of war in the 1950s, the building of the Berlin Wall in 1961, the Cuban missile crisis, and Vietnam, mounting the barricades in 1968 and protesting atomic missiles in the 1980s, and a decade later the deployment of German military air power in Bosnia, and U.S. intervention in the Persian Gulf. Whatever Borchert's original intent, "from the 1960s onward," writes Gordon Burgess, *The Man Outside* "had become . . . a by-line for pacifism."[24] Surrounded by nameless allegorical characters, Borchert's Beckmann could be adapted to meet the times. Linked to Anna Gehrke, the black market, and the postwar "crisis of masculinity,"[25] Liebeneiner's Beckmann could not.

By the time Liebeneiner's film appeared in theaters, the genre of the "returnee film" (*Heimkehrerfilm*) and the "rubble film" (*Trümmerfilm*) had become the stuff of ironic commentary. In Robert Stemmle's *Berliner Ballade* (1948), the imaginary Berlin of 2048 is juxtaposed with "archival material from 1948" and a voiceover expresses the likely dismay of many in the audience: "not another *Heimkehrerfilm!*" And in Rudolf Jugert's *Film ohne Titel*, a screenwriter, an actor, and a director debate what kind of film will attract audiences. If anti-Nazi films that explored questions of guilt were unpopular, they agreed, then the "rubble film" and the "returnee" film would certainly not fill movie houses.[26] Once tragedy, these genres were now the subject of satire; their time had come and gone.

As one reviewer of *Liebe 47* put it, "it is the theme, the atmosphere, the ambience of war and postwar that [audiences] are rejecting." The past the film depicted was "too present and not yet removed enough to spark historical interest . . . It is a time of spiritual restoration. We've had enough upheaval."[27] "Should we now start to rip open old wounds?"[28] Critical reviews and low box-office receipts suggest that when *Liebe 47* asked the question, the answer was no. Anna and Beckmann told a story that began in 1943—when Beckmann lost his knee cap at Stalingrad and Anna lost her virtue in a hail of bombs—but by 1949, Germans had progressed "from Stalingrad to currency reform," and there were many indications that for West Germans, the postwar years were over.[29]

Genre Confusion

Critics noted that Liebeneiner's film was plagued by his unsuccessful attempt to mix and match styles and film aesthetics. More than one reviewer commented that the realistic portrayal of Anna's plight did not mesh with the surrealistic excesses of Beckmann's nightmares. Indeed, according to news reports, the final dream sequence—that goes on for a full fifteen minutes—sent audiences racing for the exits.[30] Even when Beckmann is awake, for long periods he's filmed in close-up, his surroundings less important than his words and his tortured gaze. In the flashbacks that portray Anna's story, context is always as important as text. In the mid-1950s, the movie would enjoy at least something of a renaissance, applauded by Film Clubs, the organizations of West German cinema enthusiasts that railed against what they saw as the mediocrity of most German movies. Clubs showed classics of the Weimar era and representative cinema of the Soviet Union and eastern Europe, and some added to this repertoire *Liebe 47*, hailing it as Liebeneiner's "masterwork" and one of the "most remarkable postwar German movies."[31] The announcement for one film retrospective cited Liebeneiner's staging of Beckmann's cabaret appearance as an invocation of the "expressionism of the prewar period, the last stop before the Hitler era," and the dream sequences as evidence that the "surrealism of the twenties was still alive somewhere," as outmoded as it might appear to audiences in the mid-1950s.[32] What was of historic interest to cinephiles, however, dismayed reviewers in 1949 who decried Liebeneiner's mishmash of "newsreel footage, documentary film, theatrical expressiveness, and a fantastic surrealism," demonstrating only the "stylistic uncertainty of contemporary German film."[33] The film suffered from genre confusion. As one reviewer quipped, Liebeneiner was left sitting not between two stools (*Stühlen*)—the colloquial German expression that signifies indecision—but between two *styles* (*Stilen*).[34] A mixture of an "art film" that aimed for aesthetic sophistication and a "problem film" that portrayed Anna with "brutal realism," some critics concluded, *Liebe 47* succeeded as neither.

Gender Trouble

Publicity materials for *Liebe 47* prepared by the distribution company encouraged the owners of movie theaters to push the film as a story of "Woman Standing Alone—The Film Theme of our Times." Theater owners were advised to use their display windows to announce a film about "Her Front," the front of the war at home in which women had survived "separation, isolation, fear, and peril." Film posters should foreground Krahl's face, emphasizing that her story was at the crux of the "emotionally moving contents of the film."[35] But by March 1949, apparently this was subject matter that moviegoers wanted to see as little as stories of POWs, rubble, scarcity, and the black market.

Political transformation paralleled economic change, and by the time *Liebe 47* opened, the four women and sixty-one men elected to draft a "Basic Law," the constitutional foundation for a democratic West Germany, had almost completed their work. Article 3 guaranteed that "women and men have the same rights." When Dorothea Groener-Geyer, head of an alliance of women's organizations in Stuttgart, wrote to protest those who opposed the measure, she expressed sentiments that Anna Gehrke would voice three months later when *Liebe 47* opened. Groener-Geyer linked women's experience in the war and the postwar years with demands for equal rights:

> After Stalingrad, there is no aspect of life in which the actions of German men have protected German women from want, misery, and poverty. After our men fell victim to the obsessions of a man and followed him from Berlin through Paris to Stalingrad and then back again, and did not have the energy to contain the delusion of power of that obsessed individual, thus gambling away the sovereignty of our state, leaving our cities in ruins, destroying our homes, and leaving millions homeless and with no basis for their existence, the equality of women has been accomplished de facto. Nothing human or inhuman is foreign to her any longer; she has been spared no terror.[36]

Advocates of women's equality carried the day, but by early 1949 what Elizabeth Heineman describes as the "hour of the woman," defined by experiences of "bombing raids, evacuation, flight, rape, widowhood, and hunger"—a list that, with one exception, describes the stations of the cross through which Anna Gehrke progresses—tolled no longer.[37] The same issue of the Hamburg paper *Die Welt* that carried a lengthy review of *Liebe 47* in early May also offered its readers the full text of the "Basic Law." Anyone who read it saw that Article 3 was followed by Article 6, specifying the constitutional protection of marriage and affirming the ideology of maternal responsibility and domesticity that would be ubiquitous in the next decade. A past in which gender relations were disrupted and men had failed to protect women gave way to visions of a restored social order in which the "hour of the man" would ring loud and clear. The story of the "woman on her own," promoted by the film's distribution company, gave way to stories of mothers in families, the new *Lebensraum* in which West Germany should flourish. By the early 1950s, the woman at the center of sociological analyses, political debates, and the popular imagination stood in the kitchen, not amidst urban ruins, and she did her own work as a mother, not the work of men.

Anna is not much of a nurturing presence. Even as she clothes Beckmann, revealing an emotional vulnerability when she glimpses in him a memory of her husband, the moment is fleeting. Barely losing a beat, she is bellowing at him, reminding him of the "hell" that still rages inside her because her husband—and Beckmann—went off to fight a senseless war. Reviewing her limited options, she disparages "marriage, [and] being provided for." She may lack the "faith to be a nun," but she forcefully rejects marriage. By the end of the movie, she's been transformed in Beckmann's dreams, but in the final scene where she announces that she'll spend the night on Frau Puhlmann's couch, she's still nowhere close to an altar.

Compare Anna with the female protagonist in what is perhaps the best known "rubble film," Wolfgang Staudte's 1946 *The Murderers Are among Us*. When the concentration camp survivor Susanne Wallner arrives in Berlin, finding her way amidst the ruins she passes a pieta-like statue—mother and child—which the bombs have miraculously spared. The camera lingers on it after Susanne leaves the frame, making sure we haven't missed the association of one Madonna with another. Susanne too has war stories to tell, but in the postwar world, she finds not Anna's hell but redemption in work. Unlike the male protagonist, Hans Mertens, she is ready to leave the past behind, and her incarceration in a concentration camp on political, not racial or religious grounds, has left no scars. In no time at all she's clearing away glass shards and the painful memories that haunt Hans, and her work as a graphic artist leads her to design a poster for a campaign to "save the children," not just the man. The movie exemplifies, writes Robert Shandley, the "domestic melodrama" that conflates "domestication with societal integration, [and] a maternal-familial code."[38]

In *Liebe 47*, we learn little of Anna's relationship with her daughter, and she asks nothing of Beckmann's feelings for his lost son. Her hapless room is hardly home sweet home. She spends as much time accusing Beckmann as she does comforting him. And if, as one reviewer put it, her odyssey from one man to the next "taught [audiences] to comprehend why so many German women [...] filled with fear had to jump the moral tracks," this lesson was out of synch with the growing political, social, and cultural pressures to return to some version of normalcy.[39] What one reviewer hailed as a "terrific, convincing piece of the present"[40] was in fact a piece of the past that more and more Germans sought to leave behind.

In the 1950s, women on the silver screen would appear in the dirndl of the *Heimatfilm,* the tiara and ballroom gown of the costume drama, or the stylish fashions of films that celebrated, poked fun at, or critically examined the "economic miracle." The "woman of the rubble" vanished. The war appeared repeatedly in West German films, but the war at home and the postwar privation that Anna describes are rarely visible. In films that portrayed men in uniform in the immediate postwar years, like Beckmann, returning veterans often needed looking after, and recovery began in heterosexual unions orchestrated by women. But by the middle of the 1950s, movie actors in uniform were fully able to take care of themselves and fulfill their role as protectors of women in the bargain. For the most part, the war on the home front remains off camera, women have no place at the front, and the divide between front and home front that the war obliterated is reconstructed. Men, not women, told war stories.[41]

The "woman of the rubble" would return against the background of second-wave feminism in the Federal Republic and the "new German cinema"—as Hanna Schygulla, the sexually supercharged protagonist of Rainer Maria Fassbinder's 1979 *Marriage of Maria Braun*; and in the same year in Helma Sanders-Brahms' mother-daughter tale, *Deutschland, bleiche Mutter* as a protofeminist, liberated by the departure of men for the war at the front and shattered by the postwar restoration of patriarchy. More recently, in 2003 she starred as the patiently waiting Penelope of Sönke Wortmann's blockbuster, *Das Wunder von Bern*, the wife who tells us nothing of what she experienced during the war but who understands how to guide her husband, a POW who returns only in 1954, to a kinder, gentler, patriarchy. Anna has yet to make a comeback.

Celluloid "Documents of the Past"

One review of *Liebe 47* concluded that "we should all have seen [this] film."[42] Not many West Germans took this advice, but nearly sixty years later, we would do well to follow it. "In ten or twenty years," commented another reviewer, films like *Liebe 47* would "perhaps earn recognition as documents of the past."[43] As the contributions to this volume testify, he was right. Liebeneiner's "quite fantastic film" is anything but "perfectly ordinary" and it is a "document of the past" that can tell us much about the immediate postwar years—in which prominent figures in the Nazi cultural hierarchy could make pacifist films, women claimed a right to tell their war stories on equal footing with men, men were rocked by a "crisis of masculinity," and rubble defined the real and figurative landscape of postwar German cities. The film's commercial failure yields evidence of another sort, suggesting that four years after the bombs had ceased to fall and the shooting had stopped, these were parts of a past that West Germans no longer wanted to see at the movies.

Notes

1. Wolfgang Borchert, *The Man Outside*, trans. by David Porter (New York: New Directions Books, 1971), p.82.
2. Borchert, *Man*, quotations from pp.84, 89–90, 92–3, 100, 111, 115–117, 134–135.
3. Ralf Trinks, *Zwischen Ende und Anfang: Die Heimkehrerdramatik der ersten Nachkriegsjahre (1945–1949)* (Würzburg: Königshausen & Neumann, 2002); and Peter Pleyer, *Deutscher Nachkriegsfilm 1946–1948* (Münster: C.J. Fahle, 1965), p.143.
4. Ulrike Weckel, "Spielarten der Vergangenheitsbewältigung: Wolfgang Borcherts Heimkehrer und sein langer Weg durch die westdeutschen Medien," *Tel Aviver Jahrbuch für deutsche Geschichte* 31 (2003): 125–161.
5. I have benefited greatly from what others have written about the movie. See Gordon Burgess, *The Life and Works of Wolfgang Borchert* (Rochester, New York: Camden House, 2003), pp.167–171; Massimo Perinelli, *Liebe '47—Gesellschaft '49: Geschlechterverhältnisse in der deutschen Nachkriegszeit. Eine Analyse des Films Liebe 47* (Hamburg: Lit Verlag, 1999); Bettina Greffrath, *Gesellschaftsbilder der Nachkriegszeit: Deutsche Spielfilme 1945–1949* (Pfaffenweiler: Centaurus-Verlagsgesellschaft, 1995), pp.153–154, 197–199; Robert R. Shandley, *Rubble Films: German Cinema in the Shadow of the Third Reich* (Philadelphia: Temple University Press, 2001), pp.71–75; and Annette Brauerhoch, *"Fräuleins" und GIs: Geschichte und Filmgeschichte* (Frankfurt am Main: Stroemfeld Verlag, 2006), pp.288–296.
6. Borchert, "The Kitchen Clock," in *The Man Outside*, pp.177–179.
7. Brauerhoch, *"Fräuleins,"* pp.293–294.
8. This and all other translations from the dialogue are my own. The film is not available commercially. For this essay, I used a copy of the film that was given to me for "research purposes" by the distribution company that holds the rights to it.
9. Frank Biess, *Homecomings: Returning POWs and the Legacies of Defeat in Postwar Germany* (Princeton, NJ: Princeton University Press, 2006), pp.71–76.
10. Robert G. Moeller, *Protecting Motherhood: Women and the Family in the Politics of Postwar West Germany* (Berkeley, CA: University of California Press, 1993), p.22.

11. "Glanz und Elend des Deutschen Films," *Die Zeit*, April 14, 1949.
12. Gertrud Runge, "Absage an die Traumfabrik," *Die Zeit*, March 10, 1949.
13. Willy H. Thiem, "Drinnen im Zimmer," *Abendpost*, April 24, 1949. See also the review in *Münchener Allgemeine*, June 5, 1949.
14. Hans-Christoph Blumenberg, *Das Leben geht weiter: Der letzte Film des Dritten Reichs* (Berlin: Rowohlt, 1993).
15. "Verrat an Wolfgang Borchert," in *Giessener Freie Presse*, March 19, 1949.
16. Review in *Der Spiegel*, March 12, 1949: 23–24.
17. Wilhelm Müller-Scheld, "Wolfgang Liebeneiners 'Liebe 47,'" in *Augsburger Tagespost*, February 17, 1949.
18. Klaus Kreimeier, *The Ufa Story: A History of Germany's Greatest Film Company 1948–1945*, translated by Robert and Rita Kimber (New York: Hill and Wang, 1996), pp.275, 232, 345–346.
19. In general, Robert G. Moeller, "Germans as Victims? Thoughts on a Post-Cold War History of the Second World War's Legacies," *History and Memory* 17 (2005): 147–194.
20. Moeller, *Protecting Motherhood*, pp.34–37.
21. Recent research indicates that some 34,000 Germans remained in Soviet captivity after 1949–50. The exaggerated claims of the West German state reflected the tendency to lump together counts of POWs and those missing in action—all of whom could be assumed to be POWs. Biess, *Homecomings*; pp.189–190, 204; and Robert G. Moeller, "Heimkehr ins Vaterland: Die Remaskulinisierung Westdeutschlands in den fünfziger Jahren," *Militärgeschichtliche Zeitschrift* 60 (2001): 403–436.
22. Robert G. Moeller, *War Stories: The Search for a Usable Past in the Federal Republic of Germany* (Berkeley, CA: University of California Press, 2001), pp.88–122; and Svenja Goltermann, "Im Wahn der Gewalt: Massentod, Opferdiskurs und Psychiatrie 1945–1956," in *Nachkrieg in Deutschland*, ed. Klaus Naumann (Hamburg: Hamburger Edition, 2001), pp.343–364.
23. Moeller, *War Stories*, pp. 123–170; and Johannes von Moltke, *No Place Like Home: Locations of Heimat in German Cinema* (Berkeley, CA: University of California Press, 2005), pp.135–169.
24. Burgess, *Life and Works*, pp.222–223; and Weckel, "Spielarten."
25. Heide Fehrenbach, *Cinema in Democratizing Germany: Reconstructing National Identity after Hitler* (Chapel Hill, NC: University of North Carolina Press, 1995), pp.95–97; and Dagmar Herzog, *Sex after Fascism: Memory and Morality in Twentieth-Century Germany* (Princeton, NJ: Princeton University Press, 2005), pp.66–69.
26. Shandley, *Rubble Films*, pp.152–153, 174–176; von Moltke, *No Place Like Home*, p.73.
27. "Überholte Filme," in *Wirtschaftszeitung*, July 16, 1949; and "Zwischenfall mit Hintergründen," in *Die neue Zeitung*, May 28, 1949.
28. "Zwischenfall."
29. Martin Broszat, Klaus-Deitmar Henke, and Hans Woller, eds., *Von Stalingrad zur Währungsreform: Zur Sozialgeschichte des Umbruchs in Deutschland* (Munich: R. Oldenbourg Verlag, 1988); and in general, Naumann, *Nachkrieg*.
30. "Protest gegen L47," in *Frankfurter Abendpost*, May 27, 1949; review in *Abendzeitung*, May 25, 1949; "Zwischenfall"; Gerhard Sanden, "Das Grosse Experiment," *Die Welt*, May 10, 1949.

31. "Borchert-Liebeneiners 'Liebe 47,'" in *Neue Tagespost* (Osnabrück), November 5, 1956; an announcement of the Film Club in Soest, *Soester Anzeiger*, March 24, 1956; and in general, on the film clubs, Fehrenbach, *Cinema*, pp.169–201.
32. Otto Beer, "Begegnung mit den Schatten," *Stuttgarter Zeitung*, ugust 28, 1956; also "Schwarze Not," *Stuttgarter Zeitung*, May 4, 1985.
33. Groll, "Borchert, Liebeneiner und der Zeitfilm," *Süddeutsche Zeitung*, May 28, 1949.
34. Groll, "Borchert"; Willi Fehso, review in *Neue Zeitung*, March 10, 1949; also, Danielle Krüger, "Borchert-Stück als Love-Story," in *Hamburger Rundschau*, May 9, 1985; and E.O. Jauch, "Nicht Draussen vor der Tür," *Szene Hamburg*, May 1985.
35. Publicity materials in Nachlass Wilhelm Borchert, Handschriftenabteilung, Staatsbibliothek Universität Hamburg. My thanks to Alan Rosenfeld for calling my attention to these materials.
36. Dorothea Groener-Geyer to Parliamentary Council, January 2, 1949, Bundesarchiv (Koblenz), Z5/111.
37. Elizabeth Heineman, *What Difference Does a Husband Make? Women and Marital Status in Nazi and Postwar Germany* (Chapel Hill, NC: University of North Carolina Press, 1999), p.79; and in general, Perinelli, *Liebe' 47*.
38. Shandley, *Rubble Films*, p.36.
39. Herzog, *Sex*, pp.101–140; also Fehrenbach, *Cinema*, pp.92–117.
40. Hannes Schmidt, "Gültiger Realismus," *Die Welt*, March 8, 1949.
41. Jörg Echternkamp, "Mit dem Krieg seinen Frieden schliessen: Wehrmacht und Weltkrieg in der Veteranenkultur 1945–1960," *Jahrbuch für Historische Friedensforschung* 9 (2000): 78–93; Robert G. Moeller, "What Did You Do in the War, *Mutti*? Courageous Women, Compassionate Commanders, and Stories of the Second World War," *German History* 22 (2004): 563–594; and idem, "Kämpfen für den Frieden: 08/15 und westdeutsche Erinnerungen an den Zweiten Weltkrieg," in *Militärgeschichtliche Zeitschrift* 64 (2005): 359–389.
42. "Gültiger Realismus."
43. "Überholte Filme."

CHAPTER TEN

"KAMPF DEM KAMPF": AESTHETIC EXPERIMENTATION AND SOCIAL SATIRE IN *THE BALLAD OF BERLIN*

Claudia Breger

Introduction

According to Manfred Barthel's filmhistorical memoir *So war es wirklich*, Robert A. Stemmle's *Berliner Ballade* was a "milestone" event in the German postwar film landscape.[1] Based on a highly successful Berlin cabaret performance by Günter Neumann, who also wrote the screenplay, the film outdid almost all other rubble films at the box office.[2] Despite some irritation with the cabaret-inspired form, the contemporary critical response was overall positive as well, and *Berliner Ballade* was awarded a special prize "for the brilliant [*geistvolle*] depiction of German postwar circumstances" at the 1949 Biennale Film Festival in Venice.[3] This contemporary acclaim contrasts starkly with the dominantly negative terms in which the film has been discussed in more recent film scholarship. *Berliner Ballade* is, of course, not the only immediate postwar film to meet with such critical dismissal. But even in the context of general rubble film reception "as a kind of miscarriage, both in terms of film and intellectual history,"[4] *Berliner Ballade* has scored particularly badly. Seldom discussed at any length, the film tends to be summarily criticized as politically reactionary, alternatively as an example for emerging anticommunism under Allied censorship,[5] as exemplifying contemporary longings for the return of state order,[6] or as a "power fantasy" and "narrative redemption of the *Reichshauptstadt*" at the end of the rubble period.[7] I find these readings to be inadequate for at least two reasons. First, they entirely bypass the film's formal complexity and unique experimental character that ought to have caught the attention of film scholars who have generally criticized the conservative aesthetics of immediate postwar German film.[8] And second, a close reading of the ways in which *Berliner Ballade* constructs postwar society and its Nazi past shows that the quoted political evaluations of the film are clearly mistaken.

Before developing this claim, I wish to contextualize my "revisionary" reading. I am not interested in revisiting the qualities of this or any other rubble film as part of a historiographic endeavor to displace the Holocaust from its central position in Germany's political memory or to question the overall failure of postwar culture to come to terms with the past. I do recognize, however, that recent scholarship has qualified established accounts of this memory culture. Of the often celebrated New German Cinema it has been observed that even the generation of directors who started out blaming "Dad's cinema" for its inadequate depiction of the past ended up reiterating the previously dominant focus on German soldiers and postwar reconstruction rather than fully addressing Nazi racial politics and the Holocaust.[9] With such a sobered account of later German cinema in mind, a closer look at rubble film uncovers comparatively promising beginnings. While the notion of a "Zero Hour" has served as a legitimatory phantasm downplaying personal and ideological continuities between Nazi and postwar German societies, it can be taken seriously in the sense that the end of the Third Reich provided a radical challenge to the entire system of coordinates through which the majority population had organized its beliefs, norms, and collective identity.[10] The resulting skepticism included cinema's generic codes, with narrative film functioning as "the primary suspect."[11] A number of rubble films suggest that in response to these disorientations, contemporaries in fact attempted new beginnings in both aesthetic and political terms.[12] At least a few of them, including *Berliner Ballade*, did indeed, *pace* Shandley, "confront the institutions, traditions, and assumptions that led to the catastrophe that was postwar Europe."[13]

This is not to suggest that we should replace summary condemnation with a new heroic account that downplays the limits of rubble film. These limits do include the relatively minor attention paid to anti-Semitism and genocide. Among the few notable exceptions is the DEFA production *The Blum Affair* for which Stemmle wrote the screenplay.[14] Nevertheless, the relative nature of the announced new beginnings is indicated by well-documented personal continuity, for which Stemmle and Neumann provide cases in point. Although there are some indications of their critical distance vis-à-vis Nazi ideology, both of them remained active in cultural production after 1933; Stemmle wrote and directed numerous German films during the Third Reich.[15] While he was primarily involved in those parts of the Nazi industry that have been retrospectively classified as entertainment rather than propaganda, the precarious nature of these distinctions is indicated by titles like the 1941 comedy *Quax, the Crash Pilot*, for which Stemmle wrote the screenplay.[16] As I discuss below, the satire in *Berliner Ballade* can be related to the ideologically charged production of military masculinity in *Quax* not exclusively in terms of rupture, but may suggest moments of continuity.

Nonetheless, I submit that both aesthetically and politically, *Berliner Ballade* presents a serious postwar endeavor to work through the legacy of fascism as well as arguably the filmmakers' own histories of cultural implication. With respect to aesthetics, rubble films have been primarily discussed for their continuity with UFA cinema and distinguished negatively from international trends in the 1940s, especially Italian neorealism.[17] New departures tend to be framed as a return to German Expressionism or an exchange with contemporary noir aesthetics, as influenced by the legacy of Expressionism.[18] For many rubble films, these styles are doubtlessly central; *Berliner Ballade*, however, presents a different picture. With its primary reference point in the cabaret (as developed in Weimar and revived after 1945), its aesthetics is highly intermedial. In the world of film, its broad range of intertextual relations and stylistic inspirations includes Weimar art cinema, the popular genres of musical, revue, and comedy as well as the practices of montage developed by 1920s socialist cinema.

This multifaceted, experimental aesthetics creates the space for a complex social critique. Importantly, it would be mistaken to describe this critique as radical. Rather, the film's attacks on dominant mentalities are presented in a way that made them acceptable to broader audiences. Ideologically, the film's narrative is clearly informed by a general skepticism regarding *any* grand political promises, which reflects a widespread contemporary response to the collapse of Nazi ideology. The film also participates in the often complementary recourse to moral categories as a medium of social improvement. However, this use of moral categories does not advance a conservative agenda marked by residual militarism, Christian religion, and family values. Appealing instead to (the precarious faculties of) human "reason," the film articulates a liberal critique of precisely these dominant conservative sources of collective identification in postwar (West) Germany. In particular, *Berliner Ballade* analyzes fascism as an authoritarian ideology and investigates its possible genealogy in Prussian militarism. The film's critical humor has more than one target, including, in surprisingly sharp ways, the Allied occupation powers themselves. Nevertheless, its overall dominant focus is the "regular" German, as embodied in the protagonist "Otto Average Consumer"[19] whose unheroic figure is characterized as that of an easily manipulated Nazi fellow traveler in need of political and psychological reform. In its humorously moralistic ways, *Berliner Ballade* recommends such a democratic awakening.

Narrative Matters: Cinematic Cabaret

Berliner Ballade is based on motifs from Neumann's 1947 political revues *Alles Theater* (It's all theater) and, in particular, *Schwarzer Jahrmarkt* (Black Market). For film critics, this intermedial genealogy has remained a source of irritation. Contemporary reviews ambivalently commented on what they perceived to be a precarious transposition.[20] Less interested in the matter, more recent criticism unconsciously carries forward negative assessments of this intermedial experiment.[21] Yet one can more profitably discuss the film's cabaret-inspired form in the context of aesthetic modernism, in particular the search for new techniques that could provide alternatives to traditional forms of narrative.

As Shandley points out, *Berliner Ballade* presents a "series of skits that are separated by vignettes," and which are only loosely connected through the figure of the protagonist.[22] Otto's role as an average man "without qualities" turns him into a filter through which the film unfolds its panorama of postwar society. Otto returns from the war, finds his half-destroyed apartment occupied by shady contemporaries, reacts apathetically to the conditions of cold and hunger, suffers from the prevailing illness of forgetfulness, works different jobs, betrays the ways in which the fascist past lurks under the surface of change, gets married, suffers from marital ennui and is eventually killed—almost, for in a final twist he is resurrected as an agent of reason at his own funeral. In this way, the film breaks up the tight narrative structure of cause and effect that naturalizes coherence and provides orientation, or, as Hayden White famously argued, the integration of individual desire into a moral order.[23] This does not mean that morality is absent. Otto's concluding act as an agent of reason is presented precisely as an explicit moral performative when he specifies what his contemporaries ought to bury instead of him. But this apparent closure does not "naturally" follow from his character development throughout the film. Rather, Otto's stand-up skit following his quasi resurrection presents a moment of nonrealist utopian break from the actual conditions presented throughout the film. It is humorously bracketed again, only a moment later, when Otto quickly abandons his new role of a moral agent, sneaking away with his wife to continue their private life—which is, for all the spectator knows, fairly unhappy.

With its slapstick moments, cabaret vignettes and montage sequences, *Berliner Ballade* presents the postwar city through an aesthetics of spectacle. From Laura Mulvey's classical investigations into Hollywood film and the study of the early "cinema of attractions" to discussions of avant-garde as well as comedy and musical aesthetics, film theory has emphasized the potentially subversive character of spectacle, its ability to undermine the ideological work of narrative that interpellates the spectator into hegemonic fantasy.[24] Because this general claim can be too facile, it is crucial to investigate the concrete aesthetic configuration of individual events in a particular film, not least in terms of their often productive interplay with specific aspects of narrative. Therefore, rather than discussing spectacle in opposition to narration, I find it more productive to analyze the ways in which spectacle in *Berliner Ballade* enables a self-conscious, explicit practice of narrative representation. Paraphrasing Eisenstein, we can say that the "montage of attractions" in *Berliner Ballade* liberates the film from a narrowly plot-based script by highlighting narrative *discourse*, that is, the fact that it is "a tendentious selection of, and comparison between" events.[25] Like the Soviet Cinema of the 1920s, *Berliner Ballade* openly acknowledges its status as a rhetorical act of intended persuasion. Unlike the former's Marxist practitioners, however, the post-1945 German film team lacked faith in a new ideological program. Stemmle and Neumann knew the primary targets of their satire, namely, residual German fascism in postwar society, but positive alternatives or even the terms of critique seem to have been far less clear. In this situation, highlighting narrative discourse allowed them to explore diverging discourses and ambivalences. Playing with narrative, the film experiments with different explanatory models (for example, idealist versus materialist narratives) and brackets moral claims without entirely undoing them.

The film's most prominent tool of overt narration is its "conferencier." The images of *Berliner Ballade* are presented by an almost constantly present heterodiegetic voiceover narrator who functions as the film's primary agent of narrative linkage. As Sarah Kozloff's study *Invisible Storytellers* outlines, cinematic voiceover historically points back to the medium's very beginnings as a form of popular entertainment in the context of the variety.[26] The live commentator often employed in these cinematic events embodied, as Tom Gunning suggests, early cinema's explicitly performative aesthetics, dominated by the openly communicative "act of showing and exhibition."[27] With the advent of narrative integration, this aesthetics was cast as "primitive." As a descendent of the live commentator, cinematic voiceover remained suspicious; only postmodernism would eventually redeem its challenge to the illusionist, presumably unmediated storytelling of what became known as classical narrative cinema.[28]

While homodiegetic narration was considered to be somewhat more acceptable and became fairly common in the 1930s and 1940s (namely, in film noir), heterodiegetic voiceover was critiqued not least in left-wing circles as an authoritarian device. Apparently unembodied and therefore easily accepted as authoritative, heterodiegetic voiceover seemed to voice directly the film's ideological agenda.[29] In 1940s fiction film, it was mostly used as either a traditional storyteller voice (in epics or Westerns) or as a way of borrowing the supposed authority and authenticity of documentaries or newsreels.[30] *Berliner Ballade* plays with this latter form. In the beginning of the film, we are interpellated into a science fiction communication scenario, as the voiceover, directly addressing the film audience, explains that they are about to see museum footage, documentary evidence of how Berlin looked a hundred years ago in 1948. As the spectator soon realizes, however, this documentary claim amounts to little more than an excuse for unfolding the film's cabaret aesthetic; it is exuberantly mocked by the ways in which the film's narration unfolds.

Before the announced "museum" footage begins, a few shots on "the Berlin that you," the imagined 2048 spectator, "know," distance the 1948 rubble scenario. As stated above, Shandley interprets these images of a reconstructed city to articulate a discourse of redemption, but arguably, this initial scenario already has a parodistic element. It unfolds hyperbolically with the narrator's comments on the recent inclusion of the "suburbs" Magdeburg and Küstrin into the city as well as the replacement of the legendary *Grunewald,* Berlin's major forest, by the new international airport. According to Shandley, our narrator projects authority with his "calm, gentle male voice" (174), but his nonchalant tone often verges on chatter. When he introduces the film's shift from the initial futuristic scenario to the 1948 city as a look at Berlin "in the good old days," the wording provides a first hint at his subsequently developed ironic, often inadequate and banalizing mode of describing images. By introducing a confrontation between two truth claims—that of the presumably authoritative narrator and that of the "documentary" images—*Berliner Ballade* anticipates the self-reflexive and ironic use of film voiceover that is now too often associated with postmodernism strictly.

More significantly, the initial documentary claim is disturbed immediately after the film's shift back to 1948. In the process of introducing the concept of "average consumer," the narrator addresses a man that we see hurry away with two big bags of potatoes: "Hey you—[...] tell me, are you an average consumer?" As the man turns around to answer the call from offscreen, the fiction of historical documentation melts into a moment of spatiotemporal copresence. The narrator is even metonymically embodied as we see a hand offering a cigarette to the man with the two bags. Thus bribed, the pedestrian confesses that he "organized" these potatoes before the narrator graciously allows him to continue on his way. The narrator thereby corrupted his presumed historiographic authority by posing ambiguously as both legal authority and yet one who possesses relevant "American" currency (cigarettes).

This scene is only the first in the film's many instances of metaleptic confusion of narrative levels. By playfully transgressing the frame of spatiotemporal distance between voiceover narrator and on-screen actors, the film mocks the narrator's authority. Throughout *Berliner Ballade*, the issue of narrative control is thematized, partially to emphasize the narrator's power as manipulator of images and partially to question his omnipotence. Thus, scenes in which the narrator arbitrarily interferes with the events on screen are counterbalanced by others in which he apologizes to the spectator for the apparent limits of his knowledge or is literally subjected to the power of the apparatus as the flow of his account is interrupted by the operation of a camera on the diegetic level.

Already underlined by the narrator's almost constant presence, the process of representation is thus dramatized as both manipulative and arbitrary. Emphasizing the narrator's lack of reliability, the technique enables the spectator to retain a moment of critical distance vis-à-vis the didactic components of the narrative even while being repeatedly seduced by the pleasure of surrendering to (obvious) manipulation. The film's narrative mixture of manipulation and resistance is highlighted by the ambiguities of address performed in the process of metaleptic transgression. We see this already in the narrator's conversation with the potato "organizer," who, after their initial exchange, mistakenly responds to the narrator's renewed address to the audience. Impatiently, the narrator asks him to go about his business. While the fictive narrative frame of historical attraction promises the 1948 spectator imagined distance from the screened world, the systematic confusion of narrative levels teasingly realigns her with her manipulated on-screen contemporaries.

In the subsequent presentation of Otto, the "true" average consumer who must do without dubious "potato" connections after having just returned from the war, the camera conspicuously takes up this play with distance and identification. First, Otto is filmed from high above, as a miniscule figure in Berlin's rubble landscape. When a moment later a series of close-ups contours him as an individual, the narrator perpetuates the established distance through a self-reflexive comment on genre, explaining to his fictive 2048 audience that a hundred years ago, spectators presented with these images must have been afraid that this would be "another returning soldier [*Heimkehrer*] film." We are soon aligned with this veteran's gaze, however, as Otto, apparently confused, looks at the ruins of the glorious Reich capital that, the narrator explains, he no longer recognizes.

This play with distance and alignment allowed the film to sell its critique of postwar society to broader audiences. Through the balance of safe distance from and tentative identification with the protagonist, the German audience was enabled to laugh at its "average" on-screen representation. Neither hero nor villain, the continuously inadequate protagonist is gently ridiculed rather than condemned. His female roommate who has established a fashionable dating agency in Otto's old apartment calls him a *reiner Tor*, that is a "complete" or "pure fool." The lexical ambiguity points to the limits of the film's memory politics insofar as it offers a seductive notion of innocence qua foolishness. Pathetic, but still sympathetic enough to enable audience identification at a distance, the figure wins its critical significance as a recognizable image of average German consumption of politics—a cinematic portrait of a "good" (Nazi) citizen staged as a vehicle for enticing the average spectator to think critically about her own political consumption. The price for this focus is that the film does not provide sustained reflections on the average fascist murderer. Yet for those who were willing and able to see, *Berliner Ballade* hints at this problematic as well. Looking for work, Otto studies various job descriptions posted on an advertising pillar. Among other ads, the column features one announcing that "The perpetrator is among us" and, next to it, another one with the title "murderer wanted." The playful intertextual allusion to Staudte's *The Murderers Are among Us* turns into a subtle hint at otherwise backgrounded questions as Otto carefully reads and apparently contemplates the "murderer wanted" ad before he turns toward another ad announcing a night porter position for which he then in fact applies.

Average Political Consumption: The Fellow Traveler as *Untertan*

To be sure, "average consumption" is not merely a metaphor for politics in the film. *Berliner Ballade* takes the question of material loss and need, hunger and cold, as seriously—and humorously—as everything else. However, it is interesting to observe how literal and metaphorical layers of meaning are superimposed, for example in the following sequence: The lack of food—more precisely: sugar—makes Otto suffer from an illness that the commentator describes as widespread, the loss of memory. Otto's condition is first introduced in a slapstick scene in which the narrator repeatedly interrupts himself in order to call back the protagonist who subsequently forgets his food, ration card, and duty to pay in the process of leaving a grocery store. Afterward, we observe Otto's encounter with a "shady" man on the street who introduces himself as an old acquaintance and immediately starts talking about another old friend who recently did not recognize, or probably did not want to recognize him any longer. Since there are apparently good reasons to feign forgetfulness vis-à-vis this man with sunglasses and a cigar, could Otto's apparent memory loss be induced by factors other than a lack of sugar as well? Without connecting its respective illusions into a coherent moral narrative, the film foregrounds the complex link between German postwar suffering and memory (loss). The film's depiction of selective memory is a subtle—perhaps too subtle— variation of the theme explored in Neumann's revue, *Black Market*: "Typically German! There you see it again. First, they burn half the world to ashes. Then, they ask for compassion!"[31]

Politically, Otto earns his surname, Average Consumer, by buying whichever political commodity placed before him at any given time. The film parodies this disposition in a sequence on postwar politics in Berlin where the four parties in each of the four sectors go about reorganizing life with, as the narrator puts it, "sizable idealism and equally sizable official cars." The film's skepticism concerning any institutionalized politics unfolds in the parallel staging of two complementarily aggressive speeches Otto attends. Filmed from below amidst laurel paraphernalia that is rented from the same supplier, first an East Berlin communist and then a Western politician accuse each other of being Allied marionettes.[32] Otto loudly applauds both, shouting "bravo" and "yes." The film highlights the foolish nature of his enthusiasm by delaying his response, focusing attention on his belated jubilation in an already silent room. A little later, the average consumer is almost killed because "he wanted to keep in with everybody." In a bar, he is scared by a fight between two former German army commanders who develop their revanchist war fantasies through identifications with the Eastern and Western Allies respectively. Literally torn back and forth between them after unassertively protesting their war rhetoric, he offers his hand to both of them at the same time and gets knocked out.[33]

With respect to the Third Reich, Otto's failure to resist is characterized in a flashback sequence earlier in the film. At the occasion of Otto's return home, we see what the narrator designates as his memory in short scenes encapsulating each of the war years. In 1940, Otto turns up the radio to listen to the war news with apparent excitement (the narrator comments: *es wurde gesiegt*, "there were victories"), but in 1942, "it became dark," and Otto's enthusiasm waned. The narrator's passive syntax stages the lack of personal responsibility that Otto may feel, but the sequence nonetheless thematizes his compliance. Thus, we watch him lighting a candle under the portrait of Hitler in his apartment as the electric light goes off: "People [*Man*] turned on the light and bowed their heads, not least because of the block leader." Back then, the narrator relates, the work of Alfred Rosenberg announced its presence in the front of his bookshelf, hiding Thomas Mann behind it. In the diegetic present, he adds, shortly after the flashback sequence, the order is reversed. Visibly, "the *Buddenbrocks* had conquered myth," but the moment of structural continuity suggests that Otto's surface antifascism is no more reliable than his conformity during the war years. Becker and Schöll claim that flashback techniques in rubble film overall served to create "moral self-certainty" by enabling identification with the (ethical moments in the) past.[34] *Berliner Ballade* attempts precisely the opposite here. The continued presence of the postures of the past is targeted as the danger that postwar society needs to come to terms with.

The defining moment of Otto's fellow traveling is fear. Fear of block leader and neighbors makes him pose as a good Nazi, but fear also motivates his one attempt to actively resist when in 1943, he tries to escape military conscription by doing "what many did back then." He poses as physically unfit by ruining his health with a cocktail including excess caffeine, perished fish, and frantic last-minute exercise. Ironically displacing the propaganda discourse of jubilatory service for the fatherland, the narrator comments, "and his heart was beating faster and faster [*höher und höher*]." However, Otto's deflection from the norms of militarist masculinity remains fruitless at this advanced stage of the war. Although he passes out during the examination, the next shot shows him, in a parallel position, on the ground in front of a military officer, having apparently fallen on command, only in order to get up and proceed with the drill. The montage suggests that despite his contrary intentions, it is precisely Otto's (performance of) weakness that makes him into the perfect subject of military discipline.

Arguably, the scene condenses the discourse of masculinity in *Berliner Ballade*. Otto's theatrical performance merely accentuates the general fragility of his undernourished body; his soft-spokenness and overall lack of initiative or self-directed activity feminize him within the discursive frame of European modernity's hegemonic gender order. The implicit charge is explicated in several scenes. While employed as night porter in a clothing store, the average consumer fails to notice the approaching robbers because he is carried away by dreams. "To be a grand lady once," the narrator interprets his longing, as Otto admires his phantasmatically well-dressed self in the mirror of a (male) display dummy of his own average looks. Earlier in the film, Otto braves the cold winter in the three walls of his bombed-out room by staying in bed and dreaming of blond pastry shop ladies. With his head wrapped in thick layers of clothes, he is mistaken for a woman by a solicitor disrupting his sleep. As the narrator suggests, her critical response to his "unmanly" lack of initiative "left him cold, just like his oven. That is what happened to almost all average consumers at the time. They followed the example of the animals: they camouflaged themselves and hibernated." On the one hand, Otto's failure of masculinity is thus presented as understandable. Rhetorically displacing the matter of "leaving someone cold" into the literal realm, the narrator develops a materialist discourse affirming the priority of bodily needs. On the other hand, the following sentence confronts this logic by associating its laws with the animal realm; the spectator's laughter at Otto's pathetic persona is mediated by a norm of exclusive masculinity, if ironically female-embodied, qua heroic resistance to adverse conditions.

The film's analytical focus on this theme of masculinity suggests a moment of continuity between *Quax, the Crash Pilot* and *Berliner Ballade*. In 1948 as in 1941, a norm of heroic strength serves as the standard against which actual male performances fall short. Rather than entirely dissolving the symbolic fabric that sustained fascism, its postwar analysis recycles some of its components. Nonetheless, this recycling now sustains a different configuration of gender politics. First, it should be noted that femininity functions not only as a target of laughter (in Otto), but also quite abundantly as an object of desire in *Berliner Ballade*. Multiple scenes portray Otto's sultry dreams, and cabaret inserts complete the panorama of the modernist city Berlin with extended depictions of bar culture and sex work. These scenes underline the film's difference not only from the sexually repressed, if moderately homoerotic, visual politics of *Quax*, but also from the fascist politics of heterosexual desire as developed in the era's politicized revues.[35] While narrative containment of these femininity spectacles is not absent, this containment works less to condemn sexual promiscuity than to ridicule concepts of romantic love and institutionalized monogamy. After getting married in a hurry, Otto is punished with average marital hell. Secondly, the content of normative masculinity has undergone a shift. Instead of the failure to perform heroically in a militaristic context (as in *Quax*), we are now presented with a failure to perform heroic resistance to militaristic masculinity. Otto's performance of weakness functions as the way military discipline enters his body rather than presenting a suitable strategy to escape militarism. However, the film's critical emphasis is precisely on this issue of subjection—and in developing it, the film also provides us with a critique of fascist masculinity.

The theme was established already in the beginning of the film when upon his return to Berlin, Otto contemplated the ruins of the "victory alley," the collection of royal and heroic monuments built in *Tiergarten*,

Berlin's central park, at Wilhelm II's behest in 1895 and later appropriated for Albert Speer's city planning. With Otto, the spectator gazes at Prussia's fallen heroes, including Frederick the Great. In foregrounding these Prussian ruins, *Berliner Ballade* underlines a prominent theme of postwar discourse. In response to the Nazis' use of Prussian icons, contemporaries debated the Prussian links to fascism. The Allies' decision to level the alley as well as their official dissolution of Prussia in 1947 reflects the evolving critical stance toward the historical state, a stance that would constitute the dominant, albeit not unchallenged discursive position in both East and West Germany during the first postwar decades.[36] *Berliner Ballade* underwrites these anti-Prussian sentiments, but the film also suggests that the official stance of symbolic rupture may fall short of solving the problem. The camera cuts back and forth between Otto's face and the objects of his gaze. Old Fritz may have lost his arm, but he still dominates the sky from the perspective of the average consumer seated on some rubble. Retrospectively reminiscent of Staudte's broadly acclaimed 1951 film version of Heinrich Mann's *Der Untertan* (known in English as The Subject or The Emperor's Lackey), the camera investigates Otto's subject position through multiple close-ups of statuary from an extremely low angle. As we look at the shot sequence of Otto-statuary-Otto, we witness the objects' impact. Initially, he looked skeptical. Then, overwhelmed by their continued aura of power, he straightens, salutes, and lifts his hat in reverence to the heroes of the past, until he is interrupted by a woman who presents the returning soldier with a picture of her missing husband, reminding him of the deadly realities of the war waged in the name of past and future German glory.

The narrator, who had momentarily retreated during this scene of dramatic immediacy underlined by military music in the soundtrack, now takes over again, summarizing and contextualizing the significance of the incident by emphasizing that the presence of the past in Otto's mind is mirrored in the appearance of the city. Although it has been presumably cleared of "everything that is militaristic, Prussian and monarchist," closer investigation reveals that "the lampposts still have all kinds of designs of yesterday." In quick succession, a montage sequence of low-angle shots again accompanied by military music shows how deeply the heritage of fascist militarism is written into the symbolic body of Berlin, from "Emperor William Street" and "King's Alley" to "Hindenburg Wall" and "Battle Lake." Later in the film, we are once more reminded that this presence of past symbolic inscriptions has marked the bodies of the city's inhabitants as well. On a bus, Otto gets in trouble for requesting a stop by ringing the conductor's bell. Supported by other passengers' subdued calls for "order," the conductor confronts Otto with charges of *Fahrgastzersetzung* ("passenger sabotage," a word play on the Nazi term *Wehrkraftzersetzung*, "sabotage of military strength"). Otto initially tries to defend himself argumentatively, but under pressure, he once more lapses back into the routine of military drill; a short slapstick scene shows him going up and down as the image of the conductor is superimposed by that of his former military officer.

Conclusion: *Kampf dem Kampf*

At the end of the film, the same actor who played the conductor plays the cemetery official, showing up in Prussian uniform and leading the ceremony accordingly. During Otto's stint as a moral agent, the official is thrown into the grave because he refuses to bury "hatred" as suggested by the reborn average consumer. Otto himself promises to bury his fear and the other bystanders agree to do the same with egotism, indifference, and so on, but as the film suggests here, the legacy of militarism is perhaps not conquered by goodwill alone. No less significantly, however, the Prussian climbs out of the grave again. Indignantly cleaning his uniform, he now reluctantly performs the symbolic gesture requested. Rather than with radical eradication, the film answers militaristic hatred with harmless comical coercion. Politically pacifist, its symbolic politics in general is articulated in one of the cabaret song numbers that interrupt the narrative flow of the plot, but are nonetheless thematically integrated, contributing to the film's narrative discourse.

The occasion for this song is a discussion between Otto and the man who supplies, on a rent-per-day basis, the laurel paraphernalia for the different party speeches our protagonist has applauded. Recalling all the different causes his equipment has served over the years, the small businessman concludes that *Kampf* (battle, fighting) is always bad. As Otto reflects on these words, the close-up on his face is slowly fading into the cabaret scene. Its montage of images contrasts a romantically German nature scene, in which an all-male chorus performs the "Battlesong against Fighting" from Neumann's revue "It's all Theater,"[37] with various contemporary illustrations of social bellicosity, for example, signs calling for a "war on lice." The song targets the "brave German man," who even after the war still enjoys his "Lilliputian-fights" against moths, taxes, Bavarians, corruption, existentialism, and capitalism, as well as, of course, for the soccer championship. The song's title and concluding call ("When will we finally fight against fighting?") self-reflexively captures the paradoxical gesture at the heart of the film's symbolic politics. Aware of the critique's complicity with what it critiques, the film renounces purist paradigms, both in its aesthetics of bricolage and its politics of navigating different modes of political critique. Timid about embracing radical gestures of all sorts, the filmmakers' battle against fascist battle culture comes with a conciliatory touch. The film's stance against fascist militarism is nonetheless clearly articulated. With its call against "German battle culture," the musical insert thematically parallels, and thereby reinforces, Otto's closing moral address to the Prussian official. With respect to the themes identified as targets of "German battle culture" in the song, however, the interplay between the different elements of the film is more ambiguous. Arguably, Otto's concluding stance against the egotism of his corrupt roommate is bracketed by the song's distancing reflection on the battle ardor of anticorruption calls, as well as the narrator's own participation in such activity. (The spectator is reminded of the earlier scene with the "potato organizer" when, in the song, the gesture of offering American cigarettes illustrates the theme of corruption.) Through its self-reflexive narrative practice, does the film implicitly justify black market activity in the name of human need and desire? In any case, *Berliner Ballade* insists that the answer is precisely not the "strong state" for which ironically the film's black marketeer himself calls, after babbling, completely drunk, about his own status as an "anti-social element."[38]

Ridiculing this call as yet another authoritarian fantasy, the film instead turns, in its very last minute, for help to the liberal notion of human reason. As Otto, the eternal fool, sneaks away from his shortlived stint as moral agent, the narrator resumes, saying that "the average consumers were allowed to live on and the seemingly inevitable world catastrophe" precipitated by fighting Allies with the help of unregenerate Germans "could be averted, for, at the last minute, a force entered the equation that no one had counted on: human reason. This happened in 1949, if I am not mistaken." For the 1948 spectators of *Berliner Ballade*, this concluding performance of narrative authority had an obviously performative character. The film's promise of "redemption" (Shandley) was based on a demand to contemporary actors in both politics and society. Finally, this promise articulates a fantasy of global traffic rather than revanchist imperialism. If the spectator connects the narrator's concluding words back to the initial 2048 scenario, she will remember that the promised "vital and important metropolis"[39] was distinguished by its international airport, where in an imagined world beyond the cold war, planes would stop over daily on the route from New York to Moscow. Assuming, of course, that the narrator is not mistaken. Perhaps his rhetorical tentativeness in the concluding passage of the film underlines not only his obvious lack of command over the future, but also the fragile foundation of his promise in a discourse of enlightenment that contemporary philosophy was beginning to suspect of its dialectical complicity with fascism. But fragile as it may have seemed already back then, for the film team producing *Berliner Ballade* in postwar Germany, all intelligible alternatives to this liberal plea seem to have been even more suspicious.

Notes

1. Manfred Barthel, *So war es wirklich: Der deutsche Nachkriegsfilm* (Munich: Herbig, 1986), p.38. In 1965, Peter Pleyer still described the film as the most consequential political satire of the German postwar production until 1949; *Deutscher Nachkriegsfilm 1946–1948* (Münster: C.J.Fahle, 1965), p.130.
2. See Robert R. Shandley, *Rubble Films: German Cinema in the Shadow of the Third Reich* (Philadelphia: Temple University Press, 2001), p.174.
3. Barthel, *So war es wirklich*, p.40. I would like to thank Ralf Pierau for confirming this and other details, for which the available secondary literature gives conflicting versions, based on his unpublished *Staatsexamensarbeit* "R.A.S.: Grundlegung zu einer Monographie unter besonderer Berücksichtigung seines Schaffens bis 1930" (University of Magdeburg, 1993).
4. Thomas Brandlmeier, "Von Hitler zu Adenauer: Deutsche Trümmerfilme," in *Zwischen Gestern und Morgen: Westdeutscher Nachkriegsfilm 1946–1962*, ed. Hilmar Hoffmann and Walter Schobert (Frankfurt am Main: Union Druckerei, 1989), pp.32–59, here 34.
5. Brandlmeier, "Von Hitler zu Adenauer," pp.36–37.
6. Wolfgang Becker and Norbert Schöll: *In jenen Tagen...Wie der deutsche Nachkriegsfilm die Vergangenheit bewältigte* (Opladen: Leske and Budrich, 1995), pp.70–71.
7. Shandley, *Rubble Films*, pp.177, 175. Bettina Greffrath's dissertation *Gesellschaftsbilder der Nachkriegszeit: Deutsche Spielfilme 1945–1949* (Pfaffenweiler: Centaurus, 1995) mentions the film mostly as an example for rubble film's tendency toward excusing the individual and featuring politics in merely negative terms (pp.158, 245).
8. At the same time, the lack of appreciation for the aesthetic experiments in *Berliner Ballade* can ironically be attributed to the conservative approach to form matters within rubble scholarship itself. Focused on political and moral questions, the existing body of work does not significantly reflect the debates on film form and ideology, which have shaped film scholarship in general throughout the last decades.
9. See Thomas Elsaesser, "New German Cinema and History: The Case of Alexander Kluge," in *The German Cinema Book*, eds. Tim Bergfelder, Erica Carter, and Deniz Göktürk (London: BFI, 2002), pp.182–191, here p.183.
10. Klaus Kreimeier, "Die Ökonomie der Gefühle: Aspekte des westdeutschen Nachkriegsfilms," in *Zwischen Gestern und Morgen*, pp.8–28, here p.8.
11. Shandley, *Rubble Films*, pp.26, 47.
12. Thus also Anton Kaes, *Deutschlandbilder. Die Wiederkehr der Geschichte als Film* (München: edition text und kritik, 1987), pp.18–20.
13. Shandley, *Rubble Films*, p.4.

14. *Affaire Blum* was directed by Erich Engel in 1948. A few years later, Stemmle also shot the first feature-length film addressing the topic of interracial children in postwar society, *Toxi* (Munich: Fono-Film GmbH, 1952). The film remains highly ambivalent in its attempt to address racism while failing to imagine the social integration of Black Germans (see Heide Fehrenbach, *Race after Hitler: Black Occupation Children in Postwar Germany* [Princeton University Press, 2005]).

15. Stemmle's pre-NS theater and cabaret work showed socialist as well as avant-garde sympathies. From 1930 to 1934, he was employed as a leading dramaturge at Tobis Cinema; afterward, he worked as both screenplay writer and director for different film companies, including UFA (see Pierau, for a short published summary of his research: http://www.uni-magdeburg.de/mbl/Biografien/0984.htm; as well as the Stemmle article in *CineGraph—Lexikon zum deutschsprachigen Film* [Munich: edition text+kritik, 1984ff.; online at: http://www.filmportal.de; last access July 13, 2006]). Neumann had begun his career in different Berlin cabarets in the late 1920s. After 1933, he continued to work in the now heavily censored cabaret sector until 1937, repeatedly getting into trouble with the NS authorities for individual productions (see Bryan T. VanSweringen, *Kabarettist an der Front des Kalten Krieges. Günter Neumann und das politische Kabarett in der Programmgestaltung des RIAS 1948–1968*, trans. Regine Schulze [Passau: Wiss.Verlag Rothe, 1989], here pp.45–58).

16. Directed by Kurt Hoffmann (UFA). On this film, see Cary Nathenson: "Fear of Flying: Education to Manhood in Nazi Film Comedies: *Glückskinder* and *Quax, der Bruchpilot*," *Cultural History through a National Socialist Lens: Essays on the Cinema of the Third Reich*, ed. Robert C. Reimer (Rochester, NY: Camden House, 2000), pp.84–108; on the problematic entertainment —ideology distinction in general Eric Rentschler, *The Ministry of Illusion: Nazi Cinema and its Afterlife* (Cambridge, MA: Harvard University Press, 1996); Lutz Koepnick, *The Dark Mirror: German Cinema between Hitler and Hollywood* (Berkeley, CA: University of California Press, 2002).

17. See, for example, Brandlmeier, "Von Hitler zu Adenauer," p.35; Shandley, *Rubble Films*, pp.48–49.

18. Brandlmeier, "Von Hitler zu Adenauer," p.36; Shandley, *Rubble Films*, pp.27–28.

19. Apparently invented by Neumann, the notion is based on the postwar food rationing system; since then, the slightly derogatory term "Otto Normalverbraucher" has moved into everyday linguistic practice as a metaphor for a thoroughly average person.

20. On the one hand, the product is labeled as "photographed cabaret" rather than film proper (*Tagesspiegel*; quoted from VanSweringen, *Kabarettist an der Front*, p.117); on the other hand, it is praised by suggesting that "this is not a picturization of cabaret, but filmic cabaret and even a little more: focused film" (Gunter Groll; quoted from Barthel, *So war es wirklich*, p.39).

21. Thus, Shandley mentions the film's cabaret origins in the context of his argument that Otto remains an undeveloped character. Humor, he had already suggested summarily, "is used to distract the viewer from the film's ideological task" (*Rubble Films*, p.177).

22. Ibid.

23. See Hayden White, "The Value of Narrativity in the Representation of Reality," in *The Content of the Form: Narrative Discourse and Historical Representation* (Baltimore, MD: Johns Hopkins University Press, 1990).

24. Laura Mulvey, "Visual Pleasure and Narrative Cinema," in *Screen* 16.3 (1975): 6–18; see Tom Gunning, "The Cinema of Attractions: Early Film, Its Spectator and the Avant-Garde," in *Early Cinema: Space—Frame—Narrative*, ed. Thomas Elsaesser with Adam Barker (London: British Film Institute, 1990), pp.56–62, and, for example, *Classical Hollywood Comedy*, ed. Kristine Brunovska Karnick and Henry Jenkins (New York: Routledge, 1995).

25. Sergei Eisenstein, "The Montage of Film Attractions," in *The European Cinema Reader*, ed. Catherine Fowler (London: Routledge, 2002), pp.25–26.

26. Sarah Kozloff, *Invisible Storytellers: Voice-Over Narration in American Fiction Film* (Berkeley, CA: University of California Press, 1988), p.23.

27. Gunning, "The Cinema of Attractions," p.56, see 58.

28. See Kozloff, *Invisible Storytellers*, in particular pp.9–19, 39, 53.

29. Ibid., pp.80–81.

30. Ibid., p.74.

31. "Das ist die typisch deutsche Eigenschaft! Da sieht man's ja wieder mal! Erst legt so'n Volk die halbe Welt in Asche! Und dann komm'se mit der Mitleidsmasche!" (quoted from VanSweringen, *Kabarettist an der Front*, p.101).

32. Retrospective readings and even a few contemporary critiques suggested an imbalance in the film's treatment of Americans versus Soviets (see VanSweringen, *Kabarettist an der Front*, pp.117–118). At the time, Neumann was already employed at RIAS, the American sector's radio station, for which he would later support the cold war in cabaret fashion. The film, however, is dominated by the parallel staging of the different postwar forces, even while a few scenes specifically target Soviet militarism in analogy to Nazi militarism.

33. Brandlmeier uses this scene as evidence for his claim that the film equates fascism and communism, identifying the two combatants as a "Nazi" and a "communist" respectively (pp.36–37). However, the scene only specifies that the tie-wearing, not exactly proletarian-looking German gentlemen are proud former commanders of a tank and a "Stuka" (a Nazi war plane) respectively, who interrupt their fight to bond over their fond war memories. Rather than one-sided anticommunism, the scene seems to articulate a biting critique of both Soviet and Western Allies by making revanchist Germans identify with them. Brandlmeier's second example is a scene that parodies the political process of negotiation over Berlin. Smoking a cigar, one of the delegates at another fruitless conference falls asleep next to a globe model that catches fire because of his negligence. Brandlmeier reads his appearance as stereotypically Russian (p.37), but the sign on the wall behind him, which we saw a few shots earlier, reads "America."

34. Becker and Schöll, *In jenen Tagen*, p.147.

35. See Terri J. Gordon, "Fascism and the Female Form: Performance Art in the Third Reich," in *Journal of the History of Sexuality* 11.1/2 (January/April 2002): 164–200.

36. For an overview see, for example, Hans Dollinger, *Friedrich II. von Preußen: Sein Bild im Wandel von zwei Jahrhunderten* (München: List, 1986), pp.193–216.
37. See VanSweringen, *Kabarettist an der Front*, pp.95–96.
38. Becker and Schöll, *In jenen Tagen* (as quoted above).
39. Shandley, *Rubble Films*, p.174.

CHAPTER ELEVEN

PLANES, TRAINS, AND THE OCCASIONAL CAR: THE RUBBLE FILM AS DEMOBILIZATION FILM

Jaimey Fisher

Introduction: Continuities and Ruptures from Cinema under the Nazis

> We should finally put an end to these coarse troop manners
> (*Landsknechtmanieren*) on screen, with their ideology taught and drilled
> in barrack parlors (*Kasernenstuben*) and brown youth homes and with the
> German inwardness (and its ancillary terminology) put on full display...But
> this recent German film [*Wege im Zwielicht*] is played in exactly this key.
> This is very familiar to us and, if a little coquettish nihilism, in flat, banal
> formulations, didn't intervene now and again, Mr. Goebbels could easily
> have taken up this film in his production list. So perfectly would that fit
> right in...[1]

Scholars and critics have generally asserted that the rubble films of the late
1940s and early 1950s intended and achieved a break from the
Nazi-coordinated film industry that preceded it.[2] During the Allied-imposed
Filmpause of 1945–1946, there were many calls to abandon the relentlessly
entertaining style of the Nazi-coordinated film industry and to instigate
instead a socially critical, historically engaged, film-realist approach—and
most have characterized the mainstream cinema as moving, successfully or
not, in that direction. But the epigraph's unusually harsh review of Gustav

Fröhlich's *Wege im Zwielicht* (1947) suggests something usually neglected in the scholarship on the rubble film: the possibility of continuities between cinema made during and after the Nazi regime. Fröhlich's *Wege im Zwielicht* does, indeed, quote one of the most popular films made under the Nazis—Eduard von Borsody's *Wunschkonzert* (1940)—and how it does so and why point toward previously unexamined elements of both films. *Wunschkonzert* is what some have termed a "home-front" film, but I would suggest instead that the film belongs to a genre hitherto mentioned but not yet fully explicated, namely, the mobilization genre. Mobilization films like *Wunschkonzert* and the likewise immensely popular *Die große Liebe* (1942) initiate viewers into the increasingly militarized society and the growing personal sacrifices that would be demanded by the Nazis' "total war."[3] These films suggest mobilization rather than merely home-front films because of the very deliberate and very modern way in which they manipulate mobility, geography, and space in order to achieve their narrative goals. They deploy the military and its transportation technologies to arrange geographies both spatial and emotional: the military not only negotiates the dynamic national notion of Germany in very specific ways, but also maps, in a very deliberately sketched geography, the private emotional life of the main characters. They juxtapose and intertwine the usual subject of feature films, that is, the intimate emotional life of their protagonists, with a militarized project of national mobilization for war. They achieve this intertwinement above all by building on film's longstanding relationship to mobility in order to negotiate specific kinds of space, from civilian space transformed by military, mobilization, and mobility technologies into what I would call a new mental geography.[4]

If a new kind of mental geography had been advocated and had taken hold during the Nazis' "total mobilization" and war—that is, their particular instrumentalization of industrial modernity—then the post-war period would have, at least as one of its sundry aspects, to invoke and dismantle this geography and mapping. In this essay I want to investigate the deliberate negotiation of space or, more specifically formulated, the cognitive mapping of these early postwar films, to invoke the term used by Fredric Jameson.[5] Many of the rubble films make reference to and attempt to refigure this cognitive mapping of the Nazi social and cultural imaginary. This spatial subtext of mobility and transportation technologies was one of the subtle ways in which films of the 1940s engaged with their immediate cinematic predecessors, despite many claims of a radical break from the cinema of 1933–1945. This is precisely what a cycle of three films associated with Rolf Meyer, a director as well as the head of the production firm Junge Film-Union, achieves in its curious negotiation of postwar space. *Wege im Zwielicht, Zugvögel* (1946/47, Rolf Meyer), and *Die Söhne des Herrn Gaspary* (1948, Rolf Meyer) all offer depictions that invoke, indulge, and at least attempt to refigure the mobilization genre: all emphasize, with veterans as their main characters, a changing spatial sense through metaphors of mobility and the means of transportation technology. With these films' references to a wartime and then postwar cognitive mapping, I will attempt a reading that does not focus so much on character or cast, but rather on images of space, transportation, and general mobility within them. On the one hand, there was a clear invocation and even suspect indulgence of the kind of mobilization and the militarized mapping of the geographical and emotional landscape of cinema under the Nazis; on the other hand, there was an effort, with varying degrees of conviction and success, to dismantle it for the millions of returning soldiers who had not only learned but lived the Nazis' spatial agenda.[6]

Rethinking the Post–World War II *Heimkehrer* as Veteran

In tracing these continuities and ruptures, it is useful to start with the market that Rolf Meyer targeted: that of disoriented and often angry returning veterans, for whom certain psychologies and predispositions would persist from the wartime imaginary. There was, indeed, a large audience of this kind: by the war's end, some eleven million veterans were held in POW camps, the vast majority of whom returned to Germany. From its first images, *Wege im Zwielicht* invokes and foregrounds these veterans. Viewers first see a close-up long take of Lukas, played by the film's best-known cast member, Gustav Fröhlich, who had become a star at age 23, as Freder in *Metropolis*. Playing off his fame and reputation as a matinee idol, the shot highlights the fatigued and scarred markings of the *Heimkehrer* familiar from films like *Die Mörder sind unter uns* or *Irgwendo in Berlin*, or *Liebe '47*. When the camera pulls back, viewers see that this seeming *Heimkehrer* is wandering through a train station whose floor is thickly settled with homeless, refugees, and, as viewers see in a remarkable panning point of view, veterans. This pan eventually settles on that group of three veterans on whom the film will focus, Stefan, Peter, and Josef, all conspicuously still dressed in their wartime uniforms and playing cards on a Persil box, a symbol of their antipathy to denazification (the certificates clearing one of denazification were known as *Persilscheine*). It turns out that the film will not be, as the first shot implied, the story of a *Heimkehrer* Lukas and his struggles to reintegrate to the postwar society: Lukas is no typical *Heimkehrer*—if one at all—as he is not returning home to a ruined household, an alienated family, or with the symptoms of posttraumatic syndrome, all tropes familiar from other rubble films. Rather, he is the gentlemanly mayor of a small town. The film will focus instead on the travails of these three veterans: the film is invoking but dispensing with the standard *Heimkehrer* film, in which a single returning male protagonist finds his way back into an estranged family (*Die Mörder, Irgendwo in Berlin, und über uns der Himmel, vor uns liegt das Leben*); rather, the film will focus on the fates of this group of veterans, who have no home to which to return.

Scholars have often traced the theme of the *Heimkehrer* in the postwar rubble films and frequently focus on questions of reintegration into private households and traditional gender roles. But there have been remarkably few specific investigations of how the *Heimkehrer* was not merely an absent male retuning to the heterosexual family, but rather a former soldier— militarily conditioned and experienced—returning from a war that required a specifically mobilized psychology. There is typically consistent focus on the reintegration into the postwar society, but little on the militaristic baggage and imaginary that former soldiers and recently released POWs would have carried. For many of these soldiers, mobilization for war would have exposed them to some of modernity's most distinguishing aspects, including industrial organization, modern technology, and, perhaps most remarkably, travel to distant lands and contact with foreign cultures. Alon Confino, for instance, has written of how indelible these impressions derived from wartime travel would prove in the postwar period.[7]

Veterans had played an important role in German political culture after 1918, as well as in the discourse about German victimization, from the late teens through the mid 1940s. Their status would, following defeat in 1945, undergo a fundamental transition when the Allies raised demilitarization to the level of occupational policy.[8] As after World War I—but in a very different direction—the veterans became an important flashpoint for debates about how to "cure" Germany. Debates about the "German soldier," the "returning soldier," and the "POW" were ubiquitous in the postwar public sphere.[9] Like the many newspaper and journals articles and debates, these postwar films from the Junge Film-Union about former *Wehrmacht* troops reflect ways in which such important political and cultural undercurrents could and did return in a culture that liked to claim it had broken cleanly from those of the 1930s and early 1940s. The harsh review of *Wege im Zwielicht* above could, in fact, refer to any of these three films, as all focus on sympathetically depicted experiences of those from the barrack parlors (*Kasernenstuben*).

In these films, the plots extend the mobilization aspect of war because the veterans—often a group of veterans who remain together in the wake of their wartime camaraderie—have no home to which to return and spend the entire plots on the move. An article at the time, in fact, distinguishes between veterans struggling to reintegrate to their families and those merely meandering aimlessly, and these films follow those veterans committed to resisting such reassimilation to lawful civilian life.[10] *Wege im Zwielicht* follows a group of three veterans who are on the run from the police because they are believed to be responsible for an accidental death. *Söhne* follows two brothers who were separated by the Nazi regime: one fled to Switzerland with his father and has grown up in the lap of Swiss luxury, while the other was left to fight for the *Wehrmacht*. In the postwar period, they are reunited in Switzerland, but struggle with their extremely varied wartime experiences. *Zugvögel* follows the travails of a group of young veterans as they try to find themselves in the postwar context; the protagonist is Georg, a veteran who left the hospital too early and who learns that he will die from his untreated illness. The spatial dimensions and mappings of *Wege im Zwielicht* connect its (de)mobilization trajectory to these other two films: they all foreground transportation technologies and the cinematic pleasures therein; all eventually divulge a kind of secondary map that displaces the initial spaces of the narrative in a cognitive mapping mechanism familiar from mobilization films; and all trace the consequences of that spatial displacement for agency and desire to settle on a refigured third space, a compromise space between the two maps.

Spaces of (De)Mobilization: Train Stations as Abstract Space

In the opening sequence described above, *Wege im Zwielicht* introduces these veterans in a space associated with soldiers and troop movement since the first mobilization films, namely, the train station. The first twenty minutes of the film—those in which the plot tension is usually set up—is established in the train station and implies a certain lifestyle in it, something made note of in various reviews of the film. It is no mistake, of course, that the primary mapping of the film is in the urban train station, which has long been associated with both mobilization and war films more generally. Indispensable to German war planning and thoroughly interwoven with German troop movement, trains had entered the cultural imaginary—right down to the card playing—as they relate to mobilization, for instance in the very different depictions of mobilization by train in Jünger's *In Stahlgewittern* or Mann's *Doktor Faustus*. *Wunschkonzert*, although the film focuses on the fate and visual pleasures of a *Luftwaffe* pilot, nonetheless offers an important train mobilization sequence in which the female lead accompanies a young recruit to the train station to see him off to his military duties.[11] The long and visually striking sequence is remarkable not only because it foregrounds the train departure of soldiers going to war, but also because of its deliberate construction of the departure not so much as sad parting but as festive celebration: although families are breaking apart—husbands leaving wives, fathers leaving children—a cheerful mood pervades the entire sequence.

Even before their redeployment at war time, train stations had always served as a particular kind of contact zone: Wolfgang Schivelbusch describes how the train station served as the interface between two different modes of traffic, between the industrialized transportation technology that made modern society possible and the narrow medieval alleyways of the inner city.[12] Trains and train stations are thus indelible symbols of what Lefebvre calls abstract space, that is, formerly organic and preindustrial space changed irrevocably by modern industry. In fact, their hybrid character highlights, in Lefebvre's memorable emphasis, the production of abstract space out of older urban forms.[13] This janus-faced character of the train station is reflected in the familiar architecture of the European train station, with their grand facades backing the systematized lines of the industrial anterior. For works of the mobilization genre, the military train and militarized train station signify a number of transformative encounters that seem to elaborate the kind of interface that Schivelbusch and Lefebvre suggest: they were where the locality met the faraway, where the home front met the war front, where the private family met the national project. They were also the space/locus, as *Wunschkonzert* suggests and *In Stahlgewittern* describes, where the social relations of the private home were dissolved and welded anew into the camaraderie of the national military.

In the postwar, demilitarized train station, however, *Wege* deploys this modern transportation technology and its links to the war to underscore how this modern production of abstract space has gone awry. If the train allowed for mass movement in a new way—for mass mobility and migration—by organizing and transporting people in an industrial fashion, *Wege*'s train station represents a postwar return of the repressed masses: people are strewn about the floor, industry has broken down into illegal contraband, and open conflict violently erupts. The kind of industrialized society symbolized in the train and train station, the film suggests, has failed, something asserted even more sharply by the other setting in the initial spaces of the film's first 20 minutes, the ruins of the cathedral into which Stefan, Peter, and Josef pursue a commercial adversary, Fleck. Lukas watches from the cathedral's shadows as the band of veterans chase and confront Fleck, who throws some church cobblestones at them before tumbling down backward in the rubble. In following these black marketeers, the film cuts among high-contrast, low-key shots of the various religious icons and artifacts to highlight how society—Schivelbusch's modern balance between the railroad station and the cathedral—has broken down, an invocation of the postwar hand-wringing about the prevalence of secularism and moral nihilism.[14] When the police appear to investigate, the band flees to the church and jump on a train, where they happen to encounter Lukas again. Convinced he will report them, they also flee from him by jumping off the train in the countryside, a symbolic flight from industrial society that ultimately saves them.

Military Airfields versus the Rural Village: The Double Mappings of (De)Mobilization Films

With its train station full of homeless veterans, cathedral ruins used by black marketeers, and then crowded train ride overflowing with wayward masses, the film's first 20 minutes sketch a destroyed postwar space underscoring the failures of militarization and mobilization. This mapping that invokes the city, mobility, and war becomes all the starker once the film suddenly shifts to a secondary narrative map in the countryside. In the *Geopolitical Aesthetic*, Fredric Jameson argues that the cinematic operations of cognitive mapping become intensified when it is revealed that there is a secondary map behind the presumed spatial order of things: a second, initially unknown layer permits a shift to a different landscape (literally) of agency.[15] I would suggest that the mobilization films, which are, as Jameson might put it, "more spatial" than many other films, realize this kind of remapping over the course of their narratives[16]: both the war-time mobilization and postwar demobilization films remap previous notions of space, unfolding a double layering of space that can permit an effective refiguration of characters, plots, and desires through such spatial shifts.

As with mobilization films like *Wunschkonzert* and *Die große Liebe*, *Wege* offers an initially covert secondary space onto which it will map the protagonists and the scenario sketched in the first segment of the film. In *Wunschkonzert* and *Die große Liebe*, however, the secondary map was the militarized geography of Europe at war, a secondary map that undercut, in each case, a private courtship. In *Wege*, the trajectory is the opposite: the first twenty minutes show the fallout from the war and the venality of postwar veterans, veterans who remain with their comrades in the lingering, demolished, and discredited industrial spaces of the postwar period. That there will be a stark transition from this life to the secondary map in the country is reinforced in a transitional sequence that occurs right around the typically transformative 20-minutes point, when the three veterans hop off the train. Once they jump from the train and find themselves stuck in the countryside, a montage of short episodes ensues that shows them roaming with no particular destination or goal.

This montage sequence of *Wege*, however, opens with a scene that underscores the struggles with demobilization as well as a central aspect of the Nazi imaginary, namely, air power. Having departed the train and on their own in the unfamiliar countryside—thus indulging the military imaginary of travel in distant and lovely lands—the three veterans approach abandoned bombers on an airfield in a memorable shot that invokes the visual pleasures of both in *Wunschkonzert* and *Die große Liebe*. As they get close to one bomber, however, a sudden, offscreen voice, in American English, warns them off the plane, and they quickly run out of the frame. With the attraction of these visually striking bombers, the film is reinforcing the veterans' military habits and the persistence of them in the postwar period: when left uncertain, the veterans would revert to the military, military technology, and the association of air power with World War II confirmed in *Wunschkonzert* and *Die große Liebe*, a parallel to be confirmed below in a direct quote by *Wege im Zwielicht* of *Wunschkonzert*. Once displaced from the train station and train, they seem, in this context, to be seeking what Virilio, following Bergson, terms the unique "perceptual luxuries" of wars as well as wartime films.[17] But the rest of the montage sequence then reenacts the process of demilitarization and the uncertainty of demobilization after it: since they have been admonished by a faceless Allied authority, they hurry off, wander around, searching unsuccessfully for work in the unfamiliar postwar landscape. It is at this point that they arrive, coincidentally, in the small town of which Lukas is mayor, something viewers learn as Lukas returns and is greeted with a complaint about a destroyed bridge that a farmer in a horse-drawn cart needs to move his wares. This sequence arranges the scenario that will help the veterans find their way back to honest work and happiness: Lukas offers them work on the bridge as an opportunity to prove themselves. It also begins to assert the film's covert secondary map since Lukas, who seemed to be just another *Heimkehrer* wandering in the urban landscape, is actually the mayor of a small town onto which the film subsequently remaps its initially troubled modern scenario.

In a manner even more explicit than the plane scene above, the sequence in which the three veterans stumble on the secondary map of Lukas's small town cites *Wunschkonzert* and, I would argue, the mobilization genre directly. When the veterans first find their way into Lukas's town, they are seeking shelter from a rainy night and let themselves into the steeple of the town's church. Two of the veterans sleep until the third, Josef, wakes them up abruptly by playing the church organ, an act, undertaken in the middle of the night, that gives away their whereabouts immediately. A veteran in a church who suddenly plays the organ references a scene in *Wunschkonzert* in which a group of three soldiers hide in a church in France waiting for their comrades to return from an attack. There is, however, thick fog and the smoke of battle, such that one of the soldiers in the church decides to play the organ and to guide the lost *Wehrmacht* soldiers their way back to safety. The organ-playing soldier, who is promptly killed by Allied artillery targeting the source of the music, connects the primary and secondary maps of *Wunschkonzert*'s mobilization spaces: in the film's first part, the same individual, before his mobilization, had entertained his Berlin apartment house with Beethoven piano pieces. In this manner, *Wunschkonzert* apotheosizes the high culture of the home *Volksgemeinschaft* but also deliberately refunctionalizes it for war and, ultimately, consecrates it with a soldier's death in a church. *Wege* references this scene but also refigures it in a way revealing for the demobilization genre. Here the organ playing is a cultural luxury after the war, giving vent to a musical urge that had to be repressed—adamantly not, as in *Wunschkonzert*, fulfilled—during the fighting. This cultural indulgence in fact negotiates the way of the veterans into the small town, negotiates between the primary map of failed mobilization and militarization in the Hannover train station and the secondary map of the church, small town, and humble bridge rebuilding.

This reading of the primary and secondary maps—as well as their asso-ciation with metaphors of mobility and transportation technologies—is confirmed in an extended sequence about Peter, the clown of the three veterans. This sudden subplot, occurring at about fifty minutes into the film, lasts some five minutes in an eighty-minute film, but seems abruptly introduced as well as subsequently out of place. The most plausible interpretation, it seems to me, is one that emphasizes its deliberate repetitive symbols, namely, the train and the bomber. Once the three veterans are enjoying their country idyll, happily working on the bridge and Stefan falling in love with Edith, Lukas's secretary, an abrupt sequence intercedes that threatens their relocated and redirected camaraderie. The film cuts suddenly back to the train, this time to a meticulously clothed, carefully coiffed, and heavily made-up young woman who is completely unfamiliar to viewers. It turns out that she is bound for the same small town, in search of her long-lost boyfriend Peter, who gratefully hosts her in his rustic room and primitive bed, at which she, in her urbane tastes, cringes. She soon convinces Peter to leave his provincial work and friends and return to Hannover, and within the same day has him sitting back on the (now emphatically negatively coded) train. From this sudden development, however, the sequence rehearses an almost direct repetition of the earlier plot and spatial points: regretting his decision to abandon his friends and return to Hannover, Peter jumps from the train, leaves behind the promise of the city and abstract space it implies, and returns to the country to finish the work on the bridge. The repetition even includes, as it did in the montage sequence mentioned above, his passing an abandoned bomber on an airfield, but this time he walks right by without even hesitating and without having to be warned off it by the Allied authorities. Repetition and variance, as Raymond Bellour has observed, are a central part of filmic narrative's registering change and generating meaning, and the sequence rehearses the transition from the film's primary mapping in industrialized society to the secondary mapping in the country.[18] The variation within the repetition comes in Peter's willfully choosing it this time: he is not fleeing the train in desperation as they were in the original sequence, and he does not need to be convinced to stay away from military technology.

The sequence thus reiterates their conscious relocation on the secondary map of the countryside, but it also shows how desire and power has similarly been remapped in accordance with the emphatically geographical demobilization above. Peter's girlfriend Liselotte embodies, of course, the desire for that kind of sophisticated urbanity he has renounced in this subplot, so his subsequent desire is likewise rerouted through the secondary map of the film's cheerful country setting. He cedes his desire to remain with his friends and to finish the project they have undertaken for Lukas, much as the group of veterans cedes their modern military ways for the small town. Power is thereby likewise rerouted by the secondary map of the countryside: at the train station, Lukas seemed weak and ineffective, just another *Heimkehrer* limping across the postwar landscape, while in the small town he is mayor and benevolent patriarch to the young veterans. Although there is some unconvincing dramatic tension around Edith, his secretary in whom both he and Stefan have a romantic interest, the main trajectory of the plot is clear: moving the three veterans from the *Bahnhofsleben* in Hannover to the country allows them to reconcile to postwar society— and to return to life back in the German city. The film's excursion to the countryside—the narrative trajectory from a primary map of failed mobilization and militarization to a secondary map in the countryside that negates trains and planes in favor of horse-drawn wagons—ultimately allows a successful reentrance into society, namely, studying in Essen. It is a successful reentrance that is figured as a second, improved demobilization of the three comrades who have finally left their uniforms behind. The film's memorable closing image revisits and refigures, as the entire film has, the opening sequence in the train station: viewers see a long shot of the repaired bridge from down river, such that the degenerate train station is replaced with the wholesome infrastructure of the country.

In this very last shot of a film with "Wege" in the title, viewers do not see even any characters they recognize, just anonymous carriages and trucks crossing the bridge, as if to enforce that the entire filmic journey has indeed been about reforming the train station for the rural bridge, about the vagaries of postwar traffic.

Further Demobilization Remappings in the Junge Film-Union's Veteran Films

This kind of narrative remapping through traveling veterans—one that indulges the military's wartime imaginary while reforming it—structures two of the other films made by Rolf Meyer and the Junge Film-Union in this period. The two other films operate similarly, both in terms of their protagonists (veterans), their narrative trajectory (also involving travel and multiple narrative maps), and even parallel scenes of indulging but then swearing off the perceptual luxuries of transportation technologies made popular in the cinema of the Third Reich (as with the airplane and train in *Wege im Zwielicht*). *Die Söhne des Herrn Gaspary* focuses on two brothers who were separated before the war when their father, author of a book critical of the Nazis, fled with one of the boys to Switzerland. From there they had very different fates: Hans grew up wealthy, happy, and (as the film is careful to depict) skiing in Switzerland, while Günther remained in heavily bombed Hamburg, fighting in the war, and then landing in a POW camp. The secondary map here is that of Germany itself, which, over the course of the narrative, wins out over cosmopolitan, affluent, but ultimately soulless Switzerland, where the film starts and which offers many visually pleasurable scenes of driving and skiing among the mountains before ultimately turning on them.

After an opening sequence with the father Robert and his son Hans enjoying themselves on a drive after skiing—they even come across Christina, a Danish skier whom both brothers will pursue—father Robert brings his other son Günther and his estranged wife to the Swiss slopes for a reunion of the boys. But it becomes clear by the end of the film that this is a fantasy life in which there is no future for either of them. The contrast between the brothers corresponds to the topography of the film, to the contrast between Switzerland and Germany, a contrast drawn with repeated references to mobility and the war: Hans, the son from Switzerland, brags to Christina how much he has been able to travel with his father, an altogether different kind of cosmopolitanism than his brother, who viewers learn, in another sequence of repetition and variance, saw the world with the *Wehrmacht*, much as Confino describes.

The centrality of the air war to German wartime experience is confirmed by one of the film's most interesting scenes that references precisely this kind of distorted cosmopolitanism as well as, once again, the nexus of air power and perception that underpins *Wunschkonzert* and *Die große Liebe*. When the newly reunited family is relaxing on a ski lodge deck, they see some planes high above, and they hear an American debating a Frenchman about what kind of aircraft they are. Günther tries to intercede and correct them, but the American says—I should know what it is, I flew one, to which Günther retorts—Well, I shot many down. The American replies—Apparently not enough, and, anyway, the Germans started all the trouble. A tense exchange between an Allied soldier and former war adversary is rare for the rubble film, as is Günther's subsequent defense of the war,—We were only trying to live, we had the whole world against us, and now we have to listen while others shoot their mouths off. He rushes out and considers leaving Switzerland altogether. The scene is highly unusual on a couple counts, not least because it gives depoliticizing and dehistoricizing vent to the complaints of many veterans; it is also no accident, as I have been arguing throughout, that the disagreement focuses on air power, underscoring the centrality of air power to German military's self understanding and the discourse of suffering during the war.

In the end, the refigured complexities of Germany win out over Switzerland on all fronts. Narrative agency and power would seem to reside with the father, who has brought his estranged wife and their son to Switzerland. Their travels through the Swiss mountains offer the film the bulk of its visual pleasures. Robert, the father, has specific plans for the future. He has invited Günther to study in Switzerland—for which he will pay, just as he pays for this trip—so that he may study with his brother Hans. Completely inverting what viewers might expect from the adoring scenes of Swiss snow, however, Hans instead decides to join Günther back in Hamburg to study there and to found a typical postwar business: they sell the father's expensive car that Hans has driven there and buy a truck that will allow them to do commercial hauling. Even the woman torn between them, the Danish skier Christina, chooses the brooding German complexity of Günther over the Swiss levity of Hans. Both authority and desire are thereby filtered through the contrasting maps of the narrative, with narrative preference, as with Stefan in *Wege*, for the suffering but recovering veteran.

The suffering, angry veteran of Meyer's *Zugvögel* is Carl Raddatz, the actor who played the protagonist fighter pilot Herbert Koch of *Wunschkonzert*. Given the success of *Wunschkonzert* and the relatively advanced age of Raddatz for the role of a young veteran, casting him for the film's protagonist, Georg, must have been, at the least, conspicuous.

Like the films above, *Zugvögel* offers viewers a group of veterans wandering the countryside, here hitching rides on passing trucks, flirting with likewise wayward young women. In a new twist on Meyer's now familiar traveling trope, however, the foregrounded mode of transportation in *Zugvögel* (despite the aeronautical implication of its title) is aquatic, namely, kayaks. Wolfgang, a young veteran, leads two comrades and two women they have met to a hidden cache of kayaks intended for him and Georg, for whom he is still waiting. Whereas *Wege im Zwielicht* replaced the panoramic view of the train with adoring shots of the countryside and *Die Söhne* afforded, in contrast to ruined Hamburg, the pleasures of mountaintop travel and skiing, *Zugvögel*'s entire middle section offers viewers the nautical exploration of postwar Germany—a novel way to avoid the ubiquitous ruins and standing in stark contrast to, and seeming deliberately directed against, the urban industrial spectacles of the 1930s and 1940s. Given that the kayaks were hidden before the war from the bombing as aspects of school-age adventure and antimodernity, they too offer an alternative mode of transportation to that modernity that ended so unpleasantly in the war.

Paddling with his comrades in his kayak, Wolfgang pulls up alongside a ship at one point and finds Georg hidden in the shadows of the ship's hold, as if Raddatz had been held in POW abeyance since *Wunschkonzert*. Georg has just returned from the POW camp, depressed, brooding, and sickly. Although Georg is clearly delighted to see Wolfgang and joins their revived kayaking group, he continues to brood, including in his first night with the group, when, next to the obligatory bonfire, he sits by himself and then returns to the group to tell a harrowing (and presumably autobiographical) story about two prisoners who suffered endlessly in POW captivity. Slowly, though, both the beauty of the landscape seen from the kayaks and the attentions of a woman, Renee, in the group soften Georg. As in *Wege im Zwielicht*, the secondary mapping onto nature helps veterans heal such that they are ready to return to land and the postwar landscape of toil. The secondary map is not the German countryside as in *Wege*, nor the Swiss Alps in *Söhne*, but instead Germany's system of rivers and canals, a forgotten nature close at hand that allows them to evade the difficulties of landlocked lives for a final indulgence in prewar-like, leisurely travel. But as with the countryside in *Wege* and Switzerland in *Söhne*, the wayward veterans learn from the secondary map in order to eventually overcome it. On their aquatic adventure, the group slowly pairs off two by two such that they are ready to relinquish their kayaks to return to the shore.

The only casualty of this return from the film's second map is Georg himself. Unlike *Wege im Zwielicht* and *Söhne des Herrn Gaspary*, *Zugvögel* rejects a happy ending for the angry young veteran on whom it focuses. Georg, viewers learn, had some unnamed illness, but frustration and despair led him to flee the hospital prematurely. His newfound joy and love on the kayak trip lead him to seek out a doctor, who informs him he left the hospital perilously early. Eventually, Georg decides to give himself over to nature and paddles out to a watery death. Wolfgang aims to save him, but cannot paddle out after him due to a dramatic (and dramatically shot) storm. Wolfgang ends up with Renee, the women who had fallen in love with Georg. The receding secondary map once again reroutes desire and authority: Renee gives up her love for Georg for the humdrum but healthy Wolfgang, whereas power seems to rest with the doctor, who became, for the context in general, an important figure of social authority.

The Long Journey to a Rediscovered "Heimat"

In two long journal articles from 1948 about veterans' returning to Germany from POW camps (one entitled "Heimkehr der Kriegsgefangenen aus England," the other "Heimkehr aus russischer Gefangenschaft"), the authors emphasize the parallels between suffering in captivity and the challenges of returning home. Both articles foreground a key difficulty of returning from the war, namely, the finding of a "second" or "third" *Heimat* back in Germany upon arrival in what will be, in many ways, an unfamiliar environment.[19] One article admits that POW camps might have grown familiar, even in some sense comfortable, so returning to find a new *Heimat* would challenge those soldiers yet again. The articles are both concerned with the kind of mental remapping—the changes in space and psychologies as well as the intertwinements of those two—that would be required in the postwar period. In this essay, I have focused on a key reason for this rediscovery and remapping of a postwar *Heimat*: that Nazism, both in its cultural imaginary as well as military execution, relied not only on organized mobility, that is, military mobilization, but also on the mental geography such mobility and mobilization wrought.

These rubble films of the Junge Film-Union suggest that the impact of this mobilization had to be worked through in a demobilization that not only sent the soldiers home, but also required a recasting of the spatial relations that the Nazi culture industry had asserted in some of its most popular products. All three of these films follow a group of veterans on travels that provide the films with many of their visual pleasures. These travels negotiate multiple maps, that is, in all cases an initial space is undercut by a second mapping that relocates both desire and power from their primary mapping. The films, at their conclusions, settle on third spaces, on compromise spaces that negotiate between the films' primary and secondary mappings. None of the films goes very far in representing these third spaces: the films depict the (literal) journeys to those spaces, journeys that afford the films the opportunity to indulge the kind of narratives offered in the mobilization genre. The actual character of these third places, the ultimate rediscovery of the *Heimat* as these two articles suggest, is something left for later. As the very harsh reviews with which I started suggest these three films extend an important aspect of the Nazi imaginary, focusing on the travels to which viewers would have grown accustomed while leaving the precise character of the new *Heimat* for the 1950s.

Notes

1. E.R., "Trümmergrau und Leuchtfarben: *Wege im Zwielicht* (deutsch). Studio am Lehniner Platz", *Berliner Blatt* 68 (August 28, 1948).
2. See, for example, Robert Shandley, *Rubble Films: German Cinema in the Shadow of the Third Reich* (Philadelphia: Temple University Press, 2001).
3. See Eric Rentschler, *Ministry of Illusion* (Cambridge, MA: Harvard University Press, 1997).
4. I have in mind here the transfiguration of place of which Jameson writes, such that this new approach to space as cognitively mapped entails rethinking the nature of place: "We are given, in *North by Northwest*, a whole series or sequence of concrete spaces which are not too rapidly to be reduced to mere *places* [...] place and place name are only the starting points, the raw material, from which a rather different realization of concrete space is produced, which is no longer scene or backdrop for an action for actors, but includes those in some new, qualitative way. The vocation of these new space signs is often so imperious as to master the individual episodes and to transform each into the occasion for a qualitatively distinct production," Fredric Jameson, "Spatial Systems in North by Northwest," in *Everything You Always Wanted to Know about Lacan But Were Afraid to Ask Hitchcock*, ed. Slavoj Žižek (New York: Verso, 1992), pp.47–72, here p.50.
5. The main reference in this context is Fredric Jameson's *The Geopolitical Aesthetic: Cinema and Space in the World System* (Bloomington, IN: Indiana University Press, 1992) as well as Jameson's essay "Spatial Systems in North by Northwest."
6. It is important to keep in mind that the kind of wartime cognitive mapping I am emphasizing in *Wunschkonzert* and *Die große Liebe* was not unique to Germany, but was, without a doubt, an aspect of culture in all the nations in which mass mobilization was a cultural factor. *Wunschkonzert* und *Die große Liebe* are the most pertinent examples for Meyer's films, however, both because

of the immense popularity of those two films at a time when Hollywood films, for instance, were banned in Germany and because a film like *Wege im Zwielicht*, in a way I shall examine below, references the wartime popular films directly.

7. Alon Confino has written of the tourist aspects of German soldiering during World War II: Alon Confino, "Traveling as a Cultural Remembrance: Traces of National Socialism in West Germany, 1945–1960," *History and Memory* 12 (2000): 92–121. In the postwar period, Confino cites evidence that the Nazi years were remembered as a tourist heyday, confirming the intersection of soldiering for the Nazis and touring for one's own pleasure (p.102). The film *My private War* (*Mein Krieg*, directed by Harriet Eder and Thomas Kufus, 1990) offers documentary evidence of the importance of travel for the experience and memory of soldiers and veterans. At the end of the film, a number of veterans comment on how much they appreciated seeing foreign lands, even during wartime, and how much it meant to them to revisit places where they had been engaged in combat. I thank Wilfried Wilms for drawing my attention to this film and its links to these wartime popular entertainments.

8. James Diehl, *The Thanks of the Fatherland* (Chapel Hill, NC: University of North Carolina Press, 1993), p.46.

9. For a specific example, "Militarism und Soldatentum," *Süddeutsche Zeitung* 44 and then a follow-up piece "Noch einmal: Militarismus und Soldatentum," *Süddeutsche Zeitung* 59 (July 22, 1946),which returns to discuss the earlier piece because the paper had received so much mail pertaining to it. For an example of articles about former POWs and conditions in the camps, see Paul Herzog, "Heimkehr aus russischer Gefangenschaft," *Die Wandlung* 3.1 (1948): 71–79 and Hermann Sinsheimer, "Heimkehr der Kriegsgefangenen aus England," *Deutsche Rundschau* 71.6 (1948: 194–199). On the guilt question as it intersected militarism, see Helmut Lindemann, "Die Schuld Der Generäle," *Deutsche Rundschau* 75.1 (1949): 20–22 as well as Hermann von Müller, "Entartung Des Krieges," *Deutsche Rundschau* 75.9 (1949): 800–806.

10. Hermann Sinsheimer, "Heimkehr der Kriegsgefangenen aus England," p.194.

11. The film *My private War* (*Mein Krieg*) also confirms these very common experiences of train-station mobilization for German soldiers during World War II. The film's visual track is constituted primarily by amateur films shot by *Wehrmacht* soldiers, and a number of these amateur filmmakers-soldiers-shot sequences depicts families and friends on trains headed for the front.

12. Wolfgang Schivelbusch. *Railway Journey: The Industrialization of Time and Space in the 19th Century* (Berkeley, CA: University of California Press, 1977; 1986), p.174.

13. Henri Lefebvre, *The production of space*, translated by Donald Nicholson-Smith (Cambridge: Blackwell, 1991), p.49.

14. For a good overview of the debates, and anxiety, about nihilism after the war, see Stephen Brockmann, *German Literary Culture at the Zero Hour* (New York: Camden House, 2004).

15. This notion of a character coming up on a secret second map is crucial to the cognitive mapping that Jameson traces in *The Geopolitical Aesthetic*. See, for example, p.15 or p.33.

16. "How an essentially spatial medium like film could in any meaningful way be supplementarily described as being more or less spatial, as somehow significantly becoming spatialized (after having presumably once been less so) is a matter of great tact, but not at all, I think, meaningless nonsense." Jameson, *Geopolitical Aesthetic*, p.75.

17. Paul Virilio *War and Cinema: The Logistics of Perception* (New York: Verso, 1991), p.9.

18. Raymond Bellour, "The Obvious and the Code," in *Narrative, Apparatus, Ideology*, ed. Philip Rosen (New York: Columbia University Press, 1986), pp.98–99.

19. Herzog, "Heimkehr aus russischer Gefangenschaft," p.71 and Sinsheimer, "Heimkehr der Kriegsgefangenen aus England," p.196.

CHAPTER TWELVE
THE SOUND OF RUINS

Lutz Koepnick

Tullio Crali's famous 1939 painting "Nose Dive on City" shows a pilot as he steers his plane straight into a metropolitan landscape. True to Futurism's veneration of velocity and aviation, Crali pictures this approach as an experience of extreme intoxication, an ecstasy of visual perception that collapses stable frames of reference and fuses temporal and spatial dimensions into one single trajectory. While the city's buildings dramatically extend beyond the frame of the image and thus suggest a violent explosion of perspectival order, the cockpit of the plane itself no longer seems to function as a site protecting pilots from the intensity of speed and endowing them with omnipotent control over their plane's path through space. Note the plane's apparent absence of a roof, displacing any desire to use modern technology as a detached viewing apparatus able to offer framed impressions of the world below. The plane's metal bars enclosing front and side windows are painted in such a way that they bleed into the architectural structures of the city, indicative of a blurring of all distinctions between interior and exterior spaces, between a pilot's stillness in relation to his machinery and the flux of things rushing by.

"I feel my breast open like a great hole," Filippo Tommaso Marinetti wrote about the experience of flying in 1912, "and all the azure of the sky, smooth, cool, and torrential, / pours joyously in. / I am an open window, in love with the sun / and flying toward it!"[1] What we observe in Crali's painting gives new meaning to Marinetti's joy in merging with the primordial. Instead of merely exploding the confines of bourgeois subjectivity, carrying the subject beyond itself, and allowing for a union with the elements, aviation in Crali helps express a violent desire to liquidate the icons of modern civilization, to blast asunder what permits aviation in the first place. As represented on Crali's canvas, aerial warfare enables a mind-blowing fusion of body and machine, sight and motion, viewer and viewed. It transforms the pilot's body into a perception machine in search of the ultimate thrill. Body and plane here appear as each other's prosthesis, whereas plane and city emerge as a vortex-like unity. Human perception might thus be liberated from the body's inherent sluggishness and gravity. Yet as the current position of Crali's plane suggests, this kind of liberation culminates in nothing other than both the city's and the pilot's physical destruction. The transformation of the body into a high-speed perception machine defines death and destruction as a source of the most exhilarating stimulation. Aerial warfare, as depicted by Crali at the onset of World War II, energizes a new kind of technological sublime, one which seeks to erase all boundaries between frame, framer, and framed, and one in which art's desire for redemption goes hand in hand with the prospect of ruined cityscapes.

Though Crali hoped to define aerial warfare as a hallucinatory total work of art, his image remained tied to the limitations of its medium. It pictures the impact of speed onto our registers of visual and tactile perception, yet it of course excludes the sonic dimensions of a nose-dive, the overwhelming acoustics of a fighter plane racing toward, firing at, and ultimately crashing into a target at ground. Postwar cinema has sought to bridge this lacuna many times over, assaulting the viewer's ears with a multiplicity of shrill, high-pitched, whistling, and deafening sounds so as to impress the perceptual reality of aerial warfare onto the spectator's senses. But it is in Francis Ford Coppola's *Apocalypse Now* (1979), in the infamous scene depicting a U.S. raid on a Vietnamese village, that we can no doubt witness the most faithful translation of Crali's vision into the language of film. Coppola might replace the exhilarating speed of Crali's fighter plane with the relative slowness of a helicopter squadron; urban density with the impenetrability of the jungle; the dash of a deadly nose-dive with the choreography of air attack and ground landing. The scene's aim, however, is nothing other than to present the ruining of terrestrial targets as an experience of intoxication, a blurring of perceptual registers that is no different than the high produced by certain drug uses. For Lieutenant Colonel Bill Kilgore (Robert Duvall) and the members of his Ninth Air Cavalry, aerial warfare is nothing less than a total work of art. It mobilizes perception in unprecedented ways, it intoxicates the senses with feelings of perceptual omnipotence, and—whether it results in the rapturous shooting of civilians from above or in exhilarating surfing opportunities amid flying bullets—it carries the subject beyond the stultifying orders of the everyday. Coppola's cinematography, editing, and sound choreography pulls all the stops of cinematic artistry in order to both allow the viewer to see the world through Kilgore's eyes and mark the Colonel's transformation of aerial warfare into a spectacle as utterly perverse. And needless to say, it is the diegetic use of Richard Wagner's "Ride of the Valkyrie," that is, Kilgore's blasting of German opera through the attached loudspeakers of his helicopter gunship, that here is meant to offer an immediately recognizable sign for the Colonel's deranged megalomania. Intermixed with the sounds of spinning rotor blades, firing machine guns, and target hits, Wagner's music—on a narrative level—functions like a drug for the members of the Ninth Air Cavalry as much as it is meant to scare to death the villagers, to knock out their senses even before they will be hit by bullets and rockets from above. On a metanarrative level, by contrast, the purpose of these sounds is to engage the viewer in a rather remarkable kind of triangulation, namely, to draw direct lines between Wagner's aesthetic visions and practices, the Nazi use of Wagner as a mouthpiece of chauvinistic politics, and the neocolonial craze of air raiding remote villages with the most advanced tools of destruction. Aerial warfare is Wagner with other means. Kilgore's men project what is violent about nineteenth-century German music onto the targets of U.S. imperialism. Their bullets and rockets are meant to be as ruinous as Wagner's attempt to unify sensory experience in one grand operatic spectacle.

Coppola's use of Wagner as both a sign and a catalyst of destructive obsessions drew on a well-established tradition in postwar Hollywood cinema that had identified key pieces of the composer's music as quasi-automatic referents for megalomaniac violence, for what drives people beyond themselves and causes them—like Coppola's flying gunship soldiers—to wreak havoc from seemingly detached and supercilious positions. Though Wagner's compositional techniques had been essential in the development of the classical Hollywood film score in the 1930s and 1940s, after the end of World War II his music—with the exception of the "Wedding March" from *Lohengrin*—came to underscore scenes of radical evil, paranoid delusion, and perverse self-redemption. Whether it emanated from diegetic sources or from the nondiegetic soundtrack, Wagner's music after Hitler signified a fascistic undermining of humanistic values as the foundation of bourgeois individualism and liberal democracy. Think, for instance, of a harrowing scene in Edward Dmytryck's 1958 *The Young Lions*. When the idealistic German officer Christian Diestl, played by a strikingly blond Marlon Brando, at some point toward the end of World War II visits the home front, all he finds is a more or less deserted landscape of rubbles—a vast field of ruined houses produced by Allied aerial bombing attacks. The camera first tracks Diestl's walk through the ruins from a considerable distance, so distant that we focus our gaze much more on the figure of a little boy in the foreground than the shape of the officer in the far. Before long, however, the camera cuts closer to Diestl, his head turning left and right as if in search for something hidden amid the ruins. When he finally looks toward the camera and the camera cuts back to a medium shot of the boy, we are to understand that Diestl's own gaze has momentarily come to rest on the boy's body in the foreground. In a protracted and quite painful shot, we see the boy—his arm resting on crutches in order to compensate for a missing leg—desperately trying to climb over a wooden pole that blocks his way. After a few seconds we cut to a somewhat longer shot showing both the boy as he is trying to scoot his body over the pole and Diestl as he observes the boy from his position in the background, clearly not willing to help out in any way whatsoever. Finally, Diestl walks up to the boy, yet instead of lending a hand or speaking a word he greets him with a military salute, not rigidly, but nevertheless quite inappropriately. Throughout the entire scene, we hear motifs from the "Funeral March" of Wagner's *Götterdämmerung*, at times modulated into a gloomy minor key, at times stretched out into a prolonged layering of violin and percussion sounds. The music's point cannot be mistaken: instead of heroizing the agents of war and destruction, Wagner here is to bespeak the self-destructive aspects of the Nazi cult of heroism and warfare as well as the cold antihumanism of self-declared superhumans such as Diestl. Wagner, the scene suggests, is what drove Germans to attack other nations in the name of national superiority, and a cynical twilight of the gods—a total ruin of any moral compass—is what Germans in the end inflicted upon themselves as a result of their quest for total dominance. The ruins we see are Wagner's ruins—a product of nineteenth-century excess and megalomania—as much as they show Wagner in ruin—evidence of German nationalism after its violent self-annihilation.

Postwar cinema abounds with scenes in which Wagnerian soundtracks engage the viewer in a curious process of historical triangulation, asking us to understand the ruins of aerial warfare—whether on German ground or elsewhere—as a consequence of and penalty for what we might want to call with Walter Benjamin aesthetic politics, that is, the remaking of political action into an aesthetic experience. Though the ruins themselves may strike the viewer as utterly void of meaning, Wagnerian tones infuse such images with complex historical memories and moral messages. Understood as a direct translation of aesthetic form into a language of domination and destruction, Wagner's music signifies a spilling of affect and spectacle into the political whose violent transgression is to be recontained by an aesthetic of modesty and self-restraint, a discriminating handling of sights and sounds that is to reestablish the ground for moral accountability and communal integration. Instead of manipulating our emotions and hitting the listener over the head, this aesthetic wants to index the ruinous effects of Wagnerian total art within formal arrangements that allow simultaneously for affect and distance, emotion and critical cognition. Wagner may have aimed at fusing sound and sight into one encompassing experience defying—like Crali's pilot—existing borders and frames. The prevalent use of Wagnerian soundtracks in postwar cinema, however, seeks to frame and reframe the master's music and aesthetic visions from the standpoint of a semi-Brechtian, albeit often quite ambivalent, aesthetic of interruption and distanciation, of juxtaposing image and sound so as to complicate the viewer's affective response. In films such as *The Young Lions*, the sight of the ruined city not only reveals what is ruinous about Wagner and his twentieth-century legacy, it also suspends the Wagnerian foundations of classical narrative film, the way in which Hollywood cinema is virtually unthinkable without its Wagnerian fusion of sound and image into seamless unity. To see cities in ruins while hearing the "Funeral March" here is to witness the self-destruction of operatic nationalism as much as it is to recognize a profound crisis of classical cinema itself, of Hollywood's desire to translate the nineteenth-century total work of art into a template of twentieth-century popular entertainment. To see the rubbles of Berlin cannot but draw our attention to the ruins of Hollywood as well.

*   *   *

Hanns Eisler once noted that music is "*par excellence* the medium in which irrationality can be practiced rationally."[2] Music today, he added with his eyes on the practices of the commercial amusement industry, relies on highly scientific and managerial considerations so as to exploit people's emotions most effectively. In mainstream postwar cinema, the use of Wagnerian music as an atmospheric backdrop to images of aerial warfare and destruction, seems to run counter to Eisler's ruminations. Wagner's compositions, in particular recurrent motifs of *Götterdämmerung*, highlight what is irrational about German music and culture. Rather than invite the viewer to indulge in excessive emotions and to embrace the ruins of war as a spellbinding site of the sublime, the function of the Wagnerian soundtrack is to lodge reason and enlightenment—a rationalist discourse on political madness and just retribution—in the viewer's very affective response to the film. Music here becomes the medium in which we, to stay within the bounds of Eisler's dichotomy, can practice rationality in irrational ways, namely, detach our emotions from how the Wagnerian undertones of Nazi warfare allowed the irrational to radiate triumphant. It exposes to view what is irrational about the transformation of the political into a total artwork, and it allows the viewer to draw firm lines between the Wagnerian affects of war perpetrators—be they idealistic Nazi officers or deranged air cavalarists—and our own emotional investments into the medium of film.

But how do ruins sound when seen and experienced, not through the perceptual registers of those dropping bombs from the air and being responsible for mass destruction, but through the eyes of those trying to make do with the rubble? What musical means does postwar cinema choose in order to orchestrate the plight of those shocked and awed by the leveling force of aerial warfare and damage?

As is well known, German postwar cinema literally emerged from the rubble, the very first feature film after the war—Wolfgang Staudte's, *The Murderers Are among Us* (1946)—commencing with a shot in which the camera slowly ascends from a grave so as to show us an image of a devastated street in Berlin. As it gains altitude, the camera's canted angle is reminiscent of the stylized cinematography of Expressionist cinema. What we get to see in this very first shot of German postwar cinema, however, has little to do with the exaggerated shapes and aesthetic distortions of Weimar film: a street flanked by the shells of ruined tenement buildings; a man in black coat and hat approaching the camera as if directly transplanted to Berlin from a contemporary American film noir; a destroyed tank in the midground, a cross erected on top of one of the two makeshift graves in the immediate foreground. As the man approaches the viewer, the camera will pan to the left in order to track his lonesome walk, first revealing the sight of some kids who play in a dirty puddle and then—following the man's gaze—the sign of an entertainment place promising "Tanz · Stimmung · Humor" (dance, atmosphere, humor). Though this dance bar seems to attract a joyous crowd, our wanderer remains unaffected. His face communicates aloofness and disdain, while the detached movements of his body express the profound disorientation of a man shell-shocked by the experience of war, of something that denies the very ground of experience and renders the individual silent. The film's soundtrack strangely adds to the man's strangeness, for what we hear— from the very first image appearing on screen—is not a mourning orchestral score or the eerie sounds of some atonal modernist composition, but rather the barely tolerable clatter of honky-tonk music, a musical idiom clearly coded "American." Though the final seconds of this first shot identify this music to be diegetic, that is, as emanating from the dance bar, in the very beginning of the shot we cannot but consider it as extradiegetic. As it reemerges from the rubbles of aerial bombing, postwar German cinema thus immediately confronts the viewer with a dual destabilization of the cinematic frame, a questioning of the integrity and closure of diegetic space. Similar to how the camera's canted angle draws our awareness to the act of filmmaking itself, the film's soundtrack—in diegeticizing and hence embodying what at first appears to be nondiegetic and void of embodiment—asks the viewer to traverse spatial demarcations and fundamentally to distrust the framing power of the cinematic image. Already utterly out of place within the narrative space itself, the soundtrack's lighthearted honky-tonk music produces a profound sense of displacement in the spectator as well. It situates and suspends our act of viewing in a rather undefined location in between narrative and extranarrative space, a perceptual nonplace, and in doing so it questions cinema's ability to frame reliable views and transparent windows onto the real. To live among ruins is to live in a world in which the visual and the auditory no longer add up to a whole anymore. It is to inhabit a present in whose context the dream of perceptual synthesis—that telos of Wagner's operatic visions, of Crali's nosedive, of Kilgore's aerial attack—has come to naught.

Disjunctive soundtracks such as the one in *The Murderers Are among Us* occupy a prominent position in postwar filmmaking in order to encode the trauma of those who outlived the firestorms of aerial warfare. Rattling at the autarky of the cinematic frame, the juxtaposition of sights and sounds came to represent the fragmented and numbed perception of those shell-shocked by the violence of warfare, as much as it provided a means to withstand picturing ruins, neoromantically as it were, as a site of the sublime, a sight that overwhelmed the subject with a devastating, albeit fascinating, kind of beauty. Think, firstly, of Roberto Rossellini's *Germania Anno Zero* (1948), tracking the fate of young Edmund Köhler amid the rubbles of postwar Berlin. The film begins with passing images of urban ruins and will eventually show the shambles of the Berlin Reichstag building, including the skeleton of its completely devastated cupola. Urgent symphonic music emanates from the soundtrack, yet this score—in the spirit of Rossellini's neorealist stance—is directly pushed into the acoustical background by the presence of a sober voiceover detailing the quandaries of ordinary families as they try to make a living in the debris of the present. In allowing nondiegetic music and voices to guide our paths to the diegetic space of Berlin ruins, Rossellini at once stirs and restrains the viewer's affect. Similar to a later scene, in which we witness Edmund playing a recording of Hitler's voice to British souvenir hunters while the camera eerily pans across the bombed-out rooftops of Berlin tenement buildings, in the opening of the film too Rossellini, by severing sounds from their sources and transgressing the boundary between the diegetic and the nondiegetic, engineers a cinematic uncanny—a language of audiovisual disruption that unsettles the viewer and displaces any desire to consume the sight of ruins as objects of aesthetic pleasure and pure melodramatic intensity.

Think, secondly, of the disturbing combination of historical newsreel footage, enacted material, and nineteenth-century piano music in Helma Sanders-Brahms's *Germany, Pale Mother* (1979). In a rather remarkable scene, Sanders-Brahms uses aerial footage of Berlin as shot right after the end of the war, the camera somewhat shaky due to the plane's unsteady course, the colors rather faded due to the appropriation of older film stock. Throughout this prolonged shot, we hear pensive piano music evoking feelings of loss, renunciation, and unspeakable mourning. Suddenly, however, we cut to an enacted shot showing a man playing on a dilapidated piano in some unidentified exterior setting. Because the piano's legs are missing, the man sits on the floor in order to work the keyboard in what is an image of both tragic and comic proportions. Initially, he seems to continue the music of the nondiegetic soundtrack, yet before long his play turns into meaningless tinkling, a childish hammering generating what amounts to no more than cacophonic sounds. Whereas in other sequences of the film, shot/countershot techniques stitch historical material into the fictional world and thus produce a rather hybrid visual aesthetic, what we encounter in this particular scene is a disjunct and dysfunctional acoustical countershot. The postwar landscape of ruins here not only—as in Staudte and Rossellini—disrupts classical film's utopian harmony of images and sounds, it also demolishes both the visual and the acoustical from within their respective domains. Nothing here wants to add up to a unified whole anymore, nothing invites for unproblematic acts of melodramatic identification, because the ruins of aerial warfare have corrupted our belief in the power of images as much they have disfigured the melos that once absorbed viewers into totalizing spectacles of affective identification.

Staudte, Rossellini, Sanders-Brahms: no matter how different their narrative arrangements and stylistic preferences, what their work shares is the view of aerial warfare and destruction as an injunction against any highflying aesthetic of audiovisual synthesis, against an aesthetic trying to liquefy the boundaries of art and presenting war as a sublime event of first rank. As they, in different ways indeed, mobilize their film's sound and image tracks against each other, these directors pursue nothing other than to explode into atomized parts—into ruins—the legacy of Wagner's vision of the total work of art. The ruins of World War II, in this kind of work, not only embody the fateful outcome of nineteenth-century aesthetic excess and twentieth-century political megalomania, but they allegorize the very need to turn Wagner's project of the total work of art—the rational practice of advanced irrationality—into a pile of ruins. To recognize the traumas and trepidations of those subjected to aerial bombing and destruction is to renounce the nineteenth-century hopes for aesthetic synthesis; to blast asunder the Wagnerian legacy is to wrest hope and passion away from those who sought to mobilize passion and hope for the project of total warfare. What is disjunctive about the way in which directors such as Staudte, Rossellini and Sanders-Brahms capture the ruins of Berlin, then, aspires to nothing less than to give form to the catastrophe of an age in which both the beautiful and the sublime have lost their validity, a postwar age in which the task of the aesthetic has been reduced to recording negatively its own limitation and impossibility. What may look and sound idiosyncratic in this kind of work is nothing other than the attempt to recognize the very powers that have ruined what is individual and idiosyncratic in the name of aesthetic totalization. Music here emerges as a medium keenly trying to contain its own irrationality as much as to keep in check the affective intensities of the visual. To hear the sound of ruins is to experience what denies any hope for experiencing perceptual synthesis; it attests to the fact that sound and image no longer add up to a whole anymore, as much as it communicates the impossibility of thinking of the acoustical or the visual as autonomous and unified realms of signification. The ruinous split that severs sound from sight goes right through the domain of hearing and the field of seeing itself.

* * *

And, then, there is of course the case of Werner Herzog, the enfant terrible of postwar German cinema, never hesitant to provoke prevailing codes of political and aesthetic correctness, ever eager to realize his seemingly eccentric artistic visions, and persistently refusing to contain our desire for the aesthetic or the sublime even in face of the most horrendous catastrophes. In one of his early essay films, *La Soufrière* (1977), Herzog visits the evacuated town of Basse Terre on the Caribbean island of Guadeloupe, a town threatened by annihilation due to the imminent explosion of the island's volcano La Soufrière. In this thirty minute feature, we see Herzog roaming through the town's deserted streets, capturing human habitats in anticipation of their pending wreckage, but also searching for a few individuals who resist the evacuation order and hold out in spite of the looming catastrophe. Herzog's voiceover and images present Basse Terre simultaneously as uncanny and as bordering the sublime: a town in whose streets nature takes over again, displaces the structures of civilizational activity, and thus engenders a curious return of something that seemed long forgotten; a town, also, in which the threat of destruction dwarfs any remaining human presence and allows Herzog (and the viewer) humbly to recognize our own frailty and smallness. But the true hero of Herzog's tale is no doubt the volcano itself: nature gone wild, preparing to inundate Basse Terre like a bomber squadron in a devastating wave of fire and ashes. And it is Richard Wagner's music—all-too-familiar sections of the *Götterdämmerung*'s "Funeral March" and of the prelude of *Parsifal*—that we repeatedly hear from the soundtrack whenever we see images of smoke emanating from the mountain's crevasses or of the volcano at large as shot from a small aircraft. In light of the ruinous tradition of Wagnerian soundtracks sketched out in the preceding papers, the use of Wagner in this film is clearly puzzling and provocative. Why Wagner? Doesn't Herzog, in scoring scenes of looming natural disaster with the German composer's at once redemptive and disastrous sounds, aestheticize catastrophe and anestheticize our perception thereof? Doesn't Herzog, in capturing the natural history of destruction as a sublime spectacle of first rank, return us to whatever postwar cinema sought to undo, namely, a kind of aesthetics that knows of no boundary between the frame, the framed, and the framer and hence celebrates—like Crali, like Kilgore—the production of ruins as a Wagnerian total work of art?

Herzog, clearly, is and has never been a director holding up the flag of the unfinished project of the Enlightenment and allowing moralizing agendas to contain the parameters of his aesthetic visions. His understanding of what twentieth-century culture inherited from nineteenth-century opera no doubt differs from Alexander Kluge's modernist dismantling of the operatic and the melodramatic, summarized in Kluge's well-known pronouncement that "in every opera that deals with redemption a woman is sacrificed in the fifth act."[3] In contrast to the dispassionate rationalist Kluge, Herzog seeks to trade in grand melos, in gestures of sacrifice, and the futility of redemption, even in face of the most ghastly ruins left by man-made and natural disasters. Herzog's films are driven by negative theology: wreckage and destruction, a grisly entropy of meaning, is what the course of time is all about. To live amid ruins is our normal state of affairs; to elude what could help us transcend the permanent catastrophe of our present is the most basic condition of modern existence; and to take stock of what might ultimately destroy us is the only moral stance we can hope for in our otherwise amoral and agonistic universe. So why this need, one might ask, to even dramatize (or aestheticize, as most of his critics lambaste) the sight of pending disasters and ruins? Why evoke the affective baggage of nineteenth-century German opera and its overdetermined grasp for the redemptive when screening scenes of twentieth-century destruction? Why the prelude of Wagner's *Parsifal*—this fanfare of innocence, purity, and redemption—when framing images of the uncontained power of disaster?

In 1991, Herzog visited the burning oilfields in Kuwait after the military operations of Gulf War I had ceased earlier that same year. He and his film team captured devastating footage of raging oil fires amid the forsaken landscape of the desert; of highly trained specialists trying to contain the fires like heroes of ancient myths; of Kuwaitis who had been tortured or experienced painful losses during the war and now no longer appear able to find words to articulate their desolation. The resulting film, *Lessons of Darkness*, premiered at the Berlin Film Festival in February 1992, unnerving viewers and critics alike with its at once distanced and spectacular images of the postwar inferno as well as with its emotionally manipulative and overwhelming soundtrack, the amalgamation of Grieg, Mahler, Prokofiev, Schubert, Verdi, and—of course—Wagner into a sweeping requiem. Once again, the opening bars of the prelude of *Parsifal* and Siegfried's funeral music from *Götterdämmerung* take center stage, in particular during sequences in which we look down on burning fires from an aerial perspective and thus seem to assume some kind of visual mastery, a safe distance transforming Kuwait's disaster into a stunning spectatorial experience. This striking discrepancy between image and sound—the citing of Wagner's redemptive *Parsifal* while showing scenes of apocalyptic doom—has caused scholars such as Roger Hillman to reproach Herzog for transforming postwar Kuwait into his own private Bayreuth, for obscuring political realities for apolitical purposes, and for thus replaying the agendas of no one less than Leni Riefenstahl.[4] Accordingly, Herzog's quest is to transform the ruins of modern warfare into a new kind of total work of art. Herzog cites Wagner so as to aestheticize the political and hence replay the way in which CNN and other news media during the actual combat period allowed viewers across the world to take on the perspective of frontline combatants and, in fact, of the very machineries of destruction.

The discontent of Hillman and other critics is no doubt understandable. Herzog's use of Wagner in Kuwait is clearly troubling and provocative; it breaks certain representational taboos and addresses the viewer in ways most of us would like not to be addressed. What we expect is a modernist aesthetic of disruption and emotional restraint; a filmic language tactfully expressing mourning, loss, and melancholia, yet keeping in check the filmmaker's own subjectivity. What we get instead is grand opera indeed: a choreography of sights and sounds that will unsettle our affects and sweep us off our feet. What we get is a potent requiem in which Herzog's negative theology appears finally to come full circle and bonds our perception to images and sounds of utter destruction, that is, encourages us to understand the sublime beauty of catastrophe and ruinous disaster as the sole source of meaning in an otherwise meaningless world. Does it, though?

In contrast to the work of Staudte, Rossellini, and Sanders-Brahms, Herzog's audiovisual aesthetic in *Lessons of Darkness* is clearly driven by the assumption that affect and style are of utter importance in any attempt of coming to terms with traumatic experiences. Rather than embracing a modernist aesthetic of montage and interruption, which would allow the viewer to work through individual loss and collective devastation, Herzog wants us to reconnect to, or in fact relive, past traumas, not in order to embark on a masochistically entertaining ride through hell on earth, but in order to partake of a reciprocal process of projection. We are to absorb scenes of disasters with the affective registers of our own bodies as much as the ruins of history are supposed to take us in and help us play out our unsettled emotional economy. Yet in doing so, Herzog's intention is not to make us empathize and hence identify with what threatens to destroy us. Nor is it, by means of allusions to the aesthetic tradition of the sublime, to bestow the viewer with illusions of mastering histories of destruction, to situate us like pilots high above the grounds of past and present devastation. Instead, like *Parsifal* itself, Herzog's aesthetic rests on the assumption that recovery from acute trauma is a homeopathic process, one in which the subject needs to take in controlled doses of what afflicted the body in the first place so as to learn how to move beyond suffering by learning how to move with it.[5] Only the spear that cut the wound can also heal it. If much of German filmmaking in the postwar period, in particular during the heyday of New German Cinema in the 1960s and 1970s, was energized by an injunction to compensate for German society's proverbial inability to mourn, Herzog's homeopathic use of Wagner departs from the critical models of mourning and melancholia as the master tropes of approaching traumatic pasts. His aim is not to master the unmasterable through affective distance and cognitive reflexivity, but to expose our senses to what overtly or secretly troubles our minds and continues to cause displeasure. We may quarrel about the dose of poison necessary to outpoison the remnants of a poisonous past. But to think of Herzog's aesthetic as apolitical, or even worse, as a replay of Riefenstahl's rhetoric of visual mastery and omnipotence, completely misses the point. To listen to *Parsifal* while seeing images of ruins, for Herzog, is to learn how to live and keep moving in face of the ubiquity of disaster. It is to learn how to abandon moralizing gestures of distance and mastery in the hope of overcoming the kind of melancholic self-lacerations that have characterized much of postwar discourse. Unlike Coppola's Kilgore, Herzog is far from considering war theaters such as Kuwait or Vietnam as his own private Bayreuth, yet unlike Staudte, Rossellini, and Sanders-Brahms, Herzog is also far from believing that an anti-Wagnerian aesthetics of montage and affective interruption can be of much help to come to grips with catastrophic events.

The sights and sounds of ruins fascinate in his films, not because they represent the ultimate futility of all human endeavors, but because Herzog wants us to employ our sense of fascination to explode the kind of melancholia associated with traumatic fixations. Herzog's lesson of darkness is that we can only move beyond the case of Wagner, that is, beyond the deadly conflation of the political and the aesthetic in modern culture, if we first move through Wagner's music. Whether he exposes us to smoking volcanoes or burning oil fires, Herzog's aesthetics of ruins is driven by the assumption that we—to recall Nietzsche's famous diatribe— must first be Wagnerites, and hence take in catastrophic history and modernity in concentrated form, before we can cure ourselves from what is diseased and destructive about any notion of redemptive total art.[6]

In a brief segment of Kluge's 1983 *The Power of Emotions*, we follow a firefighter to the prop room of a Halberstadt theater during the massive air raid on Kluge's home town in April 1945. Normally kept from seeing the apparatus that makes grand opera possible, the firefighter seizes the moment in order to take a look at what has always fascinated him when being in the audience: the chalice used in the staging of *Parsifal* to represent the most redemptive of all objects, the grail. While the fires of the raid rage all around him, the firefighter takes hold of this container, removes its cover—and, to his utter surprise, finds the goblet to be empty. Wagner's promise of redemption, he must learn, was fake; it triggered hopes and emotions that turn out to be as ruinous as the bombs dropped on the city of Halberstadt. Ever eager to render visible what is behind the sheen of the world of opera, Kluge makes use of a mismatched musical soundtrack in order to score this scene of disillusionment. As if this already quite stagy scene needed additional devices to prevent the spectator from being absorbed into the film's diegetic world, Kluge sets the firefighters' quest for Wagner's grail, not to music of Wagner's *Parsifal* itself, but to Sibelius's *Four Legends*. The British air raids may finally explode into pieces what has always been corrupt about Wagner's vision of total art, but the master's music appears to be still so seductive that it must be evacuated from the film in order to do justice to the firefighter's disappointment. The refusal to play Wagner amid the ruins of World War II here aspires nothing less than to redeem the viewer from Wagner's phony staging of redemption, from the total work of art's promise to restore sensory synthesis and displace politics with aesthetics.

Herzog's universe has no such redemption to spare. The dead here are really dead, and neither survivors nor viewers can ever afford to think they could master the traumas and ruins of the past. Herzog's grail is as empty as Kluge's goblet of fire, yet unlike Kluge's fire marshal, Herzog's protagonists and spectators know all along that modern history rests on a deadly conflation of the redemptive and the ruinous. To consider Herzog's Wagnerian soundtracks as a neoromantic grasp for the guttural, the primal, and the immediate strangely overlooks the way in which Herzog's negative theology is itself historically mediated. Whether he conjures images of deadly volcanoes in the Caribbean or of burning oil fires in Kuwait, Herzog's Wagnerian soundtracks draw our awareness to the extent to which we need to see these ruins of history as afterimages and aftersounds of the catastrophe of World War II, the destruction of German cityscapes as a last ditch effort to contain the totalitarian quest of Nazi warfare. Herzog's simultaneous quest for the sublime, apocalyptic, and elegiac rewrites the aesthetics of ruins so commonplace in films of the immediate postwar era, not in order to aestheticize past or present destruction, but on the contrary, to shed light on what the dominant discourse of the postwar era rendered invisible and mute: the sights and sounds of those subjected to the destructions of warfare and aerial bombing. Read against the filmic iconography of postwar German ruins, Herzog's films—precisely because they cannot stop picturing ruins around the globe—indeed have some lessons to offer, namely, that we are mistaken to think that histories of destruction necessitate a minimalist aesthetic in order to be cast into politically sensitive representations; that we are wrong to privilege quasi-modernist and self-effacing artistic strategies as the exclusive mode of recollecting the apocalypses of twentieth-century German history.

In one of the most memorable scenes of *Lessons of Darkness*, Herzog interviews a Kuwaiti woman, her young son on her arm, about her family's war experience. "Even the tears were black," we hear Herzog's voiceover translating the woman's words, "when my child wept, his tears were black. When his nose ran, it ran black. Even the spit in his mouth was black." After thus describing the devastating effects of the oil fires on the civilian population, the woman then moves on to recall a raid by Iraqi soldiers who invaded their house and trampled her, her husband, and the son with their feet. "Look at this little fellow here," she concludes her harrowing narrative while the camera provides a two-shot close-up of mother and son, "he has not spoken a word since." Throughout this scene, Herzog's voiceover translates the woman's account into German (or English in the American release), even though we continue to hear her speak and hear the interpreter ask his questions. Rather than to appropriate and thus erase her voice, Herzog simultaneously reiterates and reframes her attempt to recollect a traumatic past, a past that refuses to be remembered. Herzog's strategy here seems to be to engage the viewer in a process of resituating and revisioning the symptomatic expressions of historical traumas. His aim is neither simply to have the woman reenact nor to show mastery over traumatic residues. Instead, by retelling the trauma of war and violence, by layering different voices on top of each other, Herzog aspires to move beyond traumatic ruptures without glossing over their lasting scars; to restructure the narratives about the war so as to change their symptomologies. As in many of his other essay films, Herzog during this scene simply allows his camera to keep running, not in order to subject the speaker to the authority of the camera's cold gaze, but to allow her to assimilate to the presence of the apparatus, to create space and time for unscripted acts of articulation, and hence to enable her to recall and utter things that otherwise might have remained unspoken. What makes this scenes so effective as a model of resituating traumatic events is not least of all based on the sudden absence of Herzog's earlier dominating musical soundtrack. Reminiscent of the way in which the arrival of synchronized sound around 1930 allowed, for the first time, to articulate silence in film, Herzog uses the seemingly hypnotic power of Wagnerian music to amplify the kind of silence from which the victim's voice struggles to reemerge. We all need to become Wagnerites first in order to move beyond the ruins that Wagner's desire for redemption, his megalomaniac vision of perceptual synthesis and aesthetic totality, has scattered across the globe. For to be such a Wagnerite means to recognize the silence that now rests at the very heart of the composer's bombastic musical idiom. It means to delineate a however limited and fragile space in which the individual's voice may find traction again and—precisely in abandoning all further hopes for redemption—speaks over the war's black tears, war's transformation of the natural and the man-made world into a site of apocalyptic doom. To move, homeopathically, with Wagner beyond Wagner is to recognize that, in the face of the rubble of modern aerial warfare, we have been given hope and language only for the sake of the hopeless, for the sake of the ones whose language is in ruins.

Notes

1. Filippo Tommaso Marinetti, *Selected Poems and Related Prose*, ed. Luce Marinetti, trans. Elizabeth Napier and Barbara Studholme (New Haven, CT: Yale University Press, 2002), p.43.
2. Hans Eisler, *Composing for the Films* (London: Dennis Dobson, 1947), p.70.
3. Alexander Kluge, *Die Macht der Gefühle* (Frankfurt am Main: Zweitausendeins, 1984), p.68.
4. Roger Hillman, *Unsettling Scores: German Film, Music, and Ideology* (Bloomington, IN: Indiana University Press, 2005), pp.146–150.
5. For more on the homeopathic in German cinema, see Eric L. Santner, *Stranded Objects: Mourning, Memory, and Film in Postwar Germany* (Ithaca, NY: Cornell University Press, 1990), pp.19–26; and Caryl Flinn, *The New German Cinema: Music, History, and the Matter of Style* (Berkeley, CA: University of California Press, 2004), pp.1–25.

6. "Through Wagner modernity speaks her most intimate language: it conceals neither its good nor its evil; it has thrown off all shame. And, conversely, one has almost calculated the whole of the value of modernity once one is clear concerning what is good and evil in Wagner, I can perfectly well understand a musician of to-day who says: 'I hate Wagner but I can endure no other music.' But I should also understand a philosopher who said: 'Wagner is modernity in concentrated form.' There is no help for it, we must first be Wagnerites..." Friedrich Nietzsche, *The Case of Wagner*, in *The Complete Works of Friedrich Nietzsche*, ed. and trans. Oscar Levy (New York: Russell & Russell, 1964), vol. 8, p.xxxi.

BIBLIOGRAPHY

Adorno, Theodor (1974 and 2005): *Minima Moralia: Reflections on a Damaged Life*, trans. E. F. N. Jephcott (London and New York: Verso).

—— (1985): "On the Question: 'What Is German?'" *New German Critique* 36., (trans. Thomas Y. Levin): 121–131.

Anderson, Benedict (1991): *Imagined Communities: Reflections on the Origins and Spread of Nationalism* (London: Verso).

Andreas-Friedrich, Ruth (1986): *Der Schattenmann. Tagebuchaufzeichnungen 1938–1945.* Nachwort Jörg Drews (Frankfurt am Main: Suhrkamp).

Arendt, Hannah (1958): *The Human Condition* (Chicago: University of Chicago Press).

Ariès, Phillipe (1976): *Western Attitudes toward Death: From the Middle Ages to the Present* (London: Marion Boyars).

Asper, Helmut G. (2000): "Zurück aus Hollywood. Fritz Kortner und sein Film 'Der Ruf,'" *Film-Dienst* 23: 52–55.

Bach, Steven (1992): *Marlene Dietrich: Life and Legend* (New York: Morrow).

Bark, Dennis L. and David R. Gress (1989): *A History of West Germany*, vol. 1, *From Shadow to Substance, 1945–1963* (Oxford: Basil Blackwell).

Barnouw, Dagmar (1996): *Germany 1945: Views of War and Violence* (Bloomington, IN: Indiana University Press).

Barthel, Manfred (1986): *So war es wirklich: Der deutsche Nachkriegsfilm* (Munich: Herbig).

Bathrick, David (1998): "From UFA to DEFA: Past as Present in Early GDR Films," in *Contentious Memories: Looking Back at the GDR,* ed. Jost Hermand and Marc Silberman (New York: Peter Lang), 169–188.

Becker, Wolfgang and Norbert Schöll (1995): *In jenen Tagen ... Wie der deutsche Nachkriegsfilm die Vergangenheit bewältigte* (Opladen: Leske and Budrich).

Behrenbeck, Sabine (1996): *Der Kult um die Toten Helden: Nationalsozialistische Mythen, Riten und Symbole 1923 bis 1945* (Vierow: SH Verlag).

Bellour, Raymond (1986): "The Obvious and the Code," in *Narrative, Apparatus, Ideology,* ed. Philip Rosen (New York: Columbia University Press), 98–99.

Bergfelder, Tim (2007): "German Cinema and Film Noir," in *European Film Noir*, ed. Andrew Spicer (Manchester: Manchester University Press), 138–163.

Biess, Frank (2006): *Homecomings: Returning POWs and the Legacies of Defeat in Postwar Germany* (Princeton, NJ: Princeton University Press).

Bluestone, Daniel (1994): "Preservation and Renewal in Post–World War II Chicago," *Journal of Architectural Education* 47.4 (May): 210–223.

Blumenberg, Hans Christoph (1993): *Das Leben geht weiter. Der letzte Film des Dritten Reichs* (Berlin: Rowohlt).

Borchert, Wolfgang (1971): *The Man Outside*, trans. David Porter (New York: New Directions).

Bornemann, John (2004): "Gottesvater, Landesvater, Familienvater: Identification and Authority in Germany," in *Death of the Father: An Anthropology of the End in Political Authority*, ed. John Bornemann (New York: Berghahn), 63–104.

Brandlmeier, Thomas (1989): "Von Hitler zu Adenauer: Deutsche Trümmerfilme," in *Zwischen Gestern und Morgen: Westdeutscher Nachkriegsfilm 1946–1962*, ed. Hilmar Hoffmann and Walter Schobert (Frankfurt am Main: Deutsches Filmmuseum Frankfurt am Main), 32–59.

Brauerhoch, Annette (2005): *"Fräuleins" und GIs: Geschichte und Filmgeschichte* (Frankfurt am Main: Stroemfeld).

Brockmann, Stephen (2004): *German Literary Culture at the Zero Hour* (New York: Camden House).

Broszat, Martin, Klaus-Dietmar Henke, and Hans Woller (Eds.) (1988): *Von Stalingrad zur Währungsreform: Zur Sozialgeschichte des Umbruchs in Deutschland* (Munich: Oldenbourg).

Buck-Morss, Susan (1999): *The Dialectics of Seeing: Walter Benjamin and the Arcades Project* (Cambridge, MA: MIT Press).

Burgess, Gordon (2003): *The Life and Works of Wolfgang Borchert* (Rochester, NY: Camden House).

Busemann, Adolf (1947): "Psychologische Untersuchungen an Hirnverletzten," *Nervenarzt* 18.8: 337–349.

Butler, Judith (2003): "Afterword: After Loss, What then?" in *Loss: The Politics of Mourning*, ed. David L. Eng and David Kazanjian (Berkeley, CA: University of California Press), 467–475.

Caruth, Cathy (1996): *Unclaimed Experience: Trauma, Narrative, and History* (Baltimore, MD: Johns Hopkins University Press).

Chamberlain, Brewster S. (1981): "*Todesmühlen*: Ein früher Versuch zur Massen-'Umerziehung' im besetzten Deutschland 1945–1946" *Vierteljahrshefte für Zeitgeschichte* 3: 420–436.

Claasen, Hermann (1947): *Gesang im Feuerofen. Köln: Überreste einer alten Stadt*, intro. Franz A. Hoyer (Düsseldorf: Schwann).

Clemens, Gabriele (1997): *Britische Kulturpolitik in Deutschland 1945–1949: Literatur, Film, Musik und Theater* (Stuttgart: Steiner).

Confino, Alon (2000): "Traveling as a Cultural Remembrance: Traces of National Socialism in West Germany, 1945–1960," *History and Memory* 12: 92–121.

Cvechovitch, Ann (2003): *An Archive of Feelings: Trauma, Sexuality, and Lesbian Culture* (Durham, NC and London: Duke University Press).

Dagerman, Stig (1988): *German Autumn*, trans. and intro. Robin Fulton (London and New York: Quartet Books).

Deleuze, Gilles (1986): *Cinema 2: The Time-Image*, trans. Hugh Tomlinson and Robert Galeta (Minneapolis, MN: University of Minnesota).

Diehl, James (1993): *The Thanks of the Fatherland* (Chapel Hill, NC: University of North Carolina Press).

Dimendberg, Edward (2004): *Film Noir and the Spaces of Modernity* (Cambridge, MA: Harvard University Press).

Dreher, Berkhard (1976): *Filmförderung in der Bundesrepublik Deutschland* (Berlin: Duncker & Humblot).

Dollinger, Hans (1986): *Friedrich II. von Preußen: Sein Bild im Wandel von zwei Jahrhunderten* (München: List).

Domansky, Elisabeth (1997): "Lost War: World War II in Postwar German Memory," in *Thinking About the Holocaust: After Half a Century*, ed. Alvin H. Rosenfeld (Bloomington, IN: Indiana University Press).

Echternkamp, Jörg (2000): "Mit dem Krieg seinen Frieden schliessen: Wehrmacht und Weltkrieg in der Veteranenkultur 1945–1960," *Jahrbuch für Historische Friedensforschung* 9: 78–93.

Edition Filme 6 (1991): *Staudte* (Berlin: Wissenschaftsverlag Volker Spiess).

Eisenstein, Sergei (2002): "The Montage of Film Attractions," in *The European Cinema Reader*, ed. Catherine Fowler (London: Routledge), 25–26.

Elsaesser, Thomas (2002): "New German Cinema and History: The Case of Alexander Kluge," in *The German Cinema Book*, ed. Tim Bergfelder, Erica Carter, and Deniz Göktürk (London: BFI), 182–191.

Fassbinder, Rainer Werner (1992): *The Anarchy of the Imagination* (Baltimore, MD: Johns Hopkins University Press).

Fehrenbach, Heide (1995): *Cinema in Democratizing Germany: Reconstructing National Identity after Hitler* (Chapel Hill, NC: University of North Carolina Press).

—— (2005): *Race after Hitler, Black Occupation Children in Postwar Germany* (Princeton, NJ: Princeton University Press).

Fiedler, Werner (1991): "Der Weg durch die Trümmer (1946)," *Edition Filme* 6, *Staudte* (Berlin: Wissenschaftsverlag Volker Spiess).

Fisher, Jaimey (1997): "Deleuze in a Ruinous Context: German Rubble-Film and Italian Neorealism," *iris* 23 (Spring): 53–74.

—— (2001): "Who's Watching the Rubble-Kids? Youth, Pedagogy, and Politics in Early DEFA Films," *New German Critique* 82 (Winter): 91–125.

—— (2004): "Kinder der Sterne: Jugend und Wiederaufbau in frühen westdeutschen Nachkriegsfilmen," *Zeitschrift für Germanistik* NF 14.1: 83–101.

Friedrich, Jörg (2002): *Der Brand. Deutschland im Bombenkrieg* (München: Propyläen).

Garrett, Stephen A. (1993): *Ethics and Airpower in World War II. The British Bombing of German Cities* (New York: St. Martin's Press).

Geyer, Michael (1997): "The Place of the Second World War in German Memory and History," *New German Critique* 71 (Spring/Summer): 5–41.

—— (2001): "America in Germany. Power and the Pursuit of Americanization," in *The German-American Encounter. Conflict and Cooperation between Two Cultures 1800–2000*, ed. Frank Trommler and Elliott Shore (New York and Oxford: Berghahn), 121–144.

Goergen, Jean-paul (2002): "Aufnahmen beglaubigter Kameraleute: *Die Todesmühlen*," *Filmblatt* 7: 19–20, 25–31.

Gollancz, Victor (1947): *In Darkest Germany* (Hinsdale, IL: H. Regnery Co.).

Goltermann, Svenja (2001): "Im Wahn der Gewalt: Massentod, Opferdiskurs und Psychiatrie 1945–1956," in *Nachkrieg in Deutschland*, ed. Klaus Naumann (Hamburg: Hamburger Edition), 343–364.

Gordon, Terri J. (2002): "Fascism and the Female Form: Performance Art in the Third Reich," *Journal of the History of Sexuality* 11.1/2 (January/April): 164–200.

Greffrath, Bettina (1995): *Gesellschaftsbilder der Nachkriegszeit: Deutsche Spielfilme 1945–1949* (Pfafferweiler: Centaurus).

Gunning, Tom (1990): "The Cinema of Attractions: Early Film, Its Spectator and the Avant-Garde," in *Early Cinema: Space—Frame—Narrative*, ed. Thomas Elsaesser with Adam Barker (London: British Film Institute), 56–62.

Heineman, Elizabeth (1999): *What Difference Does a Husband Make? Women and Marital Status in Nazi and Postwar Germany* (Chapel Hill, NC: University of North Carolina Press).

Heinrich, Böll (1961): *Erzählungen Hörspiele Aufsätze* (Köln, Berlin: Kiepenheuer & Witsch).

Hell, Julia (1997): *Postfascist Fantasies: Psychoanalysis, History, and the Literature of East Germany* (London and Durham, NC: Duke University Press).

Herzog, Dagmar (2005): *Sex after Fascism: Memory and Morality in Twentieth-Century Germany* (Princeton, NJ: Princeton University Press).

Herzog, Paul (1948): "Heimkehr aus russischer Gefangenschaft," *Die Wandlung* 3. 1: 71–79.

Israel, Nico (2000): *Outlandish: Writing between Exile and Diaspora* (Stanford: Stanford University Press).

Jameson, Fredric (1992a): *The Geopolitical Aesthetic: Cinema and Space in the World System* (Bloomington, IN: Indiana University Press).

—— (1992b): "Spatial Systems in North by Northwest," in *Everything You Always Wanted to Know about Lacan but Were Afraid to Ask Hitchcock*, ed. Slavoj Zizek (New York: Verso), 47–72.

Jarausch, Konrad Hugo, and Michael Geyer (2003): *Shattered Past: Reconstructing German Histories* (Princeton, NJ: Princeton University Press).

Jaspers, Karl (1946): *Die Schuldfrage* (Zürich: Artemis).

Jordan, Günter and Ralf Schenk (Eds.) (2000): *Schwarzweiß und Farbe. DEFA Dokumentarfilme 1946–92* (Berlin: Jovis).

Kaes, Anton (1987): *Deutschlandbilder. Die Wiederkehr der Geschichte als Film* (München: Edition text und kritik), 18–20.

—— (1989): *From Hitler to Heimat. The Return of History as Film* (Cambridge, MA: Harvard University Press).

—— Kaes, Anton, Martin Jay, and Edward Dimendberg (Eds.) (1994): *The Weimar Republic Sourcebook* (Berkley, CA: University of California Press).

Kaplan, Ann E. and Ban Wang (2004): *Trauma and Cinema: Cross-Cultural Explorations* (Aberdeen, UK: Hong Kong University Press).

Karnick, Kristine Brunovska and Henry Jenkins (Eds.) (1995): *Classical Hollywood Comedy* (New York: Routledge).

Käutner, Helmut (1992): "Demontage der Traumfabrik," in *Käutner*, ed. Wolfgang Jacobsen and Hans Helmut Prinzler (Berlin: Schulz & Schulz).

Kettenacker, Lothar (Ed.) (2003): *Ein Volk von Opfern. Die Debatte um den Bombenkrieg 1940–45* (Berlin: Rowohlt).

Koepnick, Lutz (2002): *The Dark Mirror: German Cinema between Hitler and Hollywood* (Berkeley, CA: University of California Press).

Konrad, Hans (1966): "Spuren der Steine? Zu einem Film von Frank Beyer," *Neues Deutschland* (July 6), 4. Reproduced in *Filmland DDR: Ein Reader zu Geschichte, Funktion und Wirkung der DEFA*, ed. Harry Blunk and Dirk Jungnickel (Cologne: Verlag Wissenschaft und Politik, 1990).

Koop, Volker (2004): *Das Recht der Sieger. Absurde alliierte Befehle im Nachkriegsdeutschland* (Berlin: BeBra).

Köppen, Manuel (2005): *Das Entsetzen des Beobachters. Krieg und Medien im 19. und 20. Jahrhundert* (Heidelberg: Universitätsverlag Winter).

Kortner, Fritz (1959): *Aller Tage Abend* (München: Kindler).

—— (1971): *Letzten Endes* (München: Kindler).

Koshar, Rudy (1998): *Germany's Transient Pasts: Preservation and National Memory in the Twentieth Century* (Chapel Hill, NC: University of North Carolina Press).

Kozloff, Sarah (1988): *Invisible Storytellers: Voice-Over Narration in American Fiction Film* (Berkeley, CA: University of California Press).

Kracauer, Siegfried (1995): *The Mass Ornament: Weimar Essays*, trans. Thomas Y. Levin (Cambridge, MA: Harvard University Press).

—— (1997): *Theory of Film: The Redemption of Physical Reality* (Princeton, NJ: Princeton University Press).

Kramer, Karen Ruoff (1999): "Representations of Work in the Forbidden DEFA Films of 1965," in *DEFA: East German Cinema, 1946–1992*, ed. Seán Allan and John Sandford (New York and Oxford: Berghahn Books).

Kreimeier, Klaus (1989): "Die Ökonomie der Gefühle: Aspekte des westdeutschen Nachkriegsfilms," in *Zwischen Gestern und Morgen: Westdeutscher Nachkriegsfilm 1946–1962*, ed. Hilmar Hoffmann and Walter Schobert (Frankfurt am Main: Deutsches Filmmuseum), 8–28.

—— (1992): *Die Ufa-Story. Geschichte eines Filmkonzerns* (München, Wien: Hanser).

—— (1996): *The Ufa Story: A History of Germany's Greatest Film Company 1948–1945*, trans. Robert and Rita Kimber (New York: Hill & Wang).

Kristeva, Julia (1989): *Black Sun: Depression and Melancholia* (New York: Columbia University Press).

Kuzniar, Alice (2007): " 'It's Not Often That I Want a Man': Reading for a Queer Marlene," in *Dietrich Icon*, ed. Gerd Gemünden and Mary Desjardins (Durham, NC: Duke University Press), 239–256.

LaCapra, Dominic (2001): *Writing History, Writing Trauma* (Baltimore, MD: Johns Hopkins University Press).

Latzel, Klaus (1996): *Deutsche Soldaten—Nationalsozialistischer Krieg?: Kriegserlebnis, Kriegserfahrung 1939–1945* (Paderborn: Schöningh).

Lefebvre, Henri (1991): *The Production of Space*, trans. Donald Nicholson-Smith (Cambridge: Blackwell).

Lindemann, Helmut (1949): "Die Schuld Der Generäle," *Deutsche Rundschau* 75. 1: 20–22.

Lindenberg, W. (1947): "Fehlbeurteilung Hirnverletzter," *Deutsches Gesundheitswesen* 2.7: 225–228.

—— (1948): "Ärztliche und soziale Betreuung des Hirnverletzten," *Deutsches Gesundheitswesen* 3.5: 145–147.

Lipkin, Steven N. (1999): "Real Emotional Logic: Persuasive Strategies in Docudrama," *Cinema Journal* 38.4 (Summer): 68–85.

Ludin, Malte (1996): *Wolfgang Staudte* (Rowohlt: Reinbek bei Hamburg).

Luft, Friedrich (1991): "Der erste deutsche Film nach dem Kriege (1946)," *Edition Filme* 6, *Staudte* (Berlin: Wissenschaftsverlag Volker Spiess).

Lukács, Georg (1983): *The Theory of the Novel*. trans. Anna Bostock (Cambridge, MA: MIT Press, 1971).

Lurz, Meinhold (1987): *Kriegerdenkmäler*, vol. 6 (Heidelberg: Esprit Verlag).

MacCannell, Dean (1993): "Democracy's Turn: On Homeless Noir," in *Shades of Noir*, ed. Joan Copjec (London: Verso), 279–297.

Mackeben, Theo (1948): ". . . und über uns der Himmel," *Darmstädter Echo* (April 6).

Marquardt, Axel and Heinz Rathsack (Eds.) (1981): *Preußen im Film. Eine Retrospektive der Stiftung Deutsche Kinemathek (= Preußen. Versuch einer Bilanz. Eine Ausstellung der Berliner Festspiele GmbH 15.8.–15.11.1981, Gropius-Bau Berlin, vol. 5)* (Reinbek: Rowohlt).

Mitscherlich, Alexander and Margarete Mitscherlich (1977): *Die Unfähigkeit zu trauern* (München, Zürich: Piper).

Moeller, Felix (1998): *Der Filmminister. Goebbels und der Film im Dritten Reich.* Mit einem Vorwort von Volker Schlöndorff (Berlin: Henschel).

Moeller, Robert G. (1993): *Protecting Motherhood: Women and the Family in the Politics of Postwar West Germany* (Berkeley, CA: University of California Press).

—— (2001a): "Heimkehr ins Vaterland: Die Remaskulinisierung Westdeutschlands in den fünfziger Jahren," *Militärgeschichtliche Zeitschrift*, 60: 403–436.

—— (2001b): *War Stories: The Search for a Usable Past in the Federal Republic of Germany* (Berkeley, CA: University of California Press).

—— (2004): "What Did You Do in the War, *Mutti*? Courageous Women, Compassionate Commanders, and Stories of the Second World War," *German History* 22: 563–594.

—— (2005a): "Germans as Victims? Thoughts on a Post–Cold War History of the Second World War's Legacies," in *History and Memory* 17.1/2: 147–194.

—— (2005b): "Kämpfen für den Frieden: 08/15 und westdeutsche Erinnerungen an den Zweiten Weltkrieg," *Militärgeschichtliche Zeitschrift* 64: 359–389.

Mosse, George (1990): *Fallen Soldiers: Reshaping the Memory of the World Wars* (New York: Oxford University Press).

Mückenberger, Christiane (Ed.) (1976): *Zur DEFA-Geschichte. Spielfilme 1946–1949* (Potsdam: Hochschule für Film).

—— (Ed.) (1981): *Zur DEFA-Geschichte. Spielfilme 1946–1949* [Folge II], *Filmwissenschaftliche Beiträge*, Sonderband 1.

Mückenberger, Christiane and Günter Jordan (1994): *Sie sehen selbst, Sie hören selbst: Die DEFA von ihren Anfängen bis 1949* (Marburg: Hitzeroth).

Mulvey, Laura (1975): "Visual Pleasure and Narrative Cinema," *Screen* 16.3: 6–18.

Naimark, Norman M. (1995): *The Russians in Germany: A History of the Soviet Zone of Occupation, 1945–1949* (Cambridge, MA: Harvard University Press).

Nathenson, Cary (2000): "Fear of Flying: Education to Manhood in Nazi Film Comedies: *Glückskinder* and *Quax, der Bruchpilot*," in *Cultural History through a National Socialist Lens: Essays on the Cinema of the Third Reich*, ed. Robert C. Reimer (Rochester, NY: Camden House), 84–108.

Naumann, Klaus (Ed.) (2001): *Nachkrieg in Deutschland* (Hamburg: Hamburger Edition).

"Noch einmal: Militarismus und Soldatentum," *Süddeutsche Zeitung* (July 22, 1946), 59.

Patalas, Enno (1953–56): "The German Waste Land," *Sight and Sound* 23.25: 24–27.

Paul, Gerhard (2004): *Bilder des Krieges. Krieg der Bilder. Die Visualisierung des modernen Krieges* (Paderborn: Schöningh).

Perinelli, Massimo (1999): *Liebe '47—Gesellschaft '49: Geschlechterverhältnisse in der deutschen Nachkriegszeit. Eine Analyse des Films* Liebe 47 (Hamburg: LIT).

Pierau, Ralf: "Stemmle, Robert Ferdinand Adolf (R. A.)" (http://www.uni-magdeburg.de/mbl/Biografien/0984.htm; last access August 20, 2006).

Pilgert, Henry P. (1953): *Press, Radio and Film in West Germany, 1945–1953* (n.p.: Historical Division of the Office of the Executive Secretary, Office of the U.S. High Commissioner for Germany).

Pleyer, Peter (1965): *Deutscher Nachkriegsfilm 1946–1948* (Münster: C.J. Fahle Verlag).

Pott, Sabine (2002): *Film als Geschichtsschreibung bei Rainer Werner Fassbinder* (Frankfurt am Main: Peter Lang).

Rentschler, Eric (1996): *The Ministry of Illusion: Nazi Cinema and Its Afterlife* (Cambridge, MA: Harvard University Press).

Riess, Curt (1953): *Berlin Berlin: 1945–1953* (Berlin: Mittag).

Sass, Louis A. (1992): *Madness and Modernism: Insanity in the Light of Modern Art, Literature, and Thought* (New York: Basic Books).

Schivelbusch, Wolfgang (1977 and 1986): *Railway Journey: The Industrialization of Time and Space in the 19th Century* (Berkeley, CA: University of California Press).

—— (1998): *In a Cold Crater: Cultural and Intellectual Life in Berlin, 1945–48*, trans. Kelly Barry (Berkeley, CA: University of California Press).

Schlosser, Horst Dieter (2005): *Es wird zwei Deutschlands geben. Zeitgeschichte und Sprache in Nachkriegsdeutschland 1945–1949* (Frankfurt am Main: Peter Lang).

Schulberg, Stuart (1952): "A Communication: A Letter about Billy Wilder." *The Quarterly of Film, Radio and Television* 7.1: 434–436.

Sebald, W. G. (1999): *Luftkrieg und Literatur* (München: Carl Hanser Verlag).

—— (2003): *On the Natural History of Destruction*, trans. Anthea Bell (New York: Random House).

Shandley, Robert (2001): *Rubble Films: German Cinema in the Shadow of the Third Reich* (Philadelphia: Temple University Press).

—— (2002): "Fritz Kortner's *Last Illusion*," in *Unlikely History. The Changing German-Jewish Symbiosis, 1945–2000*, ed. Leslie Morries and Jack Zipes (New York: Palgrave Macmillan), 251–261.

Sikov, Ed (1998): *On Sunset Boulevard: The Life and Times of Billy Wilder* (New York: Hyperion).

Silberman, Marc (2006): "Introduction: Cold War German Cinema," *Film History* 18.1: 3–5.

—— (2007): "The First DEFA Fairy-Tale Films: Cold-War Fantasies of the 1950s," in *Take Two: German Cinema of the 1950s*, eds. John Davidson and Sabine Hake (Oxford and New York: Berghahn).

Sinsheimer, Hermann (1948): "Heimkehr der Kriegsgefangenen aus England," *Deutsche Rundschau* 71.6: 194–199.

Sirk, Douglas (1997): *Sirk on Sirk. Conversations with Jon Halliday* (London and Boston: Faber and Faber).

Smith, Howard K. (1943): *Last Train from Berlin* (London: Cresset Press).

Steininger, Rolf (1983): *Deutsche Geschichte 1945–1961. Darstellung und Dokumente in zwei Bänden*, vol. 1 (Frankfurt am Main: Fischer).

Steinle, Jürgen (1995): *Nationales Selbstverständnis nach dem Nationalsozialismus. Die Kriegsschuld-Debatte in West-Deutschland* (Bochum: Universitaetsverlag Dr. N. Brockmeyer).

Stemmle, Robert A. CineGraph—Lexikon zum deutschsprachigen Film (Munich: Edition text+kritik, 1984ff; online at: http://www.filmportal.de; last access August 20, 2006).

Stern, Michael (1979): *Douglas Sirk* (Boston: Twayne Publishers).

Stettner, Peter (1992): *Vom Trümmerfilm zur Traumfabrik. Die Junge Film Union 1947–1952* (Hildesheim, Zürich and New York: Olms).

Sudendorf, Werner (2001): *Marlene Dietrich* (Munich: Deutscher Taschenbuch Verlag).

Trinks, Ralf (2002): *Zwischen Ende und Anfang: Die Heimkehrerdramatik der ersten Nachkriegsjahre (1945–1949)* (Würzburg: Königshausen & Neumann).

VanSweringen, Bryan T. (1989): *Kabarettist an der Front des Kalten Krieges. Günter Neumann und das politische Kabarett in der Programmgestaltung des RIAS 1948–1968*, trans. Regine Schulze (Passau: Wiss.Verlag Rothe).

Virilio, Paul (1991): *War and Cinema: The Logistics of Perception* (New York: Verso).

Völker, Klaus (1993): "'Aufklärung ist wichtiger als Verurteilung.' Zu Fritz Kortner's Film 'Der Ruf,'" *Filmexil* 3 (November): 5–12.

von Moltke, Johannes (2005): *No Place Like Home: Locations of Heimat in German Cinema* (Berkeley, CA: University of California Press).

von Müller, Hermann (1949): "Entartung Des Krieges," *Deutsche Rundschau* 75. 9: 800–806.

Weckel, Ulrike (2000): "*Die Mörder sind unter uns* oder: Vom Verschwinden der Opfer," *Werkstattgeschichte* 25: 105–115.

—— (2003): "Spielarten der Vergangenheitsbewältigung: Wolfgang Borcherts Heimkehrer und sein langer Weg durch die westdeutschen Medien," *Tel Aviver Jahrbuch für deutsche Geschichte* 31: 125–161.

White, Hayden (1990): "The Value of Narrativity in the Representation of Reality," in *The Content of the Form: Narrative Discourse and Historical Representation* (Baltimore, MD: Johns Hopkins University Press).

Wilder, Billy (1989): "The Wilder Memorandum," in *The Americanization of Germany, 1945–1949*, ed. Ralph Willett (London and New York: Routledge), 40–44.

Wilkening, Albert (1981): *Geschichte der DEFA von 1945–1950* (Potsdam-Babelsberg: VEB DEFA Studio für Spielfilme).

Willett, Ralph (1989): *The Americanization of Germany* (New York: Routledge).

Zimmermann, Peter (Ed.) (2005): *Geschichte des dokumentarischen Films in Deutschland*, 3 vols. (Stuttgart: Reclam).

Zuckerman, Solly (1978): *From Apes to Warlords* (London: Hamilton).

INDEX